# LECTURES ON THE FOURTEENTH AMENDMENT
## TO THE
## CONSTITUTION OF THE UNITED STATES

Da Capo Press Reprints in

# AMERICAN CONSTITUTIONAL AND LEGAL HISTORY

GENERAL EDITOR: LEONARD W. LEVY

*Brandeis University*

LECTURES ON THE

# FOURTEENTH ARTICLE
# OF AMENDMENT

TO THE

# CONSTITUTION OF THE
# UNITED STATES

BY WILLIAM D. GUTHRIE

DA CAPO PRESS · NEW YORK · 1970

A Da Capo Press Reprint Edition

This Da Capo Press edition of *Lectures on the Fourteenth Article of Amendment to the Constitution of the United States* is an unabridged republication of the first edition published in Boston in 1898.

Library of Congress Catalog Card Number 74-118030

SBN 306-71941-X

Published by Da Capo Press
A Division of Plenum Publishing Corporation
227 West 17th Street, New York, N.Y. 10011
All Rights Reserved
Manufactured in the United States of America

# LECTURES

## ON THE

## FOURTEENTH ARTICLE OF AMENDMENT

### TO THE

## CONSTITUTION OF THE UNITED STATES.

# LECTURES

ON THE

# FOURTEENTH ARTICLE OF AMENDMENT

TO THE

# CONSTITUTION OF THE UNITED STATES

DELIVERED BEFORE THE

DWIGHT ALUMNI ASSOCIATION

NEW YORK, APRIL — MAY, 1898

BY

WILLIAM D. GUTHRIE,

OF THE NEW YORK BAR

BOSTON

LITTLE, BROWN AND COMPANY

1898

University Press:

John Wilson and Son, Cambridge, U.S.A.

## These Lectures

UPON CONSTITUTIONAL LAW ARE DEDICATED WITH
AFFECTIONATE REGARD
TO

## JOSEPH H. CHOATE,

WHOSE SPLENDID TALENTS AND FORENSIC TRIUMPHS
ARE THE PRIDE AND INSPIRATION
OF THE AMERICAN BAR.

# PREFACE.

THESE lectures were intended to be merely an outline of the scope of the Fourteenth Amendment and a general introduction to the study of that branch of constitutional law. I appreciate that the subject is not treated scientifically, and that there are defects of order and grouping; and I realize imperfections of style, somewhat unavoidable in an oral discussion, which I would have tried to avoid in a treatise on the subject. Some of those who listened to the lectures have urged that they be published in the original form, and believe that they contain matter which will be interesting and useful to the profession. I have, therefore, ventured to publish them as delivered; but I hope in the near future to be able to prepare a more comprehensive and useful book upon this important subject.

The discussion in the lectures and the references in the notes have been confined almost exclusively to cases decided by the Supreme Court of the United States, the tribunal where all questions of individual liberty and property rights are now finally determined. There are many important cases in the state courts and in the lower federal courts which should be consulted by all students; but I have referred to only a few of these.

I have also thought it useful to annotate the whole Constitution. For this purpose, the search has been at the original source, and every volume of the Supreme Court reports has been examined. In this research and the preparation of the analytical index, I have been assisted by Mr. Theodore S. Beecher.

I desire also to acknowledge the assistance of my partner, Mr. Noel Gale, in the preparation and annotation of the fifth lecture, upon the rules of practice, and the assistance of Mr. C. L. Avery in collecting and verifying authorities in the other lectures.

W. D. G.

New York, October 3, 1898.

# CONTENTS.[1]

---

## LECTURE I.

## LECTURE II.

[1] Table of cases p. xiii.

## LECTURE III.

## LECTURE IV.

# LECTURE V.

# TABLE OF CASES.

# DWIGHT ALUMNI LECTURES.

———◆———

THE FOURTEENTH ARTICLE OF AMENDMENT TO THE
CONSTITUTION OF THE UNITED STATES.

————

## LECTURE I.

### OF THE HISTORY OF THE FOURTEENTH AMENDMENT.

THE subject of these lectures will be the Fourteenth Article of Amendment to the Constitution of the United States, which became a part of the organic law of the nation on July 28, 1868.[1] The course will be divided into five lectures, consisting of (i) a review of the causes which led to the adoption of the amendment, and of the broad purpose of its framers; (ii) the principles of construction and interpretation; (iii) the scope of the requirement of due process of law; (iv) the meaning of the equal protection of the laws; and (v) the rules of practice which must be followed in order to raise the constitutional point in the state and federal courts of original jurisdiction, and to secure a revision by the Supreme Court of the United States on writ of error or appeal.

Our constitutional history during the last thirty years, with comparatively few exceptions, may be said to be but

---

[1] Resolution proposing amendment was dated June 16, 1866. Secretary Seward issued two proclamations declaring the amendment to be in force, the first dated July 20, and the second, July 28, 1868. The wording of these proclamations was peculiar, and at once presented a serious question as to the validity of the ratification by six of the southern States. It also presented the question whether a State, having once given its consent or ratification, had power to withdraw it, as Ohio and New Jersey attempted to do. (See 14 Stat. 358, 15 Stat. 73, ibid. vi–xii App.; 30 Am. L. Rev. 894.)

little more than a commentary on the Fourteenth Amendment, which, indeed, nationalized the whole sphere of civil liberty.[1] This great amendment to the Federal Constitution has done more than any other cause to protect our civil rights from invasion, to strengthen the bonds of the Union, to make us truly a nation, and to assure the perpetuity of our institutions. Some of its provisions were already embodied in most of the state constitutions and bills of rights; but the experience of the civil war and of the period of reconstruction had convinced the people that fundamental rights could no longer coexist in safety with unrestrained power in the States to alter their constitutions and laws as local prejudice or interest might prompt or passion impel. The rights of the individual to life, liberty and property had to be secured by the Federal Constitution itself, as, indeed, they should have been when it was originally framed. The amendment, therefore, placed the essential rights of life, liberty and property in the several States of the Union under the ultimate protection of the national government.[2] It was the outward manifestation of the will of the people that equality and protection to life, liberty and property should be guaranteed as the national right of Americans. The deliberate purpose of the amendment was to enforce on every foot of our soil rules of equality before the law and the rights of person and property, and to make certain that those rules could nevermore be violated according to the views or caprice of local majorities. The limitations imposed upon the States by this amendment are universal in their application. They are directed against any and every mode and form of arbitrary and unjust state action,

[1] Burgess, Pol. Sc. & Const. Law i. 225.
[2] Hare's Am. Const. Law i. 747.

whether legislative, executive, or judicial;[1] yet they take away no power which any free government should ever employ.

At the time the Federal Constitution was ratified, in 1787–1788, jealousy and fear of a centralized national government prevailed. The student of the history of that critical period cannot fail to be impressed with the conviction that limitations upon the power of the States, such as are embodied in the Fourteenth Amendment, could not then have been secured, and that the Constitution would never have been ratified if the people had realized the extensive powers they were conferring upon the central government. In order to secure its acceptance by the States, it was necessary to give pledges that amendments constituting a bill of rights in limitation of the federal power, and thus protecting the people against the national government, would be forthwith submitted.[2] The first ten amendments, which were proposed by the First Congress in September, 1789, restrained the national government only, and were not intended to apply to the States.[3] No limitation upon state sovereignty or powers could at that time have been secured. These ten amendments originated in the apprehension of the people — in a prevailing sense of danger — that the powers conferred upon the general government might be arbitrarily exercised. A dread was felt in all parts of the country that the federal power might crush out self-government in the States. We may judge of the limited view of nationality existing during the infancy of the republic from the fact that, when pur-

---

[1] Civil Rights Cases, 109 U. S. 3, 11; Logan v. United States, 144 U. S. 263, 290 ; Scott v. McNeal, 154 U. S. 34, 45; Chicago, Burlington, &c. R'd v. Chicago, 166 U. S. 226, 233.

[2] Barron v. Baltimore, 7 Pet. 243, 250.

[3] Ibid. 247; McElvaine v. Brush, 142 U. S. 155, 158.

chasing Louisiana from France, Jefferson considered a constitutional amendment necessary in order to confer the power. But it was soon recognized that there was an overruling necessity justifying the assertion for the Union of all powers of nationality, which no mere confederation could have had, and which the Constitutional Convention itself probably did not contemplate.

The only provisions of the original Constitution which protected fundamental rights in the States were those entitling the citizens of each State to all the privileges and immunities of citizens in the several States, and guaranteeing a republican form of government in every State.[1] This guaranty of a republican form of government was called by Sumner " the sleeping giant of the Constitution."[2] Yet these provisions, because of their vagueness, were found to be insufficient to afford protection against unequal, oppressive, or spoliative legislation on the part of the States. In fact, prior to the adoption of the Fourteenth Amendment, private property might have been confiscated and vested rights denied by the States, and yet the sufferer could have found no protection in the federal tribunals. The arbitrary exercise by local legislatures, courts, or executive officers of power affecting life, liberty, or property could not be redressed or checked by the national judiciary except in the case of bills of attainder or laws impairing the obligation of contracts. The prohibition against *ex post facto* laws referred only to criminal cases.[3] Rights considered essential in our system of government and vest-

---

[1] Forsyth *v.* Hammond, 166 U. S. 506, 519.

[2] Foster on the Const., i. 209.

[3] Calder *v.* Bull, 3 Dall. 386, 390, 396, 399 ; *In re* Sawyer, 124 U. S. 200, 219; Medley, Petitioner, 134 U. S. 160, 170. As to what constitutes an *ex post facto* law, see Hawker *v.* New York, 170 U. S. 189 ; and Thompson *v.* Utah, 170 U. S. 343.

ing as matter of right in each individual, could be abridged or denied by the state legislatures and judiciary, and there was no appeal to the Supreme Court of the United States.[1] The fact that the powers of the States might be thus arbitrarily and oppressively exercised without redress constituted a grave menace to the perpetuity of the Union. This was, indeed, the inherent weakness in our original system of dual government. It was to cure this weakness, and to remove all opportunity for abuse of state power, that the Fourteenth Amendment was adopted. Mindful of the facility with which state constitutions are changed, the object of the framers of the amendment was to nationalize and place on a secure foundation the great republican principles of liberty and equality before the law, and thereby fix an immutable standard of just laws and equal rights applicable under all circumstances and at all times.[2]

The eight years following the first inaugural of President Lincoln were the most eventful and important in the history of our country. The election of 1860 had been a fierce political struggle, full of portentous indications, the culmination of thirty years of bitter strife between the advocates of the indissoluble nature of the Union on the one hand and the advocates of the doctrine of state rights and secession on the other. The South proclaimed and threatened that everything, even her allegiance to the Union, was staked upon this election. While slavery was certainly the immediate excuse for the war, there can be no reasonable doubt that a conflict of arms was inevitable

---

[1] Mr. Justice Field in Bartemeyer *v.* Iowa, 18 Wall. 129, 140.

[2] In Holden *v.* Hardy, 169 U. S. 366, 382, Mr. Justice Brown said: "The Fourteenth Amendment, which was finally adopted July 28, 1868, largely expanded the power of the Federal courts and Congress, and for the first time authorized the former to declare invalid all laws and judicial decisions of the States abridging the rights of citizens or denying them the benefit of due process of law."

as the ultimate result of the doctrine of state rights and secession. Civil war was merely a question of the particular cause or occasion.

President Lincoln sought in all ways to avert a resort to arms. In his own noble language, " Both parties deprecated war; but one of them would make war rather than let the nation survive, and the other would accept war rather than let it perish. And the war came." [1] When hostilities commenced, the abolition of slavery was not contemplated in any event. The government and the dominant party asserted no right to do more than restrict the territorial enlargement of slavery. Had Lincoln, at the beginning of the war, been asked for a pledge that emáncipation would not follow the triumph of the northern armies, I believe he would have given it. At that time the ownership of slaves greatly exceeded the value of all the railroads as well as of all the manufacturing interests in the country. Emancipation came only and avowedly as a necessary war measure. We might still be cursed with human slavery if the slave interest had not itself drawn the sword and justly perished by the sword.

During the war, the doctrine of the North had been that the Union was "one and inseparable," or, as was subsequently declared by the Supreme Court,[2] " an indestructible Union, composed of indestructible States;" that no State could secede; that all of the eleven States in rebellion were still in the Union as part of the nation, and that the war was being waged not against the southern States but

---

[1] Lincoln's second Inaugural Address, March 4, 1865, which is one of the finest pieces of prose in our language, excelling even the deservedly famous Gettysburg address.

[2] Texas *v.* White, 7 Wall. 700, 725 ; see also the earlier decisions of The Amy Warwick, 2 Spr. 143; 1 Fed. Cas. 808; *In re* Egan, 5 Blatchford, 319; 8 Fed. Cas. 367.

against insurgents within those States. It seemed to result logically from this position that, upon the restoration of peace, the rebel States were entitled to have full representation in Congress and in the Electoral College, and to regulate their own internal affairs as before the rebellion, unchecked and unrestrained by federal authority. And this was the position taken by the people of the South immediately after the cessation of hostilities. They demanded unconditional recognition, and asserted that they were entitled equally with the loyal States to participate in the control of the government they had fought so fiercely to destroy.

A bitter controversy then arose. President Johnson, on the one hand, sided with the South in the contention that the rebel States were entitled, as matter of constitutional right, to unconditional recognition and readmission into the Union; and, encouraged by his ill-advised support, the people of the southern States were unfortunately led to assume an attitude of defiance and to enact harsh and cruel laws directed against the negroes. The prevailing sentiment in the North, on the other hand, was that all the fruits of the war would be wasted unless guaranties were secured protecting white and black alike from arbitrary and oppressive state action in the South. It was also insisted that the insurgent States had forfeited their rights as sovereign States under the Constitution, and that terms should be imposed and pledges exacted upon their readmission or recognition as States of the Union.

Whatever may be thought of the merits of particular measures, the verdict of history will be that, upon the general question and policy of reconstruction, President Johnson was wrong, and the Senate and House of Representatives were right. To us of to-day it seems preposterous to contend that States can rebel and wage war against the national government, imperilling the existence of the nation itself, without the forfeiture of any rights whatever, and that, after they have failed and been reduced to submission, they are to become entitled to restoration as of constitutional right, without the slightest condition, without discipline or even reproof, without any punishment other than mere defeat, without any measure tending to prevent a renewal of insurrection.[1]

[1] In the report made by the majority of the Joint Reconstruction Committee June 8, 1866, will be found the most interesting review of the causes leading to the adoption of the Fourteenth Amendment, and the following may be quoted: " It is moreover contended, and with apparent gravity, that, from the peculiar nature and character of our government, no such right on the part of the conqueror can exist; that from the moment when rebellion lays down its arms and actual hostilities cease, all political rights of rebellious communities are at once restored; that, because the people of a State of the Union were once an organized community within the Union, they necessarily so remain, and their right to be represented in Congress at any and all times, and to participate in the government of the country under all circumstances, admits of neither question nor dispute. If this is indeed true, then is the government of the United States powerless for its own protection, and flagrant rebellion, carried to the extreme of civil war, is a pastime which any State may play at, not only certain that it can lose nothing in any event, but may even be the gainer by defeat. If rebellion succeeds, it accomplishes its purpose and destroys the Government. If it fails, the war has been barren of results, and the battle may still be fought out in the legislative halls of the country. Treason, defeated in the field, has only to take possession of Congress and the cabinet. . . . Your committee does not deem it either necessary or proper to discuss the question whether the late Confederate States are still States of this Union, or can ever be otherwise. Granting this profitless abstraction, about which so many words have been wasted, it by no means follows that the people of those States may not place themselves in a condition to abrogate the powers and privileges incident to a State of the Union, and deprive themselves of all pretence of right to exercise those powers and enjoy those privileges. A State within the Union has obligations to discharge as a member of the Union. It must submit to federal laws and uphold federal authority. It must have a government republican in form, under and by which it is connected with the General Government, and through which it can discharge its obligations. It is more than idle, it is a mockery, to contend that a people who have thrown off their allegiance, destroyed the local government which bound their States to the Union as members thereof, defied its authority, refused to execute its laws, and abrogated every provision which gave them political rights within the Union, still retain, through all, the perfect and entire right to resume, at their own will and

"Never in the history of the world had so mighty a rebellion been subdued. Never had any rebellion been followed by treatment so lenient, forgiving, and generous on the part of the triumphant government. The great mass of those who had resisted the national authority were restored to all their rights of citizenship by the simple taking of an oath of future loyalty, and those excepted from immediate reinstatement were promised full forgiveness on the slightest exhibition of repentance and good works."[1] No vindictiveness was shown, there were no reprisals, no bloodshed, no confiscation, as had so shamefully disgraced our country at the close of the War of the Revolution. "No blood was shed on the scaffold, nor, saving the abolition of slavery, was there any confiscation."[2] Europe looked with amazement upon the magnanimity of the conquerors; and foreign historians comment upon it with admiration.[3]

Many of the rebel States, instead of accepting the results of the war and endeavoring to restore peace and order under fair and impartial laws, proceeded to enact statutes of the most oppressive and cruel kind, designed to reduce the negro again to virtual slavery. On all sides were seen

pleasure, all their privileges within the Union, and especially to participate in its government, and to control the conduct of its affairs. To admit such a principle for one moment would be to declare that treason is always master and loyalty a blunder. Such a principle is void by its very nature and essence, because inconsistent with the theory of government, and fatal to its very existence." McPherson's Hist. of the Reconstruction, 87.

[1] Blaine's Twenty Years of Congress, ii. 85.
[2] Goldwin Smith's The United States, 282; see also 110–111.
[3] In his Commentaries on the Constitution, Mr. Foster well says (§ 38, p. 268): "But when we consider that, after five years of civil strife, in which so much blood and treasure was wasted, the victors did not demand, as an atonement, the sacrifice of a single life not destroyed in battle, or for a violation of the laws of war; and remember, not only the decimations in Rome and the guillotine in France, but the explosion of the Sepoys by the English in India less than ten years before, and the military executions in South and Central America to-day; their magnanimity seems, indeed, without a parallel."

evidences of an open and flagrant recalcitrancy against
the results of the war. It was also apprehended that the
war debt of the Confederate government would be assumed
by the southern States.

The cruel and unjust legislation in the rebel States,
the defiant attitude of the people of the South, their apparent determination to wield in opposition to the best
interests of the Union the tremendous political power of
eleven States banded together, revealed great dangers,
and convinced the statesmen and people of the North
that the unconditional readmission or recognition of these
States would be the extreme of folly. The loyal population felt that it would result in a revival of the doctrine of
state rights and expose the nation to all the dangers of a
new rebellion. They believed that they had a right, after
so much sacrifice of life and treasure, to exact from the
conquered reasonable pledges for the future protection of
black and white alike throughout the whole territory of
the South. They asked for nothing but an assurance
of fair and impartial laws and reasonable protection for
life, liberty and property. They demanded no constitutional limitations or restraints which they were not likewise willing to impose upon themselves in the loyal
States.

It will not be profitable at this time to discuss at
length whether the conditions exacted upon recognition
or readmission into the Union were or were not tech-
nically constitutional; nor will it serve any useful purpose to consider the many elements of provocation and
wrong on both sides. In the main, the North was right.
It was evident that new guards and protections were
necessary, and that some limitation had to be imposed
upon the power of the States. The statesmen of the

North would have been perfectly justified in compelling the adoption of the Fourteenth Amendment by force of arms or revolutionary methods. During the war, the Constitution, which, in truth, had not been framed for civil strife, frequently had to be strained, and many measures of the Executive and of Congress were of doubtful constitutionality. " The time was not favorable to considerate reflection upon the constitutional limits of legislative or executive authority. If power was assumed from patriotic motives, the assumption found ready justification in patriotic hearts. Many who doubted yielded their doubts ; many who did not doubt were silent." [1] The necessities of reconstruction put a new and even severer test upon the Constitution. It had to be adapted to changed and extraordinary conditions. And it is fortunate that the statesmen of that day had the courage and the foresight to insist upon the amendments necessary to secure our future safety and happiness.[2]

In considering the attitude assumed by the statesmen of the North under the circumstances existing immediately after the war, and in view of the fact that life, liberty and property were insecure in all the southern States, we should not overlook the great principle of the Declaration of Independence, " that whenever any form of government becomes destructive of these ends, it is the right of the people to alter or to abolish it, and to institute new government, laying its foundation on such principles and organizing its powers in such form as to

---

[1] Chief Justice Chase in Hepburn *v.* Griswold, 8 Wall. 603, 625.

[2] " The restoration of peace and order after the close of the Civil War, and the readmission of the conquered people to their former relations with the Federal government, presented the most difficult political and constitutional problem which the United States has had to solve. It was accomplished only by what was, in fact as well as in name, a complete reconstruction of the Union." Foster on the Constitution, i. § 38, p. 205.

them shall seem most likely to effect their safety and happiness." While the statement of principles in the Declaration of Independence may not, as Mr. Justice Brewer has said, have the force of organic law, or be made the basis of judicial decision as to the limits of right and duty, and while in all cases reference must be had to the organic law of the nation for such limits, yet the Constitution is but the body and the letter of what the Declaration is the thought and the spirit, and it is always safe to read the letter of the Constitution in the spirit of the Declaration of Independence.[1]

The difficult problems to be solved by Congress were five in number. They related to (1) the fundamental rights and immunities of American citizens; (2) the basis of representation in Congress and in the Electoral College; (3) the exclusion from office of some of the principal offenders in the Confederate cause; (4) the validity and sacredness of the national public debt and pensions to disabled Union soldiers; and (5) the assumption of claims for loss or emancipation of slaves or of any part of the Confederate debt.

In the Fourteenth Amendment, as recommended by Congress and adopted by the States, these problems were solved in separate sections of one amendment. It was at first suggested that some of these sections should be proposed as separate amendments; but it was finally concluded that this course was inadvisable, and all the provisions were submitted as subdivisions of one comprehensive amendment.[2] The language of the amendment is as follows:

[1] Gulf, Colorado & Santa Fé R'y *v.* Ellis, 165 U. S. 150, 160.

[2] In the report made to Congress by the minority of the Reconstruction Committee, it was said: "The several amendments suggested have no connection with each other; each, if adopted, would have its appropriate effect if

" SECTION 1. All persons born or naturalized in the United States, and subject to the jurisdiction thereof, are citizens of the United States and of the State wherein they reside. No State shall make or enforce any law which shall abridge the privileges or immunities of citizens of the United States; nor shall any State deprive any person of life, liberty, or property, without due process of law; nor deny to any person within its jurisdiction the equal protection of the laws.

SECTION 2. Representatives shall be apportioned among the several States according to their respective numbers, counting the whole number of persons in each State, excluding Indians not taxed. But when the right to vote at any election for the choice of electors for President and Vice President of the United States, Representatives in Congress, the Executive and Judicial officers of a State, or the members of the Legislature thereof, is denied to any of the male inhabitants of such State, being twenty-one years of age, and citizens of the United States, or in any way abridged, except for participation in rebellion, or other crime, the basis of representation therein shall be reduced in the proportion which the number of such male citizens shall bear to the whole number of male citizens twenty-one years of age in such State.

SECTION 3. No person shall be a Senator or Representative in Congress, or elector of President and Vice President, or hold any office, civil or military, under the United States, or under any State, who, having previously taken an oath, as a member of Congress, or as an officer of the United States, or as a member of any State legislature, or as an executive or judicial officer of any State, to support the Constitution of the United States, shall have engaged in insurrection or rebellion against the same, or given aid or comfort to the enemies thereof. But Congress may by a vote of two-thirds of each House, remove such disability.

SECTION 4. The validity of the public debt of the United States, authorized by law, including debts incurred for payment of pensions and bounties for services in suppressing insurrection or rebellion, shall not be questioned. But neither the United States nor any State shall assume or pay any debt or obligation incurred in

the others were rejected; and each, therefore, should be submitted as a separate article, without subjecting it to the contingency of rejection if the States should refuse to ratify the rest." McPherson's Hist. of the Reconstruction, 99.

aid of insurrection or rebellion against the United States, or any claim for the loss or emancipation of any slave; but all such debts, obligations, and claims shall be held illegal and void.

SECTION 5. The Congress shall have power to enforce, by appropriate legislation, the provisions of this article."

Section 1 embodies the most important and comprehensive of the provisions. It is now the strongest and broadest guaranty of fundamental rights under our system of government. To this section we shall principally devote our attention during the course of these lectures; and I shall only briefly refer to the objects accomplished by the other sections.

Section 2 relates to representation in Congress and the Electoral College. It will be recalled that in the original Constitution only three-fifths of the slaves were to be reckoned in the basis of representation. The result of the emancipation of the negroes was the contention that the southern States were now entitled to increase their basis of representation by two-fifths of the freed slaves, although they proposed to give those slaves no vote.[1] The admission of this contention would have endowed the voting population of the South with proportionately greater political power than was exercised by any part of the loyal voting population of the North. The second section of the amendment sought to prevent this result. While it was left to the States to grant or withhold negro suffrage, it was nevertheless provided that, if the right to vote were denied or in any way abridged, the basis of representation should be reduced in proportion to the number of the class excluded. Thus, each State was to be at perfect liberty to deny negro suffrage; but, if it did, then its political power in Congress and in the Electoral

[1] Blaine's Twenty Years of Congress, ii. 189.

College was to be reduced in proportion to the unrepresented negro population. This provision, surely, was fair and just. But the South would not accept it. The people there insisted upon the right not only to deny negro suffrage, but to have as full representation as if the whole colored population were voting. Had the South promptly and graciously accepted this clause of the Fourteenth Amendment and afforded some protection to the negroes, no one can doubt that the Fifteenth Amendment would never have been adopted. It is incorrect to say that the North forced negro suffrage on the South.[1] The conduct of the unreconciled and irreconcilable portion of the population of the South compelled the enfranchisement of the negro, as apparently necessary for his protection. The result, we must confess, has been extremely disappointing; and we look to the future with great apprehension. The enfranchisement of the colored race at that time was a political mistake, even in the best interest of the race itself. Enfranchisement under the Fourteenth Amendment would have come in time, and the very dangerous feature of the race feuds in the South during the last thirty years and still existing would have been avoided.

This provision of the Fourteenth Amendment as to representation was superseded in great measure by the Fifteenth Amendment, which was adopted subsequently and which established universal suffrage, so far as race was concerned. The later amendment provides that "the right of citizens of the United States to vote shall not be denied or abridged by the United States or by any State on account of race, color, or previous condition of servitude." It has been held that the Fourteenth and Fifteenth Amendments do not of themselves confer the

---

[1] Blaine's Twenty Years of Congress, ii. 262–267.

right of suffrage, and that the States are still at liberty
to impose property or educational qualifications upon the
exercise of that right.   There still remains, however, the
question whether any constitution or law requiring property or educational or other qualifications, particularly if
arbitrarily imposed so as to discriminate against any distinct class of voters, would not require a reduction of representation in Congress and in the Electoral College " in the
proportion which the number of such male citizens [ex-
cluded] shall bear to the whole number of such citizens
twenty-one years of age."   This point has not yet been
authoritatively decided.[1]   We may express the hope that

---

[1] Williams *v.* Mississippi, 170 U. S. 213.   In discussing the recent constitution of Louisiana, the editor of the Law Notes (ii. 80, August, 1898) says:
" The most important features of the new Constitution consist in the provisions for disfranchising the negroes without infringing the political rights guaranteed to them by the fifteenth amendment to the Federal Constitution.   The
framers of the Constitution swept the field of expedients, and at last hit upon a
plan that was deemed invulnerable.   Referring to the provisions presently to
be mentioned, the president of the convention, in his concluding address to the
members, said: 'What care I whether it be more or less ridiculous or not ?
Does n't it meet the case ?   Does n't it let the white man vote, and does n't it
stop the negro from voting, and is n't that what we came here for ? '   Article
197, prescribing the qualifications of voters, requires that the voter shall be able
to read and write, and shall demonstrate his ability to do so when he applies for
registration by making a written application in the English language or in his
mother tongue.   If he be not able to read and write, he shall be entitled to register and vote by making oath that he is the owner of property assessed at a valuation of not less than three hundred dollars.   If the foregoing were the only
provisions it is evident that illiterate and impecunious whites would be excluded
from the franchise along with negroes of the same class.   But another section
provides that ' no male person who was on January 1, 1867, or at any date prior
thereto, entitled to vote under the Constitution or statutes of any State of the
United States wherein he then resided, and no son or grandson of any such
person not less than twenty-one years of age at the date of the adoption of this
Constitution . . . shall be denied the right to register and vote in this State by
reason of his failure to possess the educational or property qualifications prescribed by this Constitution.'   Now on January 1, 1867, negroes could not
vote in Louisiana, and the fifteenth amendment to the Federal Constitution
was not adopted until 1870.   So that if the provision is constitutional, it effectually exempts most of the whites from the educational or property qualifications required of negroes."   This travesty of constitutional justice ought to

it will be settled by the Supreme Court at an early day, so as to avoid having it raised in some close presidential contest when the decision might be necessary to determine the election of a president. Prudence and patriotism should prompt an effort to avoid the possibility of having a national election turn upon a judicial decision, with the accompanying danger of political scandal.

Section 3 of the amendment excluded from office certain of the most prominent insurgents. It became evident, after the close of the war, that the leading members of the Confederate government and army would be restored to responsible political positions. Many of these insurgents had been in the service of the United States at the commencement of the war. As federal officers, they had taken the oath to support the Constitution of the United States. They had joined the Confederacy in violation of that oath; or, at least, so the North believed. The great mass of Confederates were pardoned the moment their arms were laid down; but the leaders, who, in official positions before the war, had solemnly sworn to support the Constitution, were considered far more guilty than the multitude who followed them. It was considered fit and proper that those leaders should be excluded from office, at least until Congress deemed it safe to remove the disability; and this section so provided.

Section 4 related to finances. The first part of the section was inserted because of the fear that, if the Confederate States were unconditionally restored to representation in Congress, they might endeavor to impair the

be brought to the test in the federal courts at the earliest moment. If such a provision can be sustained as within the power of the States to regulate the qualification of voters, the result ought to be the diminution of Louisiana's representation in Congress and in the Electoral College in proportion to the excluded negro vote.

obligations of the United States incurred in suppressing the rebellion and assail the system of pensions to Union soldiers. It was, therefore, considered essential that Congress should, so far as it could by organic law, guard the sacredness of the public debt and of the national pensions.

The greatest financial danger, however, lay in claims for loss of slaves and in the assumption by the southern States of the Confederate debt. The national credit might have been fatally impaired if the possibility of slave claims had not been removed. The necessity for protection seemed imperative. The slave claims would have amounted to between two and three thousand millions of dollars;[1] and it was believed by many that the government debt was already heavier than the nation could bear. Little was it dreamt that this debt could be borne and practically discharged by the generation that created it. If the possibility of an enormous claim on account of the emancipated slaves were not excluded, as Mr. Blaine said, "the burden would be so great that the Nation which had survived the shock of arms might be engulfed in the manifold calamities of bankruptcy."[2] The second sentence of section 4 of the amendment removed all danger from this source.

Returning now to section 1 of the amendment, the first clause provides:

"All persons born or naturalized in the United States, and subject to the jurisdiction thereof, are citizens of the United States and of the State wherein they reside."

This clause remedied a grave omission in the original Constitution, and placed citizenship on a secure and permanent foundation. The question as to the citizenship

---

[1] Blaine's Twenty Years of Congress, ii. 191.  [2] Ibid.

of free negroes, upon which there had been a difference
of opinion throughout the country and in the Supreme
Court, had to be settled, and the rule enunciated in the
famous and unpopular Dred Scott case had to be abrogated. If, as the result of the civil struggle, we were to
have a broader nationality, it was necessary that citizenship should be placed on unquestionable ground, — " on
ground so plain that the humblest man who should
inherit its protection would comprehend the extent and
significance of his title." [1] The Fourteenth Amendment
changed the origin and character of American citizenship,
or at least removed all doubt. " Instead of a man being
a citizen of the United States because he was a citizen of
one of the States, he was now made a citizen of any State
in which he might choose to reside, because he was ante-
cedently a citizen of the United States," [2] by reason of birth
on American soil or naturalization under federal statutes.[3]

The remaining portion of section 1 provides that :

" No State shall make or enforce any law which shall abridge the
privileges or immunities of citizens of the United States; nor shall
any State deprive any person of life, liberty, or property, without due
process of law; nor deny to any person within its jurisdiction the
equal protection of the laws."

By this clause, the Fourteenth Amendment secured to
every citizen of the United States the guaranty that his
privileges and immunities as such citizen should not be
abridged by any State ; and it imposed, as a further specific
restraint on state action, the time-honored provision of the
Fifth Article of Amendment, that no man should be deprived
of life, liberty, or property without due process of law, or,
what is its equivalent, *lex terræ*, the law of the land, the

---

[1] Blaine's Twenty Years of Congress, ii. 189.  [2] Ibid.
[3] See further upon this point of citizenship, *post*, pp. 56 *et seq.*

famous provision contained in Magna Charta. But the framers went further, and adopted another clause, in language new to our constitutions: " Nor shall any State . . . deny to any person within its jurisdiction the equal protection of the laws." This clause has been declared by the Supreme Court to be " a pledge of the protection of equal laws." [1]

When this section of the Fourteenth Amendment was first discussed by the Supreme Court, Mr. Justice Miller, in the opinion in the famous Slaughter House cases delivered on behalf of the majority of the court, went beyond what was required for the decision of those cases, and expressed a very narrow view of the scope of the amendment. There can be no doubt that the broader views contained in the dissenting opinions of Justice Field and of Justices Bradley and Swayne, on behalf of themselves and Chief Justice Chase, embodied a much truer statement of the purpose and scope of the amendment. In referring to the clause requiring the equal protection of the laws, Mr. Justice Miller made what seems to us of the present day the somewhat astonishing statement: [2] " We doubt very much whether any action of a State not directed by way of discrimination against the negroes as a class, or on account of their race, will ever be held to come within the purview of this provision." This narrow view has been entirely discarded by the Supreme Court in its later decisions, and the universal application of this clause of the amendment to every form of state action and legislation, political or civil, irrespective of race, is now firmly established. At the present term, the Supreme Court has said: [3] " A majority of the cases which

---

[1] Yick Wo *v.* Hopkins, 118 U. S. 356, 369.      [2] 16 Wall. 36, 81.
[3] Holden *v.* Hardy, 169 U. S. 366, 382.

have since arisen have turned not upon a denial to the colored race of rights therein secured to them, but upon alleged discriminations in matters entirely outside of the political relations of the parties aggrieved." Mr. Blaine stated in his "Twenty Years of Congress," that the earlier decisions of the Supreme Court deprived the Fourteenth Amendment of much of the power which Congress intended to impart to it; and that the members of Congress sincerely believed that it possessed a far greater scope than those decisions gave it.[1]

As what have been called the conservative — I would say almost hostile — views of Mr. Justice Miller were clearly in conflict with the intention of the framers of the amendment, and for many years dwarfed and dulled the protective power of the amendment, it will be interesting to quote from some of the speeches in Congress, and thus realize the intention of the framers. There is, moreover, to-day in many quarters a remarkable misconception of the intention and purpose of the framers of the Fourteenth Amendment. The debates upon all these questions are most interesting and convincing, and should always be consulted. It has lately been declared that, "doubtless, the intention of the Congress which framed and of the States which adopted this Amendment of the Constitution must be sought in the words of the Amendment; and the debates in Congress are not admissible as evidence to control the meaning of those words."[2]

---

[1] Vol. ii. 419; see also Prof. Burgess' Political Sc. & Const. Law, vol. i. 225 *et seq.*: "From whatever point of view I regard the opinion of the Court in the Slaughter House cases, — from the historical, political, or juristic, — it appears to me entirely erroneous. It appears to me to have thrown away the great gain in the domain of civil liberty won by the terrible exertions of the nation in the appeal to arms. I have perfect confidence that the day will come when it will be seen to be intensely reactionary and will be overturned."

[2] United States *v.* Wong Kim Ark, 169 U. S. 649, 699.

But, nevertheless, these debates are frequently referred to
and are "valuable as contemporaneous opinions of jurists
and statesmen upon the legal meaning of the words
themselves." [1]

The Fourteenth Amendment was introduced in the
United States Senate by Senator Howard, of Michigan,
on behalf of the Reconstruction Committee, of which
he was a member. This Committee consisted of nine
members from the House and six from the Senate. They
were the real framers of this great constitutional measure.
Referring to the provisions of the Constitution as it
stood before the adoption of the new amendments and
particularly to the Fifth Amendment, Senator Howard
said : [2] "They do not operate in the slightest degree as a
restraint or prohibition upon state legislation. States
are not affected by them, and it has been repeatedly
held that the restriction contained in the Constitution
against the taking of private property for public use without just compensation is not a restriction upon state legislation, but applies only to the legislation of Congress.
There is no power given in the Constitution to enforce
and to carry out any of these guarantees. . . . They
stand simply as a bill of rights in the Constitution, without power on the part of Congress to give them full
effect; while at the same time the States are not restrained from violating the principles embraced in them
except by their own local constitutions, which may be
altered from year to year. The great object of the first
section of this amendment is, therefore, to restrain the
power of the States and compel them at all times to re-

---

[1] United States *v.* Wong Kim Ark, 169 U. S. 649, 699; *Ex parte* Bain, 121
U. S. 1, 12.

[2] Cong. Globe, 39th Congress, 1st sess. part 3, pp. 2764, 2765, 2766.

spect these great fundamental guarantees. . . . The last two clauses of the first section of the amendment disable a State from depriving not merely a citizen of the United States, but any person, whoever he may be, of life, liberty, or property without due process of law, or from denying to him the equal protection of the laws of the State. This abolishes all class legislation in the States, and does away with the injustice of subjecting one caste of persons to a code not applicable to another. . . . Section one is a restriction upon the States, and does not, of itself, confer any power upon Congress. . . . I look upon the first section, taken in connection with the fifth, as very important. It will, if adopted by the States, forever disable every one of them from passing laws trenching upon those fundamental rights and privileges which pertain to citizens of the United States, and to all persons who may happen to be within their jurisdiction. It establishes equality before the law, and it gives to the humblest, the poorest, the most despised of the race the same rights and the same protection before the law as it gives to the most powerful, the most wealthy, or the most haughty. . . . Without this principle of equal justice to all men and equal protection under the shield of the law, there is no republican government and none that is really worth maintaining."

In explaining the provision for the equal protection of the laws, Senator Poland said of equality:[1] "It is the very spirit and inspiration of our system of government, the absolute foundation upon which it was established. It is essentially declared in the Declaration of Independence and in all the provisions of the Constitution. Notwithstanding this, we know that state laws exist, and some of them of very recent enactment, in direct violation of these

[1] Cong. Globe, 39th Congress, 1st sess. part 4, p. 2961.

principles. . . . It certainly seems desirable that no doubt should be left existing as to the power of Congress to enforce principles lying at the very foundation of all republican government if they be denied or violated by the States, and I cannot doubt but that every senator will rejoice in aiding to remove all doubt upon this power of Congress."

Thaddeus Stevens, the Republican leader in the House of Representatives, in presenting the proposition for the Fourteenth Amendment, stated the provisions of the first section, and then said:[1] "I can hardly believe that any person can be found who will not admit that every one of these provisions is just. They are all asserted in some form or other, in our DECLARATION or organic law. But the Constitution limits only the action of Congress, and is not a limitation on the States. This amendment supplies that defect, and allows Congress to correct the unjust legislation of the States, so far that the law which operates upon one man shall operate equally upon all."

Roscoe Conkling was a leading member of the Reconstruction Committee which framed the amendment. On the argument of the San Mateo County case in the Supreme Court, December 19, 1882, he produced for the first time the journal of the Committee. This journal has never been published. His argument, which was printed and filed, showed, step by step, how the various provisions came to be inserted, and he affirmed that the Committee intended to give them the broadest scope and operation, and not in any way to confine their benefit and protection to the colored race. In the course of his argument, Mr. Conkling said: " At the time the Fourteenth Amendment was ratified, as the records of the two Houses will show,

[1] Cong. Globe, 39th Congress, 1st sess. part 3, p. 2459.

individuals and joint stock companies were appealing for congressional and administrative protection against invidious and discriminating state and local taxes. One instance was that of an express company, whose stock was owned largely by citizens of the State of New York, who came with petitions and bills seeking acts of Congress to aid them in resisting what they deemed oppressive taxation in two States, and oppressive and ruinous rules of damages applied under state laws. That complaints of oppression in respect of property and other rights, made by citizens of northern States who took up residence in the South, were rife, in and out of Congress, none of us can forget ; that complaints of oppression, in various forms, of white men in the South — of ' Union men ' — were heard on every side, I need not remind the court. The war and its results, the condition of the freedmen, and the manifest duty owed to them, no doubt brought on the occasion for constitutional amendment ; but when the occasion came, and men set themselves to the task, the accumulated evils falling within the purview of the work were the surrounding circumstances, in the light of which they strove to increase and strengthen the safeguards of the Constitution and the laws."

In the same case, Senator Edmunds, who was a member of the Senate when the Fourteenth Amendment was discussed and recommended by that body, speaking of its broad and catholic spirit, said : " There is no word in it that did not undergo the completest scrutiny. There is no word in it that was not scanned, and intended to mean the full and beneficial thing that it seems to mean. There was no discussion omitted ; there was no conceivable posture of affairs to the people who had it in hand which was not considered."

Nowhere is there a better or clearer statement of the whole subject than by Mr. Justice Field, one of the greatest judges that ever sat in the Supreme Court, in his decision in the Railroad Tax cases in the United States Circuit Court of California in September, 1883, fifteen years after the amendment was adopted. He said:[1] "All history shows that a particular grievance suffered by an individual or a class, from a defective or oppressive law, or the absence of any law, touching the matter, is often the occasion and cause for enactments, constitutional or legislative, general in their character, designed to cover cases not merely of the same, but all cases of a similar, nature. The wrongs which were supposed to be inflicted upon or threatened to citizens of the enfranchised race, by special legislation directed against them, moved the framers of the amendment to place in the fundamental law of the nation provisions not merely for the security of those citizens, but to insure to all men, at all times, and at all places, due process of law, and the equal protection of the laws. Oppression of the person and spoliation of property by any State were thus forbidden, and equality before the law was secured to all. . . . With the adoption of the amendment the power of the States to oppress any one under any pretense or in any form was forever ended; and henceforth all persons within their jurisdiction could claim equal protection under the laws. And by equal protection is meant equal security to every one in his private rights — in his right to life, to liberty, to property, and to the pursuit of happiness. It implies not only that the means which the laws afford for such security shall be equally accessible to him, but that no one shall be subject to any greater burdens or charges than such as are imposed upon

[1] County of Santa Clara *v.* Southern Pac. R. Co., 18 Fed. Rep. 385, 397.

all others under like circumstances. This protection attends every one everywhere, whatever be his position in society or his association with others, either for profit, improvement, or pleasure. It does not leave him because of any social or official position which he may hold, nor because he may belong to a political body, or to a religious society, or be a member of a commercial, manufacturing, or transportation company. It is the shield which the arm of our blessed government holds at all times over every one, man, woman, and child, in all its broad domain, wherever they may go and in whatever relations they may be placed. No state — such is the sovereign command of the whole people of the United States — no state shall touch the life, the liberty, or the property of any person, however humble his lot or exalted his station, without due process of law; and no state, even with due process of law, shall deny to any one within its jurisdiction the equal protection of the laws."

More cases involving the application of the principles of the Fourteenth Amendment are now presented to the Supreme Court for adjudication than upon any other branch of jurisprudence. In one term, from October, 1896, to May, 1897, twenty-one cases in which the amendment was discussed were decided by the court, and in fifteen of these cases the decision turned upon the interpretation of its provisions. Hundreds of pages of the reports were devoted to the discussion of cases arising under the amendment.[1] At the term of the Supreme Court now about to end, the most important cases decided also arose under it; and some of the opinions delivered in these cases will rank

[1] At the October Term, 1897, there were nine cases in which the amendment was directly involved.

among the ablest and clearest on the subject. In fact, no period in the history of the Court has furnished abler or more comprehensive opinions upon constitutional law than the last few years.

Great cases involving constitutional rights are continually being decided, and should be carefully studied by all lawyers. The importance which the Fourteenth Amendment has attained in our system of constitutional law will then be realized. We shall also be led to appreciate the immense labors which the Supreme Court performs, and the inestimable services which it renders to the nation, sometimes unperceived and frequently unappreciated by the people at large.

It is only ten years since, at the opening of the second century of the national government under our Constitution, Chief Justice Fuller was called upon to preside over the Supreme Court of the United States. These ten years have been the period of its greatest activity. Preeminent at the bar of the West, fully equipped, as a ripe scholar and a great lawyer, for the highest trust our profession can bestow, Chief Justice Fuller has fully maintained the high character of the august and venerable tribunal of which he is the head, even as established in the decisions of Marshall and Story. His opinions found in forty-three volumes of the Supreme Court reports are more numerous in ten years than were those of Chief Justice Marshall in thirty-five, and equally momentous; and this great work has been accomplished notwithstanding the additional arduous duties incumbent upon him in the decision of all questions of practice.

Foreign observers speak with concern and reproach of what seems to them the want of symmetry in American character, of the all-absorbing struggle for material wealth, of the paucity of our literature, of our failure hitherto, as they say, to produce much of lasting value in art, philosophy, history, or oratory, particularly during the last thirty years.[1] But there is one branch of our government in which the severest critic finds nothing to censure, and which invites only praise and admiration; that branch is the federal judiciary, and pre-eminently the Supreme Court of the United States. With power to set aside unconstitutional enactments by Congress, to nullify arbitrary assumptions of power by the Executive Department or by the President himself, to send down its mandate and declare null and void unequal and oppressive legislation by the States, the members of the Supreme Court exercise their vast responsibilities with profound learning and painstaking investigation, and with an integrity which even the most venomous publication has not the temerity to impugn. Although overburdened with an immense volume of business — more than sevenfold what it was in the days of Marshall and Story — the justices are continually delivering opinions which are examples not only of exhaustive research and deep learning in jurisprudence, but of the best style in the English language. These opinions contain the highest results of logical thought, careful and laborious preparation, splendid diction, incisive and forcible expression, — qualities which are elsewhere often lacking in our contemporary literature. In these opinions, indeed, must we look for the ablest definitions of American institutions and for the best examples of American literature. The opinions in most cases rise far above the quality of the arguments submitted, and show much independent and original labor. To prove this, we have only to compare the briefs and arguments with the opinions of the court. As one

---

[1] Lecky's Democracy and Liberty, i. 105–108.

of the leaders of our bar, Mr. Phelps, has eloquently said of this august tribunal : " Having its origin in the sovereignty of the people, it is the bulwark of the people against their own unadvised action, their own uninstructed will. It saves them not merely from their enemies, it saves them from themselves." [1] Of this great court Daniel Webster said : " The Constitution without it would be no Constitution — the Government no Government." The bar should always bear in mind that the Supreme Court is the very keystone of our national and state governments, and that assaults upon it threaten the whole structure of the Union.[2]

In concluding this first lecture, may I not venture to impress upon you what seems to be the present duty of the bar ? Our fathers solved the great problems of the war and of the reconstruction period; and, in the Fourteenth Amendment, they gave us as our heritage a new Magna Charta.[3] Is it not for us to preserve and perpetuate the results of their labors and sacrifices, if only out of gratitude for signal services and patriotic devotion ? Each generation finds new needs, new difficulties, new dangers, new duties of its own. Each calling, each profession has its mission in our political and social life. There is to-day a growing tendency to invade the liberty of the individual and to disregard the rights of property, a tendency manifesting itself in many forms and concealing itself under many pretexts. This tendency, bred of envy and dis-

---

[1] See Mr. Phelps' great oration at the Centennial of the Supreme Court, New York, Feby. 4, 1890, Carson ii. 694.

[2] Washington in transmitting commission to John Jay as Chief Justice. Washington's Writings, Sparks' ed., x. p. 35. Letter to the Associate Justices of the Supreme Court. Letter to John Jay.

[3] " Fairly construed these amendments may be said to rise to the dignity of a new Magna Charta." Swayne, J., in Slaughter House Cases, 16 Wall. 36, 125.

content and of the thirst for organic change — call it socialism or communism or what you will — is the grave danger of the present, and it threatens humiliating disaster. In this tendency lies the difficult problem which we of this generation must prepare to face and to solve. Much is to be dreaded and guarded against in the despotism of the majority wielding and abusing the power of legislation, and ignorantly or intentionally undermining the foundations of the Constitution itself. I consider it to be the mission of the bar to cope with and to overcome this evil. If we confidently hope for success, it is only because the Fourteenth Amendment is the bulwark on which we place our reliance.

The supreme test is about to be applied to our form of government — whether the guaranties of the Federal Constitution are really adequate to afford full protection to the rights of property and persons, and to shield them from the effects of "those sudden and strong passions to which men are exposed,"[1] and which unchecked and unrestrained may lead to follies and crimes involving immeasurable misery and ruin. So long as the Constitution of the United States continues to be observed as the political creed, as the embodiment of the conscience of the nation, we are safe. State constitutions are being continually changed to meet the expediency, the prejudice, the passion of the hour. The Federal Constitution alone seems likely to endure. If the people, the bar, and the courts preserve it intact in spirit and in letter, our national future will be progress, happiness, and glory; but if it be mutilated, disregarded, or overthrown, that future will be decline, misery, and shame.

We must bear in mind that it is not the pulpit, nor the

---

[1] Chief Justice Marshall in Fletcher *v.* Peck, 6 Cranch, 87, 138.

press, but the law which reaches and touches every fibre of the whole fabric of life; which surrounds and guards every right of the individual; which keeps society in place; which embodies the good faith holding the moral world together; which grasps the greatest and protects the least of human affairs; "which is universal in its use and extent, accommodated to each individual, yet comprehending the whole community." [1]  We lawyers, if worthy of our profession, are delegated not merely to defend constitutional guaranties before the courts for individual clients, but to teach the people in season and out of season to value and respect individual liberty and the rights of property. It is our duty to preach constitutional morality to the rich and to the poor, to all trades and to all vocations, to all ranks and to all classes, in the cities and on the plains. For us is it to convince the people that the disregard of these inalienable rights is in conflict with their own welfare and happiness, and cannot be suffered if we are to remain a free people. To-day, more than ever, the bar is the great conservative force in American politics. We are the guardians of the Federal Constitution. *Sacer esto.* What higher duty could engage us than to teach its sacredness and its permanence — in the lofty phrase of the Roman advocate — its eternity!

[1] Blackstone's Com., i. 27.

# LECTURE II.

## THE PRINCIPLES OF CONSTRUCTION AND INTERPRETATION.

THE construction or interpretation of a constitution is not governed by the rules that apply to ordinary statutes or private writings.[1] A constitution is designed to be a frame or organic law of government and to settle and determine the fundamental rights of the individual. A national constitution is intended to endure for all time. Its provisions should not in any sense be limited to the conditions happening to exist when it is adopted, although those conditions and the history of the times may well throw light upon the provisions and reveal their true scope. Such a constitution is an enumeration of general principles and powers or of limitations upon the exercise of governmental functions, and it is not a mere code of rules to regulate particular cases. All progress and improvement would be barred and a constitution would soon become useless if it were not construed as a declaration of general principles to be applied and adapted as new con-

[1] See chapter on the "Rules of Interpretation" in Story on the Constitution, §§ 397–456, which should be studied. In Smith v. Alabama, 124 U. S. 465, 478, Mr. Justice Matthews said: "There is, however, one clear exception to the statement that there is no national common law. The interpretation of the Constitution of the United States is necessarily influenced by the fact that its provisions are framed in the language of the English common law, and are to be read in the light of its history. The code of constitutional and statutory construction which, therefore, is gradually formed by the judgments of this court, in the application of the Constitution and the laws and treaties made in pursuance thereof, has for its basis so much of the common law as may be. implied in the subject, and constitutes a common law resting on national authority. Moore v. United States, 91 U. S. 270."

ditions presented themselves.  Thus, the commerce clause
of the Constitution is constantly being applied to conditions of which the framers never dreamt.  At the time
of the adoption of the Constitution, who could have fore-
seen the railroad, the telegraph, the telephone, electricity,
the innumerable other inventions which are now so necessary to our comfort and enter so largely into our life
and commerce ?[1]  Particularly in a national constitution,
there must be capacity for expansion in order that its
principles may fit and be applied to the ever-varying
phases of business and social life in this quick and active
age when events and changes follow each other with such
startling rapidity.  Accordingly, in framing the Constitution, anything but the broadest and most comprehensive
statement of general principles was avoided.  It was
hardly safe to be specific.  As Chief Justice Marshall said
in the famous case of M'Culloch v. Maryland :[2] " A constitution, to contain an accurate detail of all the sub-

---

[1] *In re* Debs, Petitioner, 158 U. S. 564, 590, Mr. Justice Brewer said: " Up
to a recent date commerce, both interstate and international, was mainly by
water, and it is not strange that both the legislation of Congress and the cases
in the courts have been principally concerned therewith.  The fact that in
recent years interstate commerce has come mainly to be carried on by railroads
and over artificial highways has in no manner narrowed the scope of the constitutional provision, or abridged the power of Congress over such commerce.
On the contrary, the same fulness of control exists in the one case as in the
other, and the same power to remove obstructions from the one as from the
other.  Constitutional provisions do not change, but their operation extends to
new matters as the modes of business and the habits of life of the people vary
with each succeeding generation.  The law of the common carrier is the same
to-day as when transportation on land was by coach and wagon, and on water by
canal boat and sailing vessel, yet in its actual operation it touches and regulates transportation by modes then unknown, the railroad train and the steamship.  Just so is it with the grant to the national government of power over
interstate commerce.  The Constitution has not changed.  The power is the
same.  But it operates to-day upon modes of interstate commerce unknown to
the fathers, and it will operate with equal force upon any new modes of such
commerce which the future may develop."

[2] 4 Wheat. 316, 407; see also Gibbons v. Ogden, 9 Wheat. 1, 198; Strauder
v. West Virginia, 100 U. S. 303, 310.

divisions of which its great powers will admit, and of all the means by which they may be carried into execution, would partake of the prolixity of a legal code, and could scarcely be embraced by the human mind. It would probably never be understood by the public. Its nature, therefore, requires, that only its great outlines should be marked, its important objects designated, and the minor ingredients which compose those objects be deduced from the nature of the objects themselves." And ex-President Harrison has well said in his interesting book on " This Country of Ours " : " To the lay mind it may seem puzzling and not a little discouraging that a century has not sufficed to interpret the Constitution ; but the explanation is largely in the fact that constitutional provisions are general and not particular, and the court is required constantly to apply them to particulars and to new conditions." [1]

Nor should the courts attempt to define with precision the scope of a constitutional provision, although this is constantly and necessarily done in construing statutes. A definition of the scope of a constitutional provision cannot be necessary in any case. An exposition of the general meaning of the principle is all that should be attempted. The sole inquiry must be whether the particular case submitted for adjudication is or is not within the principle of the constitutional provision invoked or to be implied therefrom, for what is implied is as much a part of the instrument as what is expressed.[2] The Supreme Court of the United States has repeatedly declared that it was wiser to ascertain the scope and application of the Fourteenth Amendment by the " gradual process of judicial inclusion and exclusion, as the cases presented for decision shall

---

[1] p. 309.  [2] *Ex parte* Yarbrough, 110 U. S. 651, 658.

require, with the reasoning on which such decisions may be founded."[1] Fortunate, indeed, is it that no definitions have been attempted, particularly when the views as to the effect of the amendment were as narrow as those we find in the early decisions of the Supreme Court, which were delivered at a time when the court could not possibly foresee the great questions now presented under the amendment at every term. New conditions of society are evolving; and systems of law are being changed incessantly to deal with novel and complicated questions presented for adjudication. Much legislation submitted to willingly at the present day would have been deemed an arbitrary and insufferable interference with individual liberty a hundred years ago, when we were almost entirely an agricultural people; and the converse is equally true, that much of the public policy, statutory provisions and common law of the last century is entirely unsuited to the present day. Owing to the progressive development of legal ideas and institutions in England after the year 1215, the things for which the words of Magna Charta stood at the time of the American Revolution were very different from what they represented to King John and the barons at Runnymede.[2] The experience of the past, therefore, teaches that the courts should never attempt to deduce from abstract principles any limiting definition of fundamental rights as guaranteed by the Fourteenth Amendment. "It is sufficient to say that there are certain immutable principles of justice which inhere in the very idea of free government which no member of the Union may disregard";[3] that these principles recognize the inherent

[1] Davidson *v.* New Orleans, 96 U. S. 97, 104; see also Holden *v.* Hardy, 169 U. S. 366.

[2] Hurtado *v.* California, 110 U. S. 516, 529.

[3] Holden *v.* Hardy, 169 U. S. 366, 389.

rights of the individual, and are embodied and intended to be protected and secured by the fundamental law, and that the Fourteenth Amendment imposes upon the courts the duty to protect every individual or corporation from arbitrary denial or abridgment of those rights by the States.

As a much higher degree of care is exercised in the preparation and adoption of constitutional provisions than is bestowed upon the preparation and passage of statutes, a constitution imports the utmost discrimination in the use of language. Every provision must be given full effect, even at the expense of existing institutions. Not a single word can be discarded or ignored, or treated as surplusage. This cannot be said of statutes. In a leading case in this State, Judge Denio said: "When, therefore, we are seeking for the true construction of a constitutional provision, we are constantly to bear in mind that its authors were not executing a delegated authority, limited by other constitutional restraints, but are to look upon them as the founders of a State, intent only upon establishing such principles as seemed best calculated to produce good government and promote the public happiness, at the expense of any and all existing institutions which might stand in their way." [1]

One of the rules observed in the interpretation of statutes is that regard must be had to the evil contemplated by the law-makers and sought to be remedied, and that the particular enactment should generally be confined to remedying that evil. This is a wise rule in construing a statute; but it has no general application to a constitution. In construing constitutional provisions, the particular grievance or occasion out of which they grew is never

[1] In Matter of Oliver Lee & Co's Bank, 21 N. Y. 9, 12.

controlling. The grievance or occasion may no longer exist; but the constitution remains effective to govern and regulate analogous cases. Thus, although, as matter of fact, the protection of the colored race was uppermost in the minds of the people when they adopted the Fourteenth Amendment, nevertheless its provisions, when embodied in the organic law, became a general rule of conduct, civil and political, and established a fixed standard of principles governing individual rights and liberties applicable at all times and to all conditions.[1] In discussing a particular application of a constitutional provision, it is not enough to say that the case in question was not in the mind of Congress when the amendment was framed, nor of the people when it was adopted. In the language of Chief Justice Marshall: "It is necessary to go farther, and to say that, had this particular case been suggested, the language would have been so varied, as to exclude it, or it would have been made a special exception. The case being within the words of the rule, must be within its operation likewise, unless there be something in the literal construction so obviously absurd, or mischievous, or repugnant to the general spirit of the instrument, as to justify those who expound the constitution in making it an exception."[2]

When the language of a constitution is clear, no court should speculate as to the purpose of the framers. The words used should be given their natural and ordinary meaning. If, however, a word or term has acquired a fixed technical meaning in legal or constitutional history, it will be presumed that it has been employed in that sense.

[1] Slaughter-House Cases, 16 Wall. 36, 72 ; Ex parte Virginia, 100 U. S. 339, 347, 361 ; Holden v. Hardy, 169 U. S. 366, 382, 385 ; United States v. Wong Kim Ark, 169 U. S. 649, 676.

[2] Dartmouth College v. Woodward, 4 Wheat. 518, 644.

It may be said of the Fourteenth Amendment as Marshall wrote of the Constitution: "As men, whose intentions require no concealment, generally employ the words which most directly and aptly express the ideas they intend to convey, the enlightened patriots who framed our constitution, and the people who adopted it, must be understood to have employed words in their natural sense, and to have intended what they have said." [1] Judge Story said in his great work on the Constitution: [2] "What is to become of constitutions of government if they are to rest, not upon the plain import of their words, but upon conjectural enlargements and restrictions, to suit the temporary passions and interests of the day? Let us never forget that our constitutions of government are solemn instruments, addressed to the common sense of the people, and designed to fix and perpetuate their rights and their liberties. They are not to be frittered away to please the demagogues of the day. They are not to be violated to gratify the ambition of political leaders. They are to speak in the same voice now and forever. They are of no man's private interpretation. They are ordained by the will of the people; and can be changed only by the sovereign command of the people."

There is another rule in construing or expounding a constitution, and that is that the ancient maxim "de minimis non curat lex" has no application. The violation of a constitutional right should never be measured or met by any such plea. It is said that counsel once attempted to argue before Chief Justice Marshall that in the particular instance before the court the invasion of constitutional rights was slight, but he was sternly reminded that the

---

[1] Gibbons v. Ogden, 9 Wheat. 1, 188.
[2] Story on the Constitution, sec. 1908 (5th ed.).

case involved the Constitution of the United States, and that the degree or extent of the invasion had no bearing upon the point.[1] When a constitutional right is invaded, we are not bound to stand silent so long as moderation is practised. There can be no greater political blindness, no more dangerous policy, than to sanction the infringement of constitutional rights because the particular instance is in itself apparently harmless or seems expedient. Admit the wedge ever so little, and there is nothing to prevent its being driven home. We are not compelled to wait until the unconstitutional measure becomes ruinous confiscation or an intolerable interference with personal liberty. In respect of constitutional guaranties, we have a right to expect absolute security and protection, and the courts are under a duty to enforce the constitutional provisions guaranteeing our rights wholly irrespective of the degree of infringement. Present inconvenience, however great, present expediency, however tempting, can never justify the slightest disregard of any provision of a constitution.

It is ever the moderate and light invasions of constitutional rights that are the most dangerous. As was said in a leading case:[2] "It may be that it is the obnoxious thing in its mildest and least repulsive form; but illegitimate and unconstitutional practices get their first footing in that way, namely, by silent approaches and slight

---

[1] Thus, in the case of Sentell v. New Orleans &c. Railroad Co., 166 U. S. 698, the Supreme Court gave the most careful consideration to a case involving a claim arising out of the killing of a dog and adjudged the validity under the Fourteenth Amendment of an act providing that no owner could recover for the killing of a dog unless the dog had been placed upon the assessment rolls, and that the amount of recovery should be limited to the value of the dog on the assessment roll.

[2] Mr. Justice Bradley in Boyd v. United States, 116 U. S. 616, 635. See also Gulf, Colorado & Santa Fé R'y v. Ellis, 165 U. S. 150, 154.

deviations from legal modes of procedure. This can only be obviated by adhering to the rule that constitutional provisions for the security of person and property should be liberally construed. A close and literal construction deprives them of half their efficacy, and leads to gradual depreciation of the right, as if it consisted more in sound than in substance. It is the duty of courts to be watchful for the constitutional rights of the citizen, and against any stealthy encroachments thereon. Their motto should be *obsta principiis.*" As to our constitutional rights, eternal vigilance and uncompromising enforcement must be our rule of conduct if we are to preserve and perpetuate American constitutional institutions. We should never tolerate any infringement of constitutional rights, no matter how slight or trivial. Toleration of even insignificant violations of constitutional rights serves to weaken our sense of those rights.

Nor should we forget the warning of Junius to the people of England, uttered seven years before the American Revolution:[1] " Let me exhort and conjure you never to suffer an invasion of your political constitution, however minute the instance may appear, to pass by, without a determined, persevering resistance. One precedent creates another. They soon accumulate, and constitute law. What yesterday was fact, to-day is doctrine. Examples are supposed to justify the most dangerous measures, and where they do not suit exactly, the defect is supplied by analogy. Be assured that the laws, which protect us in our civil rights, grow out of the constitution, and that they must fall or flourish with it. This is not the cause of faction, or of party, or of any individual, but the common interest of every man in Britain."

[1] Dedication of Letters of Junius (ed. 1812), i. 2; see also Macaulay's History of England, i. 26, 28.

While the application of the Fourteenth Amendment is universal, and protects the individual from an arbitrary exercise of power by state authority, whether it be the legislature, the executive, or the judicial branch of state government, it must be borne in mind that the federal courts cannot supervise or interfere with the internal affairs of a State unless some constitutional right has been invaded by state authority. The wrongful actions of individuals, unsupported by such authority, are not to be redressed under this amendment. They constitute merely private wrongs, or crimes of the individual. The denial of a constitutional right must rest upon some state law or state authority for its excuse or perpetration if the Fourteenth Amendment is to furnish any remedy.[1] Nor is the hardship or injustice of state laws necessarily an objection to their constitutional validity.[2] The federal courts should not be driven into perplexing inquiries as to the expediency or policy of state laws — inquiries which are usually unfit and improper for the judicial department. They will not permit themselves to be made harbors in which the people are to find a refuge from ill-advised and oppressive state statutes which do not infringe or deny constitutional guaranties.[3] The remedy for evils of that character is to be sought in the state legislatures, or at the ballot box — not in the federal courts. "The rule, briefly stated, is that whenever an act of the legislature is challenged in court the inquiry is limited to the question of power, and does not extend to the matter of ex-

---

[1] Mr. Justice Bradley in Civil Rights Cases, 109 U. S. 3, 13; United States *v.* Cruikshank, 92 U. S. 542; Logan *v.* United States, 144 U. S. 263, 293.

[2] County of Mobile *v.* Kimball, 102 U. S. 691, 704; Missouri Pacific Railway Co. *v.* Humes, 115 U. S. 512, 520; N. Y. & N. E. Railroad Co. *v.* Bristol, 151 U. S. 556, 570.

[3] County of Mobile *v.* Kimball, 102 U. S. 691, 704.

pediency, the motives of the legislators, or the reasons which were spread before them to induce the passage of the act. This principle rests upon the independence of the legislature as one of the coördinate departments of the government. It would not be seemly for either of the three departments to be instituting an inquiry as to whether another acted wisely, intelligently, or corruptly." [1]

The only safeguard against the abuse of sovereign powers of legislation which do not violate constitutional guaranties is still to be found in the structure of the state governments themselves and at the polls.[2]    Although the Federal Constitution guarantees a republican form of government and the fundamental rights of the individual, it must be recognized that, provided these fundamental rights are not abridged or denied, the ultimate power to determine all questions of local government and public policy rests, after all, in the people of the States, speaking through their constitutions or legislatures.    The Fourteenth Amendment was not adopted in order to grant to Congress power to prescribe the local legislative policy or the forms or modes of process or procedure in the respective States, nor to vest in the Supreme Court general supervision over the legislation of the States, with authority to nullify such as it did not approve.    If this were not so, the Supreme Court would become the censor of practically all state statutes and the tribunal of appeal from all legislation regulating or affecting indi-

---

[1] Angle v. Chicago, St. Paul &c. Railway, 151 U. S. 1, 18; see also Ex parte McCardle, 7 Wall. 506, 514; Doyle v. Continental Ins. Co., 94 U. S. 535, 541; Soon Hing v. Crowley, 113 U. S. 703, 710; Missouri Pacific Railway Co. v. Humes, 115 U. S. 512, 520; Mugler v. Kansas, 123 U. S. 623, 661; Maynard v. Hill, 125 U. S. 190, 204; Minnesota v. Barber, 136 U. S. 313, 319.

[2] Powell v. Pennsylvania, 127 U. S. 678, 686.

vidual liberty or property rights. It was never intended that any such supervisory jurisdiction should be conferred on the federal courts by the Fourteenth Amendment, nor has it been exercised heretofore.

Growing out of the necessity for the observance of rules of comity in our dual system of state and federal governments, the doctrine is now well established that the construction placed upon any state statute or constitution by the highest court of the State is generally to be deemed conclusive upon the federal courts.[1] It may be that the federal court differs with the state court as to such construction, but the decision of the state court is nevertheless accepted. The question before the federal court is always whether the statute, as construed by the state court, is or is not repugnant to the Fourteenth Amendment, and not whether the state court erred in its construction.[2] But if the case, instead of coming from the highest court of the State, originates in a circuit court of the United States, and comes from that court to the Supreme Court a different question may be presented. In such a case, assuming that there are no controlling decisions of the state courts, the Supreme Court will review the construction or interpretation of the statute by the court below.[3] In the one class of cases, the Supreme Court ordinarily regards the decision below (*i. e.,* of the

---

[1] Forsyth *v.* Hammond, 166 U. S. 506, 519.

[2] " So far does this doctrine extend, that when a statute of two States, expressed in the same terms, is construed differently by the highest courts, they are treated by us as different laws, each embodying the particular construction of its own State, and enforced in accordance with it in all cases arising under it." Mr. Justice Field in Louisiana *v.* Pilsbury, 105 U. S. 278, 294; see also State Railroad Tax Cases, 92 U. S. 575, 617; Iowa Central Railway Company *v.* Iowa, 160 U. S. 389, 393; Merchants' Bank *v.* Pennsylvania, 167 U. S. 461, 462, and *infra,* Lecture V.

[3] Loan Association *v.* Topeka, 20 Wall. 655, 659; Fallbrook Irrigation District *v.* Bradley, 164 U. S. 112, 155.

state court) as conclusive; in the other class, it considers the point of construction, and determines, first, whether the law was properly construed in the lower federal court; and, secondly, whether, as properly construed, it does or does not invade a constitutional right. It will, therefore, be seen that it is often of vital importance to proceed in the first instance, if at all possible, in a federal court.[1]

But the rule as to accepting the interpretation of the state court is not universal. It does not strictly apply to the effect and operation of state statutes. The Supreme Court may decline to concur in the view of the state court as to the real effect and operation of a state statute or ordinance and its necessary tendency.[2] So also a statute or ordinance may be fair on its face and impartial in appearance, but be so applied and administered as to violate the guaranty of due process of law. It is the method of enforcement, not the interpretation, that is then involved; and, if such enforcement be such as to deprive the individual of his rights, adequate redress may be had in the federal courts under the Fourteenth Amendment.[3]

The Supreme Court has always declined to pass upon the constitutionality of an act unless that point is necessarily involved in the particular case presented for adjudication.[4] The jurisdiction and duties of the court are

[1] The latest case emphasizing the difference between a case coming from a circuit court and coming on a writ of error from a state court is Laclede Gas Light Company v. Murphy, 170 U. S. 78, 100.

[2] Soon Hing v. Crowley, 113 U. S. 703, 710; Yick Wo v. Hopkins, 118 U. S. 356, 366; Railroad and Telephone Cos. v. Board of Equalizers, 85 Fed. Rep. 302, 317.

[3] *Ibid;* see also Williams v. Mississippi, 170 U. S. 213, 224; Neal v. Delaware, 103 U. S. 370, 394; Ex parte Virginia, 100 U. S. 339, 347; Henderson v. Mayor of N. Y., 92 U. S. 259, 268.

[4] Powell v. Brunswick County, 150 U. S. 433, 441; Egan v. Hart, 165 U. S. 188, 194; Castillo v. McConnico, 168 U. S. 674, 679.

strictly judicial. It will under no circumstances express its opinion upon hypothetical cases or feigned controversies.[1] It will not furnish advisory opinions, even if requested by Congress or the Executive, and notwithstanding that the question submitted may be *publici juris.* In 1793 President Washington propounded to the Supreme Court twenty-nine questions of international law which were perplexing the government, and which public interests demanded should be promptly and authoritatively determined; but the Justices respectfully declined to answer the questions, and held that the court could only give opinions in litigated controversies duly brought before it.[2] Accordingly, a case must always show that there is an adversary contest in good faith, and that the party challenging the constitutionality of a state statute has a property or personal interest to protect in so doing. The court will not anticipate questions of constitutional law, however desirable it may be to settle them. It matters not that the statute might be construed as to some one else in some other case so as to cause it to violate the amendment.[3] A litigant's right is limited to the inquiry whether, in the case which he presents, the effect of the statute in question is to deprive him of individual liberty or of some constitutional right of property. That the statute may deny the right to some third party is immaterial.[4]

It is frequently a question of great difficulty and deli-

---

[1] Bartemeyer *v.* Iowa, 18 Wall. 129, 134, 135.

[2] Carson's History Supreme Court U. S. ch. xi. p. 164; This Country of Ours, by B. Harrison, 304; Gordon *v.* United States, 2 Wall. 561; s. c. 117 U. S. 697; United States *v.* Old Settlers, 148 U. S. 427, 466.

[3] California *v.* Pacific Railroad Co., 127 U. S. 1, 28.

[4] Giles *v.* Little, 134 U. S. 645, 650; Ludeling *v.* Chaffe, 143 U. S. 301, 305; Northern Pacific Railroad *v.* Patterson, 154 U. S. 130, 134; Conde *v.* York, 168 U. S. 642, 648.

cacy to determine whether a state enactment is constitutional, and it is only in a clear case that the federal
courts will nullify it. The federal courts always hesi-
tate to interfere with the legislative branch of the state
governments.[1] If there be any presumption at all, it is
that the statute is valid, and the burden of showing the
contrary must be upon those who assail its constitutionality. The authoritative statement of the rule is in this
language: "But in determining whether the legislature, in
a particular enactment, has passed the limits of its constitutional authority, every reasonable presumption must be
indulged in favor of the validity of such enactment. It
must be regarded as valid, unless it can be clearly shown
to be in conflict with the constitution. It is a well-settled
rule of constitutional exposition, that if a statute may or
may not be, according to circumstances, within the limits
of legislative authority, the existence of the circumstances
necessary to support it must be presumed."[2]

This rule of presumption, however, has certain exceptions. It is sometimes necessary for the State to prove
the facts which sustain an apparently arbitrary exercise of
power. A statute may be *prima facie* unconstitutional.
This was ruled last year in the Covington Turnpike case.[3]
For example, a statute may deny or interfere with interstate trade in a recognized article of commerce, and it may
be incumbent upon the State to show affirmatively sufficient
reasons for the exclusion of the commodity.[4] A statute
may well be held not to conflict with the Fourteenth
Amendment so far as it relates to local affairs, taxation,

[1] Fletcher *v.* Peck, 6 Cranch, 87, 128.
[2] Sweet *v.* Rechel, 159 U. S. 380, 392; see also Presser *v.* Illinois, 116 U. S. 252, 269.
[3] Covington &c. Turnpike Co. *v.* Sandford, 164 U. S. 578, 595.
[4] Minnesota *v.* Barber, 136 U. S. 313, 319.

etc.; and yet the same statute, if interfering with or taxing interstate trade, may conflict with the commerce clause.[1]  The questions, and, therefore, the presumptions, are different.

At every term of the Supreme Court, the argument is advanced that, within the province of local affairs, the powers of the state legislatures are supreme, and that the federal courts cannot interfere with the discretion or acts of the law-making power of " sovereign " States.  Of course, it must be evident that, if any such doctrine obtained, all that would be needed to deprive a man of liberty or property in violation of the Constitution would be the fiat of a legislature.  " The administration of justice would be an empty form, an idle ceremony.  Judges would sit to execute legislative judgments and decrees; not to declare the law, or to administer the justice of the country."[2]  The Supreme Court has repeatedly declared the power and the duty of the federal judiciary to look at the substance of legislation irrespective of its form or pretense, and to determine for itself whether such legislation does or does not interfere with constitutional rights; but, nevertheless, it is compelled in case after case to reiterate and emphasize the rule and to explain at length what surely ought now to be considered as settled in constitutional law. Nowhere do we find a more vigorous and forcible statement of the doctrine than in the Nebraska Maximum Rate cases,[3] decided at the present term, in which Mr. Justice Harlan, delivering the unanimous opinion of the court,

[1] Telegraph Co. *v.* Texas, 105 U. S. 460, 466; Ratterman *v.* Western Union Tel. Co., 127 U. S. 411, 424; Western Union Tel. Co. *v.* Pennsylvania, 128 U. S. 39; W. U. Telegraph Co. *v.* Alabama, 132 U. S. 472, 475; Schollenberger *v.* Pennsylvania, 171 U. S. 1, 19.

[2] Webster in Dartmouth College *v.* Woodward, 4 Wheat. 518, 582.

[3] Smyth *v.* Ames, 169 U. S. 466, 527.

said: " But despite the difficulties that confessedly attend the proper solution of such questions, the court cannot shrink from the duty to determine whether it be true, as alleged, that the Nebraska statute invades or destroys rights secured by the supreme law of the land. No one, we take it, will contend that a state enactment is in harmony with that law simply because the legislature of the State has declared such to be the case; for that would make the state legislature the final judge of the validity of its enactment, although the Constitution of the United States and the laws made in pursuance thereof are the supreme law of the land, anything in the constitution or laws of any State to the contrary notwithstanding. Art. VI. The idea that any legislature, state or Federal, can conclusively determine for the people and for the courts that what it enacts in the form of law, or what it authorizes its agents to do, is consistent with the fundamental law, is in opposition to the theory of our institutions. The duty rests upon all courts, federal and state, when their jurisdiction is properly invoked, to see to it that no right secured by the supreme law of the land is impaired or destroyed by legislation. This function and duty of the judiciary distinguishes the American system from all other systems of government. The perpetuity of our institutions and the liberty which is enjoyed under them depend, in no small degree, upon the power given the judiciary to declare null and void all legislation that is clearly repugnant to the supreme law of the land."

There is another rule of practical importance in construing statutes claimed to be in conflict with the Fourteenth Amendment. It often happens that only a part of the statute is assailed as unconstitutional; and it is then necessary to determine what effect the invalidity of that part will have upon the whole statute. The rule is that the same statute may be in part constitutional and in part unconstitutional, and that the constitutional part may be upheld and given effect provided the unconstitutional part is wholly independent and can be separated from the remaining portions of the act. But if the valid and invalid parts are mutually connected and interdependent, or if it be reasonable to assume that the legislature intended that all the provisions should take effect as a whole and would not have passed the residue independently, then the whole act must fall with the unconstitutional parts. In the Income Tax cases, Chief Justice Fuller said: " It is elementary that the same statute may be in part constitutional and in part unconstitutional, and if the parts are wholly independent of each other, that which is constitutional may stand while that which is unconstitutional will be rejected."[1] He also quoted with approval the language of Mr. Justice Matthews in the Virginia Coupon cases:[2] " It is undoubtedly true that there may be cases where one part of a statute may be enforced as constitutional, and another be declared inoperative and void, because unconstitutional; but these are cases where the parts are so distinctly separable that each can stand alone, and where the court is able to see, and to declare, that the intention of the legislature was that the part pronounced valid should be enforceable, even though the other part should fail. To hold otherwise would be to substitute for the law intended by the legislature one they may never have been willing by itself to enact." In a doubtful case, it

[1] Pollock *v.* Farmers Loan & Trust Co., 158 U. S. 601, 635.
[2] 114 U. S. 269, 304.

is always safer to set aside the statute than to attempt to eliminate the invalid provisions, for any such attempt must involve the risk of making a new law. To uphold part may confer upon a statute a positive operation beyond the legislative intent, and beyond what any one can say the legislature would have enacted if it had been aware of the illegality of the unconstitutional parts. Such action is not within the judicial province. It is not construction, but legislation, and ordaining as law what the legislative branch of the state or national government might have done, but has not done.[1]

Extreme or absurd contentions often lead to the enunciation of doctrines which greatly embarrass the consideration of cases involving substantial invasions of individual liberty. The Fourteenth Amendment was thought by certain women to have greatly extended their civil and political rights. In the second case arising under the amendment, decided the same day as the Slaughter House cases, Mrs. Myra Bradwell sought to review, by writ of error, a decision of the Supreme Court of Illinois, denying her the right to practice law, as an attorney, at the bar of that State.[2] And, a short time thereafter, a Mrs. Virginia Minor[3] attempted to sue a registrar of voters in the State of Missouri for refusing to allow her to vote at a general election. In both instances, however, the Supreme Court of the United States held that, although women were clearly citizens of the United States by virtue of the amendment, nevertheless neither the right to vote nor the right to practice law was a privilege or immunity

[1] United States *v.* Reese, 92 U. S. 214, 221; Trade-Mark Cases, 100 U. S. 82, 99; Spraigue *v.* Thompson, 118 U. S. 90, 95.
[2] Bradwell *v.* The State, 16 Wall. 130.
[3] Minor *v.* Happersett, 21 Wall. 162.

belonging to citizens of the United States. Not discouraged by these early decisions, Miss Belva Lockwood, a few years ago, made application for a writ of mandamus from the Supreme Court of the United States to the Supreme Court of Virginia, to compel her admission to the bar of that State as an attorney and counsellor, asserting that the Code of Virginia had been so construed as to exclude her upon the sole ground that she was a woman.[1] Her application was denied.

These decisions were not without importance. They announced that the Fourteenth Amendment did not add to the privileges or immunities of a citizen of the United States, but simply furnished an additional guaranty for such as already existed, and prohibited the States from abridging them.

The Fourteenth Amendment was invoked, at an early date, in behalf of the Chinese. They were held to be covered by the word " persons," which was employed in a much broader sense than the word " citizens " used in the preceding sentence of the same section of the amendment. In one of the first cases, Mr. Justice Field, sitting in the Circuit Court of the District of California, released on *habeas corpus* twenty-two women of the Chinese race, who were prohibited from landing at San Francisco under a statute obviously directed against people of that nationality.[2] Subsequently, in Yick Wo v. Hopkins, a municipal ordinance, conferring upon certain officials power to grant or withhold consent to the operation of laundries in wooden buildings, was declared void on the ground that it conferred upon those officers a purely arbitrary power,

---

[1] *In re* Lockwood, Petitioner, 154 U. S. 116.
[2] *In re* Ah Fong, 3 Sawy. 144, 157; Ah Kow v. Nunan, 5 Sawy. 552, 560. *In re* Tiburcio Parrott, 1 Fed. Rep. 481, 497.

— not a discretion in any legal sense reviewable by the courts.[1] It is interesting to compare this case with the earlier decisions in Barbier v. Connolly[2] and Soon Hing v. Crowley,[3] in which ordinances prescribing that laundries should be closed during certain hours of the night were upheld. The distinction between the two classes of cases is vital. In the one class, the ordinance in question was a reasonable exercise of the police power of the State, applying equally to all persons of whatever race in the same class. In the other instance, it was an arbitrary and unreasonable interference with individual liberty and intended to discriminate, and, in fact, discriminating, solely against the Chinese.

It was eighteen years before it was decided that a corporation was a person within the purview of the first section of the Fourteenth Amendment. This was first distinctly held by the Supreme Court in the case of Santa Clara Co. v. Southern Pacific Railroad, argued in January and decided in May, 1886.[4] And the point was reiterated at the last term in the following language: "It is now settled that corporations are persons within the meaning of the constitutional provisions forbidding the deprivation of property without due process of law, as well as a denial of the equal protection of the laws."[5] These decisions emphasized the difference

---

1 Yick Wo v. Hopkins, 118 U. S. 356; In re Hoover, 30 Fed. Rep. 51, 54. United States v. Wong Dep Ken, 57 Fed. Rep. 206, 212.

2 Barbier v. Connolly, 113 U. S. 27.

3 Soon Hing v. Crowley, 113 U. S. 703.

4 Santa Clara Co. v. South. Pac. Railroad, 118 U. S. 394, 396; s. c. below, 18 Fed. Rep. 385.

5 Covington &c. Turnpike Co. v. Sandford, 164 U. S. 578, 592; see also United States v. Northwestern Express Co., 164 U. S. 686, 689. In Gulf, Colorado & Santa Fé R'y v. Ellis, 165 U. S. 150, 154, Mr. Justice Brewer said: "The rights and securities guaranteed to persons by that instrument cannot be disregarded in respect to these artificial entities called corporations any more than

between "citizen" and "person." But it is proper to observe that corporations are not entitled to the privileges and immunities of citizens of the United States which we have just discussed. They are persons but not citizens. Moreover, the Santa Clara decision applied only to a domestic corporation of the State whose legislation was assailed as unconstitutional. In the subsequent case of Philadelphia Fire Association *v.* New York,[1] it was determined that a State could prescribe whatever conditions it saw fit for permitting a foreign insurance company to transact business within its limits, even to the extent of total exclusion, although it could not exclude an individual. This power does not, however, apply to agencies of the general government nor to corporations engaged in interstate commerce. In the language of Mr. Justice Field, in Pembina Mining Co. *v.* Pennsylvania,[2] "The States may, therefore, require for the admission within their limits of the corporations of other States, or of any number of them, such conditions as they may choose, without acting in conflict with the concluding provision of the first section of the Fourteenth Amendment. . . . The only limitation upon this power of the State to exclude a foreign corporation from doing business within its limits, or hiring offices for that purpose, or to exact conditions for allowing the corporation to do business or hire offices there, arises where the corporation is in the employ of the federal government, or where its business is strictly commerce, interstate or foreign. The control of such commerce, being in the federal government, is

---

they can be in respect to the individuals who are the equitable owners of the property belonging to such corporations. A State has no more power to deny to corporations the equal protection of the law than it has to individual citizens."

[1] 119 U. S. 110, 119.         [2] 125 U. S. 181, 189.

not to be restricted by state authority." Until the foreign corporation has, by conforming to the requirements
imposed by a State as a prerequisite, received permission to
do business therein, it is not a person within the jurisdiction of that State and entitled as such to equality before
its laws. This power to exclude foreign corporations is of
increasing importance, and, I believe, the commerce clause
of the Constitution will have to be more broadly enforced
for the protection of corporations engaged in interstate
commerce.

When prejudice in the South ran high against the lately
emancipated negro, and the broad and beneficent provisions of the Fourteenth Amendment were less thoroughly
understood than at present, attempts were made in many
States to exclude colored men from juries. Where, however, either in pursuance of a legislative enactment or
because of the arbitrary ruling of a judge, negroes were
denied the right to participate in jury service, convictions
secured against negroes by juries from which men of their
own race were thus excluded were set aside. The Supreme
Court said : " A denial to citizens of the African race, because of their color, of the right or privilege accorded to
white citizens, of participating, as jurors, in the administration of justice, is a discrimination against the former
inconsistent with the amendment, and within the power of
Congress, by appropriate legislation, to prevent; that to
compel a colored man to submit to a trial before a jury
drawn from a panel from which was excluded, because of
their color, every man of his race, however well qualified
by education and character to discharge the functions
of jurors, was a denial of the equal protection of the
laws." [1]

---

[1] Neal *v.* Delaware, 103 U. S. 370, 386.

It was shown in the first lecture of this series, that the Joint Reconstruction Committee of Congress intended that section 1 of the Fourteenth Amendment should have the broadest scope, and that it should constitute a universal rule applicable to all cases in which an attempt was made to deny, infringe, or abridge the fundamental rights and liberties of the individual, whatever his race.[1] We shall now consider more in detail the subdivisions of this section.

The first sentence provides that "All persons born or naturalized in the United States, and subject to the jurisdiction thereof, are citizens of the United States and of the State wherein they reside." This provision changed the origin of federal citizenship.[2] Prior thereto, no one could be a citizen of the United States unless a citizen of a State according to the state constitution or laws. He is now a citizen wholly irrespective of state legislation, and simply by reason of birth in the United States or naturalization under federal laws. There is, therefore, a two-fold citizenship under our system; namely, federal citizenship and state citizenship.[3] The qualifications of citizenship under state laws may be different from those required under the Federal Constitution, and there are rights as citizens of the United States which do not appertain to state citizenship.

The phrase " subject to the jurisdiction thereof " in this clause has occasioned considerable difficulty. If the parents of a child born in the United States were citizens, the meaning was clear. But what was to be the status of a child born in the United States of Indians, or of Chinese

---

[1] *Supra*, p. 22–27.

[2] *Supra*, p. 19.

[3] Slaughter-House Cases, 16 Wall. 36, 73 ; United States *v.* Cruikshank, 92 U. S. 542, 549.

or other alien parentage? In the leading case of Elk *v.* Wilkins,[1] it was decided that an Indian born a member of one of our Indian tribes still existing and recognized as such, even though he had voluntarily separated himself from his people and taken up his residence among the white citizens, but who did not appear to have been naturalized or taxed, was not born in the United States " subject to the jurisdiction thereof," and was not a citizen. He was born " subject to the jurisdiction" of his tribe. This decision left in uncertainty the legal status of all others born in the United States of alien parentage. Was their citizenship to be determined by the common-law principle of locality of birth, or was the rule of the civil law as to the allegiance of the parents to control? This question was not settled until a few weeks ago, thirty years after the amendment was adopted, thus showing how slowly constitutional law develops in the life of a nation. The common-law rule has been finally affirmed by the Supreme Court in the recent case of the United States *v.* Wong Kim Ark.[2] The Supreme Court held that a child born in this country of Chinese parents domiciled here is a citizen of the United States by virtue of the locality of his birth. The whole subject is discussed at length in the opinions in this case. The effect of this decision is to make citizens of the United States by virtue of the Fourteenth Amendment all persons born in the United States of alien parents permanently domiciled and residing here, except the children of the diplomatic representatives of foreign powers ; and, therefore, a male child born here of Chinese subjects is now eligible to the office of President, although his parents could not be naturalized under our laws.

[1] 112 U. S. 94, 98.
[2] 169 U. S. 649, 652, by Mr. Justice Gray; see also the interesting dissenting opinion of Chief Justice Fuller at pp. 705 *et seq.*

The second sentence of section 1 provides that "No State shall make or enforce any law which shall abridge the privileges or immunities of citizens of the United States."

This language presents a question of the greatest personal interest to every citizen. What are the privileges and immunities of citizens of the United States which are thus not to be abridged by the States? It must surely be those privileges and immunities which attach to citizens of the United States *as such,* and not as citizens of any particular State or Territory embraced within the Union; it must be those privileges and immunities which belong to them as citizens under the government established by the Constitution of the United States and regulated by the laws of Congress — the privileges and immunities that James Wilson would have characterized as "federal liberty." [1] Among these privileges and immunities are the fundamental rights of the individual which are mentioned in the first eight amendments to the Constitution.[2] These early amendments are known as the Federal Bill of Rights. They secure, as respects the federal government, the free exercise of religion; freedom of speech and of the press; peaceable assemblage and petition; keeping and bearing arms; immunity against the quartering of soldiers in time of peace; security against unreasonable searches and seizures; presentment and indictment by a grand jury in case of accusation of infamous crime; security against being put twice in jeopardy and being forced to testify

---

[1] Wilson's Works (ed. 1896), p. 539.

[2] The first eight amendments apply only to the federal government and not to the States. Livingston *v.* Moore, 7 Pet. 469, 551; Holmes *v.* Jennison, 14 Pet. 540, 582; The Justices *v.* Murray, 9 Wall. 274, 278; Walker *v.* Sauvinet, 92 U. S. 90, 92; United States *v.* Cruikshank, 92 U. S. 542, 552; Presser *v.* Illinois, 116 U. S. 252, 265; Eilenbecker *v.* Plymouth County, 134 U. S. 31, 34.

against one's self; due process of law; compensation for private property taken for public use; speedy public trial; confrontment with witnesses; compulsory process for obtaining witnesses and the assistance of counsel; trial by jury in suits at common law; and immunity against excessive bail, excessive fines, and unusual punishments.

Unless "the privileges and immunities of citizens of the United States" are derived from the Constitution of the United States, it is difficult to see from what source they are derived. They cannot have their origin in the constitutions or laws of the respective States, because those constitutions and laws create or declare the privileges and immunities of their own citizens, not of citizens of the United States. Moreover, the privileges and immunities created by the constitution and laws of one State are not the same as those created by the constitution and laws of another. They might differ in every State. If the true interpretation be that these privileges and immunities are such as the States grant, not only may the privileges and immunities protected by the Fourteenth Amendment be inconsistent with each other, but the protection afforded may be continually varying on account of changes in the constitutions and laws of the different States. As was well said by the Supreme Court in one of the earliest cases construing the amendment: "In regard to that amendment counsel for the plaintiff in this court truly says that there are certain privileges and immunities which belong to a citizen of the United States as such; otherwise it would be nonsense for the Fourteenth Amendment to prohibit a State from abridging them." [1]

There can be no reasonable doubt that the Reconstruction Committee understood and contemplated that among

[1] Mr. Justice Miller in Bradwell v. The State, 16 Wall. 130, 138.

the privileges and immunities they were seeking to protect against invasion or abridgment by the States were included those set forth in the first eight amendments.[1]   The Committee's report declared that it was necessary to have such "changes of the organic law as shall determine the civil rights and privileges of all citizens in all parts of the republic." In submitting the amendment to the Senate on behalf of the Committee, Senator Howard presented what he said were " the views and the motives which influenced that committee . . . and the ends it aims to accomplish." Speaking of the privileges and immunities of citizens of the United States, he said,[2] " We may gather some intimation of what probably will be the opinion of the judiciary by referring to a case adjudged many years ago." He then quoted at length from Corfield *v.* Coryell, 4 Wash. C. C. Rep. 371, 380, and proceeded to say: " Such is the character of the privileges and immunities spoken of in the second section of the fourth article of the Constitution. To these privileges and immunities, whatever they may be, — for they are not and cannot be fully defined in their entire extent and precise nature, — to these should be added the personal rights guaranteed and secured by the first eight amendments of the Constitution: such as the freedom of speech and the press; the right of the people peaceably to assemble and petition the govern. ment for a redress of grievances, a right appertaining to each and all the people; the right to keep and bear arms; the right to be exempted from the quartering of

---

[1] " It is never to be forgotten that, in the construction of the language of the Constitution here relied on, as indeed in all other instances where construction becomes necessary, we are to place ourselves as nearly as possible in the condition of the men who framed that instrument." Mr. Justice Miller in *Ex parte* Bain, 121 U. S. 1, 12.

[2] Cong. Globe, 39th Cong. 1st Sess., pt. 3, pp. 2764–2765.

soldiers in a house without the consent of the owner; the right to be exempt from unreasonable searches and seizures, and from any search or seizure except by virtue of a warrant issued upon a formal oath or affidavit; the right of an accused person to be informed of the nature of the accusation against him, and his right to be tried by an impartial jury of the vicinage; and also the right to be secure against excessive bail and against cruel and unusual punishments." After further discussion, Senator Howard continued: "The great object of the first section of this amendment is, therefore, to restrain the power of the States and compel them at all times to respect these great fundamental guaranties."

From these statements as to the declared purpose of the framers, officially and authoritatively made to the Senate on behalf of the Reconstruction Committee, it would seem to be entirely clear that the intention was that the essential rights of life, liberty and property distinctly recognized in the Constitution and in the first eight amendments should, by the Fourteenth Amendment, be made the indisputable and secure possession of every citizen of the United States, beyond the power of any State to abridge. Yet the result of judicial interpretation has been almost to uphold the contention that the clause in question is practically meaningless and superfluous, and that the States may abridge and deny many of the rights expressly recognized in and by the first eight amendments, notwithstanding the avowed purpose and intention of the Reconstruction Committee and of Congress.[1] But although

---

[1] Indeed, the true purpose and scope of this provision have been overlooked or disregarded. Thus Judge Cooley in his Principles of Const. Law, 258, says : "It may well be questioned whether the provision just considered was necessary. It is certainly not clear that there can exist any privilege or immunity of a citizen of the United States which, independent of the fourteenth amendment, is not beyond state control."

the decisions of the Supreme Court tend to support the view that the States may invade and deny many of the privileges and immunities of United States citizens thus mentioned, except in so far as they are protected by the provision requiring due process of law and equal laws, it cannot be said that the question has ever been adequately presented to the court or decided by it. The power of the States to abridge these great rights of citizens can never be conceded until the court shall expressly so decide in a case involving the exact question and adequately argued.

The point that the privileges and immunities of citizens of the United States include the rights protected by the first eight amendments was made in the case of the Chicago Anarchists in 1887, — Spies *v.* Illinois, — by Mr. John Randolph Tucker, a distinguished advocate and constitutional lawyer.[1] Chief Justice Waite mentioned the contention in the opinion of the court, but it was found unnecessary to decide the question. In April, 1892, Mr. Justice Field — dissenting in O'Neil *v.* Vermont — said that, after much reflection, he thought that the privileges and immunities of citizens of the United States were such as had their recognition in or guaranty from the Constitution of the United States. "This definition," he added, "is supported by reference to the history of the first ten amendments to the Constitution, and of the amendments which followed the late Civil War."[2] At the same time Mr. Justice Harlan, on behalf of himself and Mr. Justice

---

[1] Spies *v.* Illinois, 123 U. S. 131, 150, 170. The question was raised also in the brief of B. F. Butler in this case.

[2] 144 U. S. 323, 361; see also Hodgson *v.* Vermont, 168 U. S. 262, 272; and compare also the earlier cases of Bartemeyer *v.* Iowa, 18 Wall. 129; United States *v.* Reese, 92 U. S. 214; United States *v.* Cruikshank, 92 U. S. 542; Hurtado *v.* California, 110 U. S. 516; and Presser *v.* Illinois, 116 U. S. 252.

Brewer, said : "I fully concur with Mr. Justice Field, that since the adoption of the Fourteenth Amendment, no one of the fundamental rights of life, liberty or property, recognized and guaranteed by the Constitution of the United States, can be denied or abridged by a State in respect to any person within its jurisdiction. These rights are, principally, enumerated in the earlier amendments of the Constitution. They were deemed so vital to the safety and security of the people, that the absence from the Constitution, adopted by the convention of 1787, of express guarantees of them, came very near defeating the acceptance of that instrument by the requisite number of States."[1] In the Kemmler case, which went up from the New York Court of Appeals and involved the constitutionality of the law providing for the execution of condemned murderers by electricity, the validity of which was challenged on the ground that it inflicted a cruel and unusual punishment, Chief Justice Fuller intimated that it was not and could not be contended that the Eighth Amendment applied to the States.[2] An examination of the record in the Kemmler case and in the other cases which suggest that the first eight amendments are not applicable to the States since the adoption of the Fourteenth Amendment, will show that the real point was either not made or was inadequately presented, and that the cases turned principally upon the construction of the requirement of due process of law. Of course, before the adoption of the Fourteenth Amendment, it was well settled that the first

[1] O'Neil v. Vermont, 144 U. S. 323, 370.

[2] In re Kemmler, 136 U. S. 436, 446; see also Thorington v. Montgomery, 147 U. S. 490, 492. The remarks of Chief Justice Fuller in this case were clearly unnecessary for the decision of the cause and could hardly be considered as expressing his settled judgment. The point was again raised but not decided in Craemer v. Washington State, 164 U. S. 704; and in Krug v. Washington State, 164 U. S. 704.

eight amendments applied to the national government alone.[1]

In the famous case of Hurtado v. California, decided in 1884, the privilege and immunity conferred by the Fifth Amendment — i. e., presentment or indictment by a grand jury in a capital case — was merely mentioned in the assignment of errors, and the constitutional point we are now considering was not argued in the briefs of counsel and was not even mentioned in the opinion of Mr. Justice Matthews.[2]   This Hurtado case was a prosecution for murder under a California statute which authorized the institution of such proceedings by information and without any presentment or indictment by a grand jury. The dissenting opinion of Mr. Justice Harlan would probably have prevailed if the clear intention of the framers of the Fourteenth Amendment had been called to the attention of the court; but the dissenting opinion also was devoted entirely to construing the meaning and scope of the phrase " due process of law " without reference to the Fifth Amendment.[3]

It is impracticable to do more at this time than to suggest the point.  A full statement of the argument on either side would require very much more time than we can possibly give to its consideration during the course of these lectures.  It is, however, important to bear in mind that this great question has yet to be squarely decided by the Supreme Court in some case properly rais-

[1] Eilenbecker v. Plymouth County, 134 U. S. 31, 34, and cases cited.

[2] 110 U. S. 516, 519.

[3] Hurtado v. California, 110 U. S. 516, 538. In this case the point was barely suggested in the brief of counsel; but was in no sense properly presented to the attention of the court.  In the briefs in the case of In re Kemmler, 136 U. S. 436, the point was merely touched upon; in O'Neil v. Vermont, 144 U. S. 323, it was not raised; and in Hodgson v. Vermont, 168 U. S. 262, the discussion turned rather upon a question of procedure.

ing the point and fully presenting it in connection with the intention of the framers of the Fourteenth Amendment. To this intention of the framers, as evidenced by the extracts which have been read to you, not the slightest reference has heretofore been made in any case, so far as I can ascertain. When the proper case arises, the question ought to be treated as still open, and we may hope that the inestimable and priceless individual rights guaranteed by the first eight amendments will, in the main at least, be held to be beyond the power of any State to abridge or deny. There are many of those rights which the provision " due process of law " does not include.

# LECTURE III.

## OF DUE PROCESS OF LAW.

THE phrase "due process of law" antedates the establishment of our institutions, and is endeared to our race by antiquity and the noblest historical associations. It embodies one of the broadest and most far-reaching guaranties of personal and property rights.[1] Indeed, no words in our language signify more in respect of the rights and privileges of the individual than "due process of law."[2] The third clause of section 1 of the Fourteenth Amendment provides: "Nor shall any State deprive any

[1] Mr. Justice Johnson, speaking in Bank of Columbia v. Okely, 4 Wheat. 235, 244, decided in 1819, said: "As to the words from Magna Charta, incorporated into the constitution of Maryland, after volumes spoken and written with a view to their exposition, the good sense of mankind has at length settled down to this: that they were intended to secure the individual from the arbitrary exercise of the powers of government, unrestrained by the established principles of private rights and distributive justice." And Judge Cooley, Const. Lim.* 355, said: "While every man has a right to require that his own controversies shall be judged by the same rules which are applied in the controversies of his neighbors, the whole community is also entitled, at all times, to demand the protection of the ancient principles which shield private rights against arbitrary interference, even though such interference may be under a rule impartial in its operation. It is not the partial nature of the rule, so much as its arbitrary and unusual character, which condemns it as unknown to the law of the land."

[2] The term is one of those grand "monuments showing the victorious progress of the race in securing to men the blessings of civilization under the reign of just and equal laws, so that, in the famous language of the Massachusetts Bill of Rights, the government of the commonwealth 'may be a government of laws and not of men.' For, the very idea that one man may be compelled to hold his life, or the means of living, or any material right essential to the enjoyment of life, at the mere will of another, seems to be intolerable in any country where freedom prevails, as being the essence of slavery itself." Mr. Justice Matthews in Yick Wo v. Hopkins, 118 U. S. 356, 370.

person of life, liberty, or property without due process of law."

This pledge of individual rights and liberties is in the Constitution of the United States in a twofold sense : in the Fifth Amendment it is a limitation upon the powers of the national government ; in the Fourteenth Amendment it is a limitation upon the powers of the States.[1] Without venturing to attempt any specific definition,[2] it may be said that the general scope of the provision requiring due process of law is to secure to every person, whether citizen or alien, those fundamental and inalienable rights of life, liberty and property which are inherent in every man, and to protect all against the arbitrary exercise of governmental powers in violation and disregard of established principles of distributive justice. This protection is the object and the essence of free government, and without it true liberty cannot exist.

If there were time, it would be interesting to trace the historical origin of this term "due process of law," and the development of its meaning and scope. At first, the words undoubtedly related to those beneficent rules of procedure which had been framed to protect and shield the individual in his personal and property rights ; but at the time of the American Revolution they had come

[1] Davidson *v.* New Orleans, 96 U. S. 97, 101; Hallinger *v.* Davis, 146 U. S. 314, 319.

[2] "This phrase, 'due process of law,' has always been one requiring construction; and, as this court observed long ago, never has been defined, and probably never can be defined, so as to draw a clear and distinct line, applicable to all cases, between proceedings which are by due process of law and those which are not." Mr. Justice Miller in Freeland *v.* Williams, 131 U. S. 405, 418. In Holden *v.* Hardy, 169 U. S. 366, 389, Mr. Justice Brown said: "This court has never attempted to define with precision the words 'due process of law,' nor is it necessary to do so in this case. It is sufficient to say that there are certain immutable principles of justice which inhere in the very idea of free government which no member of the Union may disregard."

to be regarded as comprehending also the famous phrase "the law of the land." The two terms are now treated as synonymous, although "due process of law" is the more comprehensive.

The words "due process of law" mean infinitely more under our system of government than they ever did or do now in England. There the provision restricts only the king; it leaves Parliament unrestrained. "The concessions of Magna Charta were wrung from the king as guaranties against the oppressions and usurpations of his prerogative. It did not enter into the minds of the barons to provide security against their own body or in favor of the Commons by limiting the power of Parliament. . . . The omnipotence of Parliament over the common law was absolute, even against common right and reason. . . . In this country written constitutions were deemed essential to protect the rights and liberties of the people against the encroachments of power delegated to their governments, and the provisions of Magna Charta were incorporated into Bills of Rights. They were limitations upon all the powers of government, legislative as well as executive and judicial." [1]

Under the English system, the rule of Parliament is not restricted by constitutional limitations; and the maxim that "the king can do no wrong" may still prevent redress for spoliation or arbitrary denial of personal rights on the part of the executive. The theory of English constitutional law is entirely different from the theory of the American system.[2] Many English statutes would be nullified by our courts; and much of the legis-

[1] Mr. Justice Matthews in Hurtado *v.* California, 110 U. S. 516, 531.
[2] Lecky, Democracy and Liberty, i. 8, 53; Bryce's American Commonwealth, i. 35.

lation relating to Ireland would be declared unconstitutional in the United States. One hundred and five years
ago, Mr. Justice Wilson in Chisholm *v.* Georgia[1] compared our form of government with the British, and said
that the latter was but a despotism of Parliament; and
ninety years later Mr. Justice Miller in United States *v.*
Lee[2] again set forth the vast difference in the essential
character of the two systems of government, and showed
that in this country no man is so high that he is above
the law; that no officer of the national or state governments may set that law at defiance with impunity; and
that our courts of justice are established, not only to
decide upon the controverted rights of citizens as against
each other, but also to pass upon rights in controversy
between them and the government.

The twenty-ninth chapter of Magna Charta, which,
Blackstone says,[3] " alone would have merited the title that
it bears, of the Great Charter," secured every freeman in
the undisturbed enjoyment of his life, his liberty and his
property, unless forfeited by the judgment of his peers or
the law of the land. The Petition of Right in the third
year of the reign of Charles I. prayed " that freemen be
imprisoned or detained only by the law of the land, or by
due process of law, and not by the King's special command without any charge." This was, I believe, the first
use of the term " due process of law " in any of the great
constitutional measures affecting the rights and liberties
of the people of our race.[4]

No statement of the general meaning of the phrases
" due process of law " and " the law of the land " is more
often quoted than that given by Mr. Webster in the

---

[1] 2 Dall. 419, 457, 460.  [2] 106 U. S. 196, 205.
[3] 4 Bl. Com. 424.  [4] Cooley, Const. Lim. * 351.

Dartmouth College case.[1]   It defines the term in its relation to procedure as well as to substantive rights.   Mr.
Webster said: "By the law of the land is most clearly
intended the general law; a law, which hears before it
condemns; which proceeds upon inquiry, and renders
judgment only after trial.   The meaning is, that every
citizen shall hold his life, liberty, property, and immunities, under the protection of the general rules which govern
society.   Everything which may pass under the form of
an enactment, is not, therefore, to be considered the law
of the land."   Judge Story's definition is succinct and
accurate: "Due process of law in each particular case
means such an exertion of the powers of government as
the settled maxims of law permit and sanction, and under
such safeguards for the protection of individual rights
as those maxims prescribe for the class of cases to which
the one being dealt with belongs."[2]   An admirable and
learned discussion of the meaning of "due process of law"
by Mr. Justice Curtis will be found in Murray's Lessee *v.*
Hoboken Land and Improvement Co.[3]

It is important to appreciate that "due process of law"
is process according to the system of law obtaining in
each State, and not according to any general law of the
United States.[4]   In ascertaining and determining such law,
regard should be had to the usages, public policy and modes
of proceeding existing in the respective States, and these

[1] Dartmouth College *v.* Woodward, 4 Wheat. 518, 581.

[2] Story on Const. 5th ed. § 1945.

[3] 18 How. 272, 276.   The meaning of the phrase "due process of law" will be
found discussed in the following cases: Kennard *v.* Louisiana, 92 U. S. 480, 481;
Davidson *v.* New Orleans, 96 U. S. 97, 101; *Ex parte* Wall, 107 U. S. 265, 288;
Hagar *v.* Reclamation District No. 108, 111 U. S. 701, 708; Missouri Pacific Rail-
way Co. *v.* Humes, 115 U. S. 512, 519; Freeland *v.* Williams, 131 U. S. 405, 418;
Hallinger *v.* Davis, 146 U. S. 314, 317; Holden *v.* Hardy, 169 U. S. 366, 384, 389.

[4] Walker *v.* Sauvinet, 92 U. S. 90, 93; Missouri *v.* Lewis, 101 U. S. 22, 31;
Hurtado *v.* California, 110 U. S. 516, 535.

should control unless shown to be wholly unsuited to the subject matter. No violation of due process of law is involved when the law is executed according to the customary forms and established usages of the particular State, or in subordination to the principles which underlie them. As was said in a leading case:[1] "The Fourteenth Amendment does not profess to secure to all persons in the United States the benefit of the same laws and the same remedies. Great diversities in these respects may exist in two States separated only by an imaginary line. On one side of this line there may be a right of trial by jury, and on the other side no such right. Each State prescribes its own modes of judicial proceeding."[2] In another case the Supreme Court declared: "In the Fourteenth Amendment, by parity of reason, it refers to that law of the land in each State, which derives its authority from the inherent

[1] Missouri v. Lewis, 101 U. S. 22, 31.

[2] Of course, this right of a State to prescribe its own laws and procedure is subject to limitation. As Comstock, J., said in Wynehamer v. The People, 13 N. Y. 378, 392–393, 395: "To say, as has been suggested, that 'the law of the land,' or 'due process of law,' may mean the very act of legislation which deprives the citizen of his rights, privileges or property, leads to a simple absurdity. The constitution would then mean, that no person shall be deprived of his property or rights, unless the legislature shall pass a law to effectuate the wrong, and this would be throwing the restraint entirely away. The true interpretation of these constitutional phrases is, that where rights are acquired by the citizen under the existing law, there is no power in any branch of the government to take them away; but where they are held contrary to the existing law, or are forfeited by its violation, then they may be taken from him — not by an act of the legislature, but in the due administration of the law itself, before the judicial tribunals of the state. The cause or occasion for depriving the citizen of his supposed rights must be found in the law as it is, or, at least it cannot be *created* by a legislative act which aims at their destruction. Where rights of property are admitted to exist, the legislature cannot say they shall exist no longer; nor will it make any difference, although a process and a tribunal are appointed to execute the sentence. If this is the 'law of the land,' and 'due process of law,' within the meaning of the constitution, then the legislature is omnipotent. It may, under the same interpretation, pass a law to take away liberty or life without a pre-existing cause, appointing judicial and executive agencies to execute its will. Property is placed by the constitution in the same category with liberty and life."

and reserved powers of the State, exerted within the limits of those fundamental principles of liberty and justice which lie at the base of all our civil and political institutions, and the greatest security for which resides in the right of the people to make their own laws, and alter them at their pleasure." [1]  What would be a fair and just provision in one State might be oppressive and grossly arbitrary elsewhere. Each State has its peculiar interests and traditions that may call for distinct legislative policies. The federal courts must recognize that doctrines (e. g., relating to mining, irrigation, levees, etc.) obtaining justly and of necessity in the West and Southwest might be entirely inapplicable and unreasonable if enforced in the States of the East, and laws enacting them might be held to be arbitrary and void as entirely unsuited to conditions in the eastern States. But the question is more legislative than judicial. In each case, the primary inquiry must be as to what is the system of law of the particular State, and whether, according to that law, as adjudged by its courts, the procedure in question is " due process "; and the secondary inquiry must be whether in that process of law, if followed, there is any violation of the fundamental rights secured by the Federal Constitution.[2]

It must also be borne in mind that the Fourteenth Amendment does not confer jurisdiction to correct the erroneous or wilfully improper acts of state officers or courts in violation or disregard of law,[3] and that the

---

[1] Hurtado v. California, 110 U. S. 516, 535. See also Barbier v. Connolly, 113 U. S. 27, 31; In re Kemmler, 136 U. S. 436, 448; In re Converse, 137 U. S. 624, 631; Hodgson v. Vermont, 168 U. S. 262, 273; Green v. Elbert, 27 U. S. App. 325, 328.

[2] Kennard v. Louisiana, 92 U. S. 480, 481; Caldwell v. Texas, 137 U. S. 692, 698; Leeper v. Texas, 139 U. S. 462, 468; McNulty v. California, 149 U. S. 645, 647.

[3] United States v. Cruikshank, 92 U. S. 542, 554; s. c. 1 Woods, 308, 316;

grievance complained of must be sanctioned by a state statute or some other form of state authority. Ordinarily, the Supreme Court will not attempt to review and correct the errors of state tribunals in the general administration of the local laws;[1] but if a law or ordinance be systematically administered so as to violate the Fourteenth Amendment, the court will interfere.[2]

We may now review, although in a manner necessarily hasty and imperfect, some of the leading cases in the Supreme Court which have construed the clause of section 1 of the Fourteenth Amendment, that no State shall deprive any person of life, liberty, or property without due process of law. The cases are very numerous, and most of them may be grouped under four principal heads: (1) the police power; (2) the power of eminent domain or the taking of private property for public use; (3) the power of taxation; and (4) procedure, civil and criminal. These are the great branches of state legislation which particularly affect the personal liberty and the property rights of the individual.

The police power of the States primarily includes such measures as are appropriate or needful to protect the public morals, the public health, or the public safety, and to promote the good order and domestic peace of the

Virginia v. Rives, 100 U. S. 313, 318; United States v. Harris, 106 U. S. 629, 638; Civil Rights Cases, 109 U. S. 3, 11; Logan v. United States, 144 U. S. 263, 290; Green v. Elbert, 27 U. S. App. 325, 328.

[1] Arrowsmith v. Harmoning, 118 U. S. 194, 196; *In re* Converse, 137 U. S. 624, 631; Morley v. Lake Shore Railway Co., 146 U. S. 162, 171; McNulty v. California, 149 U. S. 645, 647; Marchant v. Pennsylvania Railroad, 153 U. S. 380, 385.

[2] Henderson v. Mayor of New York, 92 U. S. 259, 273; Chy Lung v. Freeman, 92 U. S. 275, 279; Neal v. Delaware, 103 U. S. 370; Soon Hing v. Crowley, 113 U. S. 703, 710; Arrowsmith v. Harmoning, 118 U. S. 194, 196; Yick Wo v. Hopkins, 118 U. S. 356, 373; Williams v. Mississippi, 170 U. S. 213, 225.

community.[1] The term is now somewhat loosely used in the most comprehensive sense, *i. e.*, so as to embrace the whole system of internal regulations of personal and property rights. It would tend to avoid confusion if the definition were confined and the use of the term were limited to those restraints upon private rights and liberties which the morals, health, or peace of the community may require, leaving other regulations that have no direct relation to morals, health, or peace, but are authorized as being in the interest of the public at large and as subserving the public policy or welfare of the State, to be characterized as general governmental powers or institutions. Rules observed by the courts in construing statutes relating to public health, morals, or peace have no application to many statutes relating to the use of property, the carrying on of trades or businesses, the exercise of franchises, etc. For example, it has often been declared that a statute under the police power is invalid unless it appear to have a real or substantial relation to the public health, morals, or peace, and that any interference with individual liberty must be justified by some vital necessity and cannot be carried beyond the scope of that necessity; but such considerations apply either remotely or not at all to many statutes, which, under the so-called police power, regulate the charges of railroad, telegraph, or telephone companies, warehousemen, the use of property in common, irrigation, levees, the exercise of the power of eminent domain, etc. Again, it has been repeatedly held that the right to exercise the police power cannot be parted with by the legislature.[2] As Chief Justice Waite said : [3] " No legis-

[1] Barbier *v.* Connolly, 113 U. S. 27, 31; Minnesota *v.* Barber, 136 U. S. 313, 328; Lawton *v.* Steele, 152 U. S. 133, 136; Schollenberger *v.* Pennsylvania, 171 U. S. 1, 15.

[2] " Whatever differences of opinion may exist as to the extent and bounda-

[3] Stone *v.* Mississippi, 101 U. S. 814, 819.

lature can bargain away the public health or the public morals. The people themselves cannot do it, much less their servants." Now, the regulation of charges of railroads is frequently said to be within the police power.[1] Yet a legislature could grant to a railroad the right, for a period of time, to charge certain rates, and such a grant, duly accepted and based on consideration, would be held to be a contract protected by the Constitution.[2] Nevertheless, it might be suggested that such a grant would be a bargaining away of the police power, because the right to regulate charges is said to spring from the police power. Many other examples might be given to show that the loose use of the term "police power" is misleading, and that it would tend to clearness if, as suggested above, the term were confined to statutes or regulations affecting the public health,[3] morals, or peace, and if such other legislation as related to the public welfare or public policy of the State were designated as within those general governmental powers inhe-

ries of the police power, and however difficult it may be to render a satisfactory definition of it, there seems to be no doubt that it does extend to the protection of the lives, health, and property of the citizens, and to the preservation of good order and the public morals. The legislature cannot, by any contract, divest itself of the power to provide for these objects. They belong emphatically to that class of objects which demand the application of the maxim, *salus populi suprema lex;* and they are to be attained and provided for by such appropriate means as the legislative discretion may devise. That discretion can no more be bargained away than the power itself." Mr. Justice Bradley in Beer Co. *v.* Massachusetts, 97 U. S. 25, 33; see also Munn *v.* Illinois, 94 U. S. 113, 125; Boyd *v.* Alabama, 94 U. S. 645, 650; Butchers' Union Co. *v.* Crescent City Co., 111 U. S. 746, 751; Holden *v.* Hardy, 169 U. S. 366, 391 *et seq.;* Kresser *v.* Lyman, 74 Fed. Rep. 765, 767. In Railroad Co. *v.* Richmond, 96 U. S. 521, 528, Chief Justice Waite said: "The maxim 'sic utere tuo ut alienum non lædas' . . . lies at the foundation of the police power."

[1] See argument of Mr. Carter, in Smyth *v.* Ames, 169 U. S. 466, 513; also Munn *v.* Illinois, 94 U. S. 113, 130; Chicago, etc., R. R. Co. *v.* Iowa, 94 U. S. 155, 161.

[2] Railroad Commission Cases, 116 U. S. 307, 325; Georgia Banking Co. *v.* Smith, 128 U. S. 174, 179.

[3] See admirable discussion of police power, In Matter of Petition of Cheesebrough, 78 N. Y. 232, 237.

rent in every form of government. A classification of this kind would simplify the consideration of many cases, and would avoid much apparent conflict. Rules which are wise and necessary in construing police powers in the narrower sense indicated would then be recognized at once as not at all relevant to the discussion of other governmental powers.[1]

In considering the validity of an enactment of a state legislature under the police power, the inquiry is whether the regulation or classification has been designed to subserve some reasonable public purpose, or is a mere device or excuse for an unjust discrimination, or for the oppression or spoliation of a particular class. Any regulation of the internal affairs of the State, fairly subserving a valid police purpose and reasonably exercised for the benefit of the community at large, will be upheld; but if it be arbitrary and have no substantial relation to the health, morals, peace, or welfare of the community, it will be nullified.[2] No precise limits, however, should be

[1] Professor Thayer says, in a note to his work "Cases on Constitutional Law," part ii. 693: "Discussions of what is called the 'police power' are often uninstructive, from a lack of discrimination. It is common to recognize that the subject is hardly susceptible of definition, but very often, indeed, it is not perceived that the real question in hand is that grave, difficult, and fundamental matter, — what are the limits of legislative power in general? In talking of the 'police power,' sometimes the question relates to the limits of a power admitted and fairly well known, as that of taxation or eminent domain; sometimes to the line between the local legislative power of the States and the federal legislative power; sometimes to legislation as settling the details of municipal affairs, and local arrangements for the promotion of good order, health, comfort, and convenience; sometimes to that special form of legislative action which applies the maxim of *sic utere tuo ut alienum non lædas*, adjusts and accommodates interests that may conflict, and fixes specific limits for each. But often, the discussion turns upon the true limits and scope of legislative power in general, — in whatever way it may seek to promote the general welfare." See also the language of Mr. Justice Shiras in Parsons *v.* District of Columbia, 170 U. S. 45, 51.

[2] Yick Wo *v.* Hopkins, 118 U. S. 356, 368; Minnesota *v.* Barber, 136 U. S. 313; Collins *v.* New Hampshire, 171 U. S. 30, 34.

placed upon the police power of a State, for no one can foresee what regulations the welfare of the community may require.[1]

ᐟ The first decision upon the police power of the States as affected by the Fourteenth Amendment was in the Slaughter House cases,[2] in which Mr. Justice Miller wrote the prevailing opinion. I have already discussed this decision in the first lecture. It was held that the Fourteenth Amendment did not interfere with the exercise of the police power by the States. In those cases, it appeared that the purpose of the statute involved was clearly to remove from the more densely populated part of the city of New Orleans noxious slaughter houses and large and offensive collections of animals necessarily incident to the slaughtering business of a large city, and to locate them where the convenience, health and comfort of the people required them to be placed. The creation of a corporation for this purpose, instead of imposing the same duties on the city itself, was deemed legal, and the provisions were held to be reasonable, fit and proper. Beyond this point as to police power, the case does not properly go; and it would probably never have excited so much attention if the opinion of Mr. Justice Miller had not reached out and discussed the broadest constitutional questions which might arise under the Fourteenth Amendment.

In the case of Lawton *v.* Steele,[3] Mr. Justice Brown

---

[1] Hawker *v.* New York, 170 U. S. 189, 192.

[2] 16 Wall. 36. In the subsequent case of Bartemeyer *v.* Iowa, 18 Wall. 129, 138, Mr. Justice Field said: "No one has ever pretended, that I am aware of, that the fourteenth amendment interferes in any respect with the police power of the State. . . . It was because the act of Louisiana transcended the limits of police regulation, and asserted a power in the State to farm out the ordinary avocations of life, that dissent was made to the judgment of the court sustaining the validity of the act." See also Butchers' Union Co. *v.* Crescent City Co., 111 U. S. 746.

[3] 152 U. S. 133, 136.

delivered a very instructive opinion as to the police power, and said: "It is universally conceded to include everything essential to the public safety, health, and morals, and to justify the destruction or abatement, by summary proceedings, of whatever may be regarded as a public nuisance. Under this power it has been held that the State may order the destruction of a house falling to decay or otherwise endangering the lives of passers-by; the demolition of such as are in the path of a conflagration; the slaughter of diseased cattle; the destruction of decayed or unwholesome food; the prohibition of wooden buildings in cities; the regulation of railways and other means of public conveyance, and of interments in burial grounds; the restriction of objectionable trades to certain localities; the compulsory vaccination of children; the confinement of the insane or those afflicted with contagious diseases; the restraint of vagrants, beggars, and habitual drunkards; the suppression of obscene publications and houses of ill fame; and the prohibition of gambling houses and places where intoxicating liquors are sold. Beyond this, however, the State may interfere wherever the public interests demand it, and in this particular a large discretion is necessarily vested in the legislature to determine, not only what the interests of the public require, but what measures are necessary for the protection of such interests.[1]  To justify the State in thus interposing its authority in behalf of the public, it must appear, first, that the interests of the public generally, as distinguished from those of a particular class, require such interference; and, second, that the means are reasonably necessary for the accomplishment of the purpose, and not unduly oppressive upon individuals. The legislature may not, under the guise of

---

[1] Citing Barbier *v.* Connolly, 113 U. S. 27, and Kidd *v.* Pearson, 128 U. S. 1.

protecting the public interests, arbitrarily interfere with private business, or impose unusual and unnecessary restrictions upon lawful occupations. In other words, its determination as to what is a proper exercise of its police powers is not final or conclusive, but is subject to the supervision of the courts."

In Barbier *v.* Connolly[1] a municipal ordinance prohibiting laundry work between 10 P. M. and 6 A. M. was sustained as valid. The court said : "The Fourteenth Amendment . . . undoubtedly intended not only that there should be no arbitrary deprivation of life or liberty, or arbitrary spoliation of property, but that equal protection and security should be given to all under like circumstances in the enjoyment of their personal and civil rights; that all persons should be equally entitled to pursue their happiness and acquire and enjoy property; that they should have like access to the courts of the country for the protection of their persons and property, the prevention and redress of wrongs, and the enforcement of contracts; that no impediment should be interposed to the pursuits of any one except as applied to the same pursuits by others under like circumstances; that no greater burdens should be laid upon one than are laid upon others in the same calling and condition, and that in the administration of criminal justice no different or higher punishment should be imposed upon one than such as is prescribed to all for like offences."[2]

[1] 113 U. S. 27, 31.

[2] The police power will be found discussed in the following cases: Matter of Application of Jacobs, 98 N. Y. 98, 108; The People *v.* Marx, 99 N. Y. 377; People *v.* Gillson, 109 N. Y. 389, 400; People *v.* Rosenberg, 138 N. Y. 410, 415; Colon *v.* Lisk, 153 N. Y. 188, 196; Slaughter-House Cases, 16 Wall. 36, 62; New Orleans Gas Co. *v.* Louisiana Light Co., 115 U. S. 650, 661; Yick Wo *v.* Hopkins, 118 U. S. 356, 367; Dent *v.* West Virginia, 129 U. S. 114, 122; Minnesota *v.* Barber, 136 U. S. 313, 328; Brimmer *v.* Rebman, 138 U. S. 78, 82; Lawton

The legislation of the State of Illinois regulating the charges of warehousemen was sustained by the Supreme Court in the famous case of Munn v. Illinois[1] and in the other so-called Granger cases. Such legislation is frequently referred to as a branch of the police power. This is one of the instances in which the term "police power" is loosely used, for it is confusing and inaccurate to denominate the governmental regulation of railroad or elevator charges as being an exercise of the police power. The point actually decided in these Granger cases was that where property is affected with a public interest, as in the case of a grain elevator or a railway, the legislature may fix by law the maximum amount which shall be charged for its use. In the cases then before the court, the charges or limits established were reasonable. The opinion, however, did not stop at this point, Chief Justice Waite proceeding to state in the Munn case: "We know that this is a power which may be abused; but that is no argument against its existence. For protection against abuses by legislatures the people must resort to the polls, not to the courts." Repeating this idea in one of the Granger cases, he said:[3] "Where property has been clothed with a public interest, the legislature may fix a limit to that which shall in law be reasonable for its use. This limit binds the courts as well as the people. If it has been improperly fixed, the legislature, not the courts, must be appealed to for the change."

The decisions in the Granger cases are sound upon the

v. Steele, 152 U. S. 133, 136; Scott v. Donald, 165 U. S. 58, 91; Davis v. Massachusetts, 167 U. S. 43, 47; Holden v. Hardy, 169 U. S. 366, 391 *et seq.*; Powell v. Pennsylvania, 127 U. S. 678, 683; Plumley v. Massachusetts, 155 U. S. 461, 479: and compare Schollenberger v. Pennsylvania, 171 U. S. 1, and Collins v. New Hampshire, 171 U. S. 30.

[1] 94 U. S. 113.                    [2] 94 U. S. 113, 134.
[3] Peik v. Chicago, etc. Railway Co., 94 U. S. 164, 178.

point actually involved, namely, that the legislature may fix reasonable maximum rates; but these dicta of Chief Justice Waite were too broad. They caused as great a sensation and created as much alarm as any decision ever delivered by any court. They obscured for several years the powers of the courts to relieve against arbitrary and unjust legislation. Owners of property feared that the rule announced was subversive of the rights of private property. Well-founded apprehensions arose that these suggestions of the Chief Justice would lead to confiscatory legislation, ruinous to many enterprises and destructive of all security of investment. Such legislation came, and vast damage resulted. It was aimed principally at railroads, which represent enormous property interests; but it was also directed against various other corporate enterprises. Finally, the regulations became so irksome and destructive, the rates imposed so arbitrary and unreasonable, that the Granger cases had to be modified and limited, and the doctrine recognized and enforced that the power of the state legislatures to regulate charges was not unlimited or without effective restraint. In the so-called Railroad Commission cases,[1] the Supreme Court had to declare, and through Chief Justice Waite himself, that "This power to regulate is not a power to destroy, and limitation is not the equivalent of confiscation." Then, in the Minnesota Railroad Commission cases,[2] the Court set aside the state law on the ground that such legislation, by authorizing the imposition of unreasonably low rates, deprived the railroad companies of property without due process of law. The power of regulation, which, according to the doctrine of the Munn case, existed in the state

[1] 116 U. S. 307, 331.
[2] Chicago &c. Railway Co. *v.* Minnesota, 134 U. S. 418.

legislatures, had to be confined by the Supreme Court within just and reasonable limits, and the jurisdiction of the courts to restrict and their ultimate power to review had to be declared. This doctrine was most clearly and unequivocally announced in the Reagan case,[1] when Mr. Justice Brewer, speaking for the whole court, delivered the opinion. This decision is the leading case upon this important and far-reaching point of jurisdiction. Last year, Mr. Justice Harlan, in the Covington Turnpike case,[2] delivering the unanimous opinion of the Supreme Court, reiterated this doctrine, and quoting from previous decisions said that " there is a remedy in the courts for relief against legislation establishing a tariff of rates which is so unreasonable as to practically destroy the value of the property of companies engaged in the carrying business, and that especially may the courts of the United States treat such a question as a judicial one, and hold such acts of legislation to be in conflict with the Constitution of the United States, as depriving the companies of their property without due process of law, and as depriving them of the equal protection of the laws." The latest case involving this question is the Nebraska Maximum Rate case,[3] decided at the present term. In this case, the Nebraska statute was set aside because it provided an unreasonably low rate of compensation to railroads.

It is now, therefore, well established that the federal courts will intervene and set aside a regulation of charges which is unreasonable, and that the reasonableness of the regulation is a judicial question.[4] Further than this, however,

---

[1] Reagan *v.* Farmers' Loan and Trust Co., 154 U. S. 362.
[2] Covington &c. Turnpike Co. *v.* Sandford, 164 U. S. 578, 592.
[3] Smyth *v.* Ames, 169 U. S. 466, 546.
[4] The opinion of Judge Seaman, in Milwaukee Electric Railway & Light Co. *v.* City of Milwaukee, 87 Fed. Rep. 577, 586, well illustrates the present aspect

they will not go. As was said in Chicago &c. Railway Co. *v.* Wellman,[1] " The legislature has power to fix rates, and the extent of judicial interference is protection against unreasonable rates." But I venture to say that the judicial power to pass upon other police regulations is not as extensive, and that the Supreme Court would decline to set aside a statute relating to public health, morals, or peace merely on the ground that it seemed to be unreasonable or unnecessarily rigid and harsh.

The decision in Munn *v.* Illinois[2] has never been expressly limited. The subsequent cases involving railroad charges have only had the effect of repudiating the dictum of Chief Justice Waite as to the unlimited power of the state legislatures to fix rates " which shall in law be reasonable." The doctrine of the Munn case has been followed in Budd *v.* New York[3] and Brass *v.* Stoeser,[4] and the court seems, by the language of these later decisions, to have affirmed the decision in the Munn case. It is notable, however, that in the Munn case two justices express dissent from the views of the court. In the Budd case the dissenting justices were three, while in the Brass case there were four justices to join in the minority opinion. If, in any of these cases, it had been shown that the rates, as fixed by the legislature, were so unjust as to take away

of the courts upon this question: " The main controversy in each of these actions is whether the ordinance of June 11, 1896, unreasonably fixes rates of fare which would deprive the complainant of its property without due process of law, and thus violates the fourteenth amendment to the constitution of the United States. . . . I am of opinion that . . . the company has not received earnings in excess of an equitable allowance to the investors for the means necessarily invested in furnishing such service ; that enforcement of the ordinance would deprive complainant of property rights, by preventing reasonable compensation for its service; and that, therefore, the ordinance clearly violates the Constitution of the United States, and is invalid."

[1] 143 U. S. 339, 344.      [2] 94 U. S. 113.
[3] 143 U. S. 517, 547, 548.      [4] 153 U. S. 391.

reasonable profit from the business of conducting grain elevators, and therefore practically to confiscate property, the Supreme Court would undoubtedly have set the law aside. In closing the opinion in the Budd case, Mr. Justice Blatchford said :[1] "In the cases before us, the records do not show that the charges fixed by the statute are unreasonable, or that property has been taken without due process of law, or that there has been any denial of the equal protection of the laws; even if under any circumstances we could determine that the maximum rate fixed by the legislature was unreasonable."

This power of a State to regulate the affairs of its own people, when exerted for any public purpose, is liberally construed and is not likely to be interfered with by the federal courts. It is not, however, without limit, and it must be founded upon some rule of natural reason. The interests of the public generally, as distinguished from those of a particular class, must justify such interference; and the means must be reasonably necessary for the accomplishment of the purpose, and not unduly oppressive upon individuals.[2]

State enactments especially affecting railroads, transportation companies, and certain particular occupations and callings have been sustained as valid regulations under the police power. The public interest may require that transportation by the dangerous agency of steam be hedged about with safeguards for the lives and property of the public that would be unnecessary and absurd if applied to other methods of traffic.[3] It may well be that the sale of explosives and chemicals which, unless in the hands of experts, are dangerous to health and life, should be at-

---

[1] 143 U. S. 517, 548.    [2] Lawton *v.* Steele, 152 U. S. 133, 137.
[3] Missouri Railway Co. *v.* Mackey, 127 U. S. 205, 210; St. Louis & San Francisco R'y *v.* Mathews, 165 U. S. 1, 26.

tended with restrictions that would be arbitrary and intolerable if imposed upon other departments of business.[1]

Thus, statutes have been sustained directing the removal of grade crossings as a menace to public safety and imposing the entire expense upon the railroad companies;[2] making railroads liable in double damages for losses occasioned through failure to erect fences;[3] depriving railway companies of the defense of contributory negligence in respect to injuries received by employees, and of the right to contract for exemption from liability for negligence;[4] requiring railroad employees to be examined at certain times as to their eyes, and the company to pay for the expenses of the examination;[5] making railroad companies responsible in damages for all property set on fire by their engines, whether directly or indirectly, and irrespective of negligence, and giving the road an insurable interest in the property to protect itself against contingent loss;[6] compelling trains operated wholly within a State to receive and let off passengers at certain designated stations;[7] compelling heating by steam instead of coal fires; abating nuisances;[8] etc., etc.[9]

The police power of the States is nowhere better illustrated than in the restrictions which have been imposed upon the manufacture of intoxicating liquors and the sale

[1] Patterson *v.* Kentucky, 97 U. S. 501.

[2] N. Y. & N. E. Railroad Co. *v.* Bristol, 151 U. S. 556.

[3] Missouri Pacific Railway Co. *v.* Humes, 115 U. S. 512 ; Minneapolis Railway Co. *v.* Beckwith, 129 U. S. 26, 31.

[4] Missouri Railway Co. *v.* Mackey, 127 U. S. 205, 209; Minneapolis &c. Railway Co. *v.* Herrick, 127 U. S. 210.

[5] Nashville &c. Railway *v.* Alabama, 128 U. S. 96.

[6] St. Louis & San Francisco R'y *v.* Mathews, 165 U. S. 1, 5.

[7] Gladson *v.* Minnesota, 166 U. S. 427, 430.

[8] Fertilizing Co. *v.* Hyde Park, 97 U. S. 659, 667.

[9] N. Y. & N. E. Railroad Co. *v.* Bristol, 151 U. S. 556; St. Louis & San Francisco R'y *v.* Mathews, 165 U. S. 1, 27; Jones *v.* Brim, 165 U. S. 180; Chicago &c. Railroad *v.* Nebraska, 170 U. S. 57.

thereof as a beverage. By a long line of decisions it has been uniformly recognized that no provision of the Fourteenth Amendment inhibits the States from regulating the liquor traffic within their boundaries. It has, furthermore, been well established that the States can impose upon the retail sale of liquors conditions which are not exacted from those who prosecute other occupations. Bartemeyer *v.* Iowa[1] was the first case in which the Supreme Court of the United States considered the effect of the provisions of the Fourteenth Amendment upon the power of the States in relation to the liquor traffic. It was intimated in the opinion of the court.that the regulations imposed could not go to the extent of destroying property employed in that business. In Kidd *v.* Pearson[2] it was said that the power of the States could not extend to a prohibition of the importation of liquor in the original packages of commerce, and this position has been lately reaffirmed.[3] In Mugler *v.* Kansas,[4] however, a statute prohibiting the manufacture or sale of intoxicating liquors, and authorizing the summary destruction of property devoted to such manufacture, was upheld as a valid exercise of the police power. The opinion of Mr. Justice Harlan in this case is one of the remarkably strong opinions upon constitutional law of that great jurist, now the senior associate justice of the Supreme Court, and a careful study of the language of the opinion is particularly recommended to all students of constitutional law.

The exercise of police power by the state legislatures

---

[1] 18 Wall. 129.        [2] 128 U. S. 1.

[3] See the subsequent case of Leisy *v.* Hardin, 135 U. S. 100; and 26 Stat. 313, c. 728, and the case of *In re* Rahrer, 140 U. S. 545, thereupon; also Scott *v.* Donald, 165 U. S. 58; Rhodes *v.* Iowa, 170 U. S. 412; and Vance *v.* W. A. Vandercook Company, 170 U. S. 438, 468.

[4] 123 U. S. 623.

may come before the federal courts for adjudication in
two aspects: the one having relation to matters wholly of
local concern, such as internal manufactures, trade, etc.;
the other having relation to matters of national concern,
such as interstate commerce, etc. In cases of the first
class, the question arises solely under the Fourteenth
Amendment; in cases of the other class, it arises under
the commerce clause of the Federal Constitution itself.
Whatever may be the power of a State over matters that
are completely internal, the local legislatures can never
regulate, prohibit, or interfere with matters that are of
national concern or that relate to interstate commerce.
Legislation of the one class may be within the sphere of
state action, or what used to be termed state sovereignty;
legislation of the other class is an encroachment upon the
sphere of the national government. Thus, in Mugler *v.*
Kansas [1] a statute regulating and prohibiting the liquor
traffic was upheld because it related to internal affairs;
but in the famous original package case, Leisy *v.* Hardin,[2]
a similar statute was declared void in so far as it interfered with interstate commerce.

With respect to matters of purely local concern and
internal traffic, the question as to what police or governmental regulations are appropriate, necessary, or wise is
confided, in great measure, to the discretion of the state
legislatures; and with this discretion the federal courts
will not ordinarily interfere under the Fourteenth Amendment. This rule was the basis of the decision in a case
involving the validity of the Oleomargarine acts of Pennsylvania. In this case Mr. Justice Harlan said:[3] "If all
that can be said of this legislation is that it is unwise, or

---

[1] 123 U. S. 623.  [2] 135 U. S. 100.
[3] Powell *v.* Pennsylvania, 127 U. S. 678, 686.

unnecessarily oppressive to those manufacturing or sell-
ing wholesome oleomargarine, as an article of food, their
appeal must be to the legislature, or to the ballot-box, not
to the judiciary." No question of interstate commerce
was then involved. Such language would never have
been used with relation to a state statute unnecessarily
oppressive to those engaged in legitimate interstate commerce.[1] In such a case the Supreme Court would not
remit aggrieved parties to the local ballot-box for redress,
but would itself decide the federal question of constitutional right, because the true character of any legislation
affecting national affairs must ultimately be determined
by it. Then the question is federal; the policy must be
national. As was reiterated in the South Carolina Dis-
pensary case,[2] the utmost good faith on the part of a State
in enacting any statute affecting interstate commerce cannot control the final determination by the Supreme Court
of the question whether the regulation is or is not repugnant to the pledge of untrammelled commercial intercourse
secured to the people by the supreme law of the land.

One of the latest decisions upon this point of due process
is Holden *v.* Hardy,[3] in which the cases arising under the
police power in connection with the Fourteenth Amendment are examined in detail in an interesting opinion by
Mr. Justice Brown. Statutes of Utah providing that the
period of employment of workingmen in underground
mines should be limited to eight hours per day were held
to be a valid exercise of the police power. This decision
does not, however, uphold all eight-hour laws. The court
said that it did not criticise the many authorities to the

[1] Schollenberger *v.* Pennsylvania, 171 U. S. 1, 16; Collins *v.* New Hampshire,
171 U. S. 30.

[2] Scott *v.* Donald, 165 U. S. 58, 91.          [3] 169 U. S. 366.

effect that state statutes restricting the hours of labor were unconstitutional. That general and broad question was not involved. It was admitted that underground mining was injurious to health, and the state limitation of hours of labor underground was, therefore, sustained.

We may now consider the power of eminent domain, or the taking of private property for public use, and the extent of the supervision of the federal courts by virtue of the amendment. The primary inquiry always is whether the use is public or not. If the use be not public, private property cannot be taken, no matter how much is offered in compensation.[1] If the use be public, the question of actual necessity is not of a judicial character, but rather one for determination by the law-making branch of the government.[2] Then comes the inquiry as to what is just compensation for the property taken.[3] The claim was made

[1] In Missouri Pacific Railway *v.* Nebraska, 164 U. S. 403, 417, it was held that, when a statute of a State, as construed by its highest court, had the effect of compelling a railroad to allow a private party to erect an elevator upon its right of way, it amounted to a taking of private property for a private purpose, and was therefore unconstitutional and void.

[2] Boom Co. *v.* Patterson, 98 U. S. 403, 406; Backus *v.* Fort Street Union Depot Co., 169 U. S. 557, 568, and cases cited. It may be interesting to note the clearness and precision of the French upon this point. In the Declaration des droits de l'homme et du citoyen, prefixed to the French Constitution of 1791, the following is recited: "The right to property being inviolable and sacred, no one ought to be deprived of it, except in cases of evident public necessity, legally ascertained, and on condition of a previous just indemnity."

[3] In his work on Natural Rights, the well-known English writer, Professor Ritchie, says (p. 265): "The Fifth Amendment to the Constitution of the United States of America declares that private property shall not be taken for public use 'without just compensation.' None of these written constitutions define the term 'just.' None of them are so rash as to attempt to answer the question of Socrates: 'What is Justice?' So that what is 'just compensation' must ultimately depend on public opinion at the time when the compensation comes to be given, as much as in Great Britain, where there is no written constitution, and where we have hitherto got on somehow without declaring our natural rights. It may also be pointed out that 'legally ascertained' or 'due process of law' is a phrase to which different ages and countries would give a very different meaning."

that there had to be a jury trial to determine the compensation. "But the Constitution of the United States does not forbid a trial of the question of the amount of compensation before an ordinary common law jury, or require, on the other hand, that it must be before such a jury. It is within the power of the State to provide that the amount shall be determined in the first instance by commissioners, subject to an appeal to the courts for trial in the ordinary way; or it may provide that the question shall be settled by a sheriff's jury, as it was constituted at common law, without the presence of a trial judge. These are questions of procedure which do not enter into or form the basis of fundamental right. All that is essential is that in some appropriate way, before some properly constituted tribunal, inquiry shall be made as to the amount of compensation, and when this has been provided there is that due process of law which is required by the Federal Constitution." [1]  It has also been held that a State, in condemnation cases, may authorize the taking of possession prior to the final determination of the amount of compensation and payment therefor. There is no longer any doubt that if adequate provision for compensation is made, authority may be granted for taking possession pending inquiry as to the amount which must be paid and before any final determination thereof.[2]

[1] Backus *v.* Fort Street Union Depot Co., 169 U. S. 557, 569; see also Bauman *v.* Ross, 167 U. S. 548, 593.

[2] Cherokee Nation *v.* Kansas Railway Co., 135 U. S. 641; Sweet *v.* Rechel, 159 U. S. 380; Backus *v.* Fort Street Union Depot Co., 169 U. S. 557, 568. The result of these decisions seems to be that the property holder is not deprived of his property without due process of law, merely because the amount of his compensation is not settled to a finality at the time of the entry of the party seeking condemnation. If the law provides a method by which the owner, on yielding possession, can have the value of his property adjusted and the necessity for its condemnation settled by some competent tribunal, within a reasonable time after the entry of the party seeking condemnation, the requirement of due process of law is satisfied.

Attention should be called to a curious and interesting feature in the development of this question. In the case of Davidson *v.* New Orleans,[1] decided at the October term, 1877, Mr. Justice Miller said that a state statute "may violate some provision of the state constitution against unequal taxation; but the Federal Constitution imposes no restraints on the States in that regard. If private property be taken for public uses without just compensation, it must be remembered that, when the Fourteenth Amendment was adopted, the provision on that subject, in immediate juxtaposition in the Fifth Amendment with the one we are construing, was left out, and this was taken."

This language of Mr. Justice Miller would seem to indicate that, in his judgment, the Fourteenth Amendment afforded no protection against the taking of private property for public use without just compensation. If his language does not mean that, what is the meaning of the suggestion? In the same case, Mr. Justice Bradley expressed the view that the opinion of Mr. Justice Miller narrowed more than it should the scope of the requirement of due process of law. He said: "I think, therefore, we are entitled, under the fourteenth amendment, not only to see that there is some process of law, but 'due process of law,' provided by the State law when a citizen is deprived of his property; and that, in judging what is 'due process of law,' respect must be had to the cause and object of the taking, whether under the taxing power, the power of eminent domain, or the power of assessment for local improvements, or none of these: and if found to be suitable or admissible in the special case, it will be adjudged to be 'due process of law;' but if found to be

[1] 96 U. S. 97, 105.

arbitrary, oppressive, and unjust, it may be declared to be not ' due process of law.' " [1]

Twenty years later, in the California Irrigation cases,[2] decided in November, 1896, the Supreme Court again referred to this point in the following language: " There is no specific prohibition in the Federal Constitution which acts upon the States in regard to their taking private property for any but a public use. The Fifth Amendment which provides, among other things, that such property shall not be taken for public use without just compensation, applies only to the Federal government, as has many times been decided. . . . In the Fourteenth Amendment the provision regarding the taking of private property is omitted, and the prohibition against the State is confined to its depriving any person of life, liberty or property, without due process of law. It is claimed, however, that the citizen is deprived of his property without due process of law, if it be taken by or under state authority for any other than a public use, either under the guise of taxation or by the assumption of the right of eminent domain. In that way the question whether private property has been taken for any other than a public use becomes material in this court, even where the taking is under the authority of the State instead of the Federal government." This was a very great advance from Mr. Justice Miller's position, but there was yet no decision that due process of law comprehended full protection against deprivation of property without just compensation.

At the same term, however, it was declared that the court was unanimously of opinion that the taking of any part of the property of a railroad company for the pur-

[1] 96 U. S. 97, 107.
[2] Fallbrook Irrigation District *v.* Bradley, 164 U. S. 112, 158.

pose of building and maintaining a structure thereon for the private use of individuals was in essence and effect a taking of private property of the railroad corporation for the private use of the petitioners, Mr. Justice Gray saying[1] that: "The taking by a State of the private property of one person or corporation, without the owner's consent, for the private use of another, is not due process of law, and is a violation of the Fourteenth Article of Amendment of the Constitution of the United States." It will be observed that in this case the court did not decide, nor, as it will be interesting to note, had it yet decided that the taking of property for a public use without just compensation was equally a violation of the Fourteenth Amendment.

Finally in March, 1897, nearly thirty years after the amendment was adopted, the Supreme Court for the first time squarely decided the point. Mr. Justice Harlan then reviewed all the authorities in a very important case,[2] and said: "In our opinion, a judgment of a state court, even if it be authorized by statute, whereby private property is taken for the State or under its direction for public use, without compensation made or secured to the owner, is, upon principle and authority, wanting in the due process of law required by the Fourteenth Amendment of the Constitution of the United States, and the affirmance of such judgment by the highest court of the State is a denial by that State of a right secured to the owner by that instrument." This decision brushes away the suggestion in Davidson *v.* New Orleans, and establishes the doctrine

[1] Missouri Pacific Railway *v.* Nebraska, 164 U. S. 403, 417.

[2] Chicago, Burlington &c. R'd *v.* Chicago, 166 U. S. 226, 241. In this case, the guaranty of " just compensation " was found to be of little practical value, for the railroad company was deprived of very valuable property rights and was allowed by the local jury one dollar as just compensation.

that " due process of law " includes an adequate restriction upon the power of the States as fully as the Fifth Amendment restricts the national government. At the present term, Mr. Justice Brewer said [1] that it was now " not open to further debate that this court may examine proceedings had in a state court, under state authority, for the appropriation of private property to public purposes, so far as to inquire whether that court prescribed any rule of law in disregard of the owner's right to just compensation." [2]

It frequently happens that although property is not physically invaded or the owner actually ousted of his possession, yet the beneficial enjoyment is materially interfered with and the value diminished by public improvements or under some exercise of state power. Neither the Fifth nor the Fourteenth Amendment compels the payment of damages in such a case, for it is regarded as but an incidental consequence of the lawful and proper exercise of a governmental power.[3]

In Eldridge v. Trezevant,[4] which involved the right of the State of Louisiana to erect levees upon the lands abutting upon navigable rivers without making compensation for the land taken, the Supreme Court of the State of Louisiana decided that such taking, damage, or destruction of property for the purpose of building a public levee was an exercise of the police power of the State and *damnum absque injuria*, because the State had a right of servitude or easement over the lands in question for the

---

[1] Backus v. Fort Street Union Depot Co., 169 U. S. 557, 565.

[2] See also *supra*, lecture ii. pp. 57–64, where it is shown that the Fifth Amendment was intended by the framers of the Fourteenth Amendment to be made applicable to the States.

[3] Mr. Chief Justice Fuller in Gibson v. United States, 166 U. S. 269, 275.

[4] 160 U. S. 452, 468.

purpose of constructing levees and roads — a right existing before the Territory of Louisiana was ceded to the United States. It was contended that the provisions of the Fourteenth Amendment limited public rights existing in the form of servitudes or easements existing prior to its adoption. Mr. Justice Shiras delivered the opinion of the court and said: " The subject-matter of such rights and regulations falls within the control of the States, and the provisions of the Fourteenth Amendment of the Constitution of the United States are satisfied if, in cases like the present one, the state law, with its benefits and its obligations, is impartially administered."[1] Yet a statute passed in the State of New York, providing for levees along the banks of the Hudson without compensation to the owner, would be unconstitutional, because no such right of servitude or easement exists under the state law.

Taxation is the next branch of the subject of due process of law. In the levying and collection of a tax, a more summary method of procedure must necessarily be followed than in ordinary suits between parties; and the character of the proceeding for the enforcement of taxes

[1] See also Kaukauna Co. v. Green Bay &c. Canal, 142 U. S. 254; Water Power Co. v. Water Commissioners, 168 U. S. 349. In Head v. Amoskeag Manufacturing Company, 113 U. S. 9, 21, the Supreme Court considered a form of governmental power, somewhat similar to the power of eminent domain, as to the regulation of property in which many have a common interest, where the development and profitable use of such property is not strictly a matter of public interest, or where its improvement is not a public work. Mr. Justice Gray announced the rule in these words: " When property in which several persons have a common interest, cannot be fully and beneficially enjoyed in its existing condition, the law often provides a way in which they may compel one another to submit to measures necessary to secure its beneficial enjoyment, making equitable compensation to any whose control of or interest in the property is thereby modified." See also Wurts v. Hoagland, 114 U. S. 606, 613, and Fallbrook Irrigation District v. Bradley, 164 U. S. 112, 158.

must depend upon the nature of the tax and the manner in which its amount is determinable. If the tax be assessed according to value, notice to the owner, at some stage of the proceeding, is necessary, because, in estimating the value, the taxing officers act judicially;[1] whereas, if the imposition be a capitation or poll tax, or a license or occupation tax, or an assessment according to frontage or acreage, no notice is usual or requisite.[2] The Fourteenth Amendment does not require the state legislatures to provide a hearing in respect of local improvements and public works or in respect of the property which shall be deemed benefited thereby. It is within the discretion of the legislative power to grant or withhold such hearing. So also the determination of the taxing district and the manner of the apportionment are within the legislative power.[3]

The requirements of due process of law in matters of taxation, assessments for local improvements, etc., are not

[1] Hagar v. Reclamation District No. 108, 111 U. S. 701, 710.

[2] The result of many cases has been the rule declared by the Supreme Court that a statute or proceeding imposing a tax or assessment upon property according to its value will constitute due process of law if the owner has an opportunity to question the validity or the amount of the tax or assessment either before its amount is determined or in subsequent proceedings for its collection. The notice need not be personal, but may be by publication. Where, for example, the statute prescribes the court in which and the time at which the various steps in the assessment shall be taken, a notice by publication to all parties interested to appear and defend is suitable, and sufficiently answers the requirement of due process of law. State Railroad Tax Cases, 92 U. S. 575, 609; McMillen v. Anderson, 95 U. S. 37; Pearson v. Yewdall, 95 U. S. 294; Davidson v. New Orleans, 96 U. S. 97; Hagar v. Reclamation District No. 108, 111 U. S. 701, 710; Kentucky Railroad Tax Cases, 115 U. S. 321; Spencer v. Merchant, 125 U. S. 345, 356; Huling v. Kaw Valley Railway, 130 U. S. 559; Palmer v. McMahon, 133 U. S. 660; Lent v. Tillson, 140 U. S. 316, 328; Paulsen v. Portland, 149 U. S. 30; Pittsburgh &c. Railway Co. v. Backus, 154 U. S. 421; Winona & St. Peter Land Co. v. Minnesota, 159 U. S. 526, 537.

[3] Kelly v. Pittsburgh, 104 U. S. 78; Hagar v. Reclamation District No. 108, 111 U. S. 701; Williams v. Supervisors of Albany, 122 U. S. 154; Spencer v. Merchant, 125 U. S. 345; Walston v. Nevin, 128 U. S. 578; Paulsen v. Portland, 149 U. S. 30.

at all times easy of ascertainment or definition, because
of the different purposes to be accomplished, and the
different rules applicable in each particular instance. An
attempt to state any general rule to cover all cases is for
this reason to be avoided. In the case of Parsons *v.*
District of Columbia,[1] Mr. Justice Shiras said: "It is trite
to say that general principles announced by courts, which
are perfectly sound expressions of the law under the facts
of a particular case, may be wholly inapplicable in another
and different case; and there is scarcely any department
of the law in which it is easier to collect one body of
decisions and contrast them with another in apparent
conflict, than that which deals with the taxing and police
powers. There is a wide difference between a tax or
assessment prescribed by a legislative body, having full
authority over the subject, and one imposed by a municipal corporation, acting under a limited and delegated
authority. And the difference is still wider between
a legislative act making an assessment, and the action
of mere functionaries, whose authority is derived from
municipal ordinances."

In Davidson *v.* New Orleans,[2] to which reference has
already been made, it was decided that assessments for
local improvements may be levied on the abutting owners,
and that the fact that their property is assessed twice
for the same improvement, and only part of it is benefited, or that a personal judgment is entered against the
owner for the amount of the tax, does not invalidate the
assessment if the owner has had notice and an opportunity to object. The determination of the persons benefited by a local improvement and of the extent to which
they are benefited depends largely upon the discretion of

[1] 170 U. S. 45, 51.          [2] 96 U. S. 97.

the legislature.   A man has no cause for complaint merely because the enforced collection of a tax does not benefit him as much as others.   As was said in one of the cases : "It may be true that he does not receive the same amount of benefit from some or any of these taxes as do citizens living in the heart of the city.   It probably is true, from the evidence found in this record, that his tax bears a very unjust relation to the benefits received as compared with its amount.   But who can adjust with precise accuracy the amount which each individual in an organized civil community shall contribute to sustain it, or can insure in this respect absolute equality of burdens, and fairness in their distribution among those who must bear them?" [1]

In Spencer *v.* Merchant [2] the Supreme Court said : "In the absence of any more specific constitutional restriction than the general prohibition against taking property without due process of law, the legislature of the State, having the power to fix the sum necessary to be levied for the expense of a public improvement, and to order it to be assessed, either, like other taxes, upon property generally, or only upon the lands benefited by the improvement, is authorized to determine both the amount of the whole tax, and the class of lands which will receive the benefit and should therefore bear the burden, although it may, if it sees fit, commit the ascertainment of either or both of these facts to the judgment of commissioners. When the determination of the lands to be benefited is entrusted to commissioners, the owners may be entitled to notice and hearing upon the question whether their

[1] Kelly *v.* Pittsburgh, 104 U. S. 78, 82.
[2] 125 U. S. 345, 356.   This resulted from the noted case of Stuart *v.* Palmer, 74 N. Y. 183; see 100 N. Y. 585; see also 170 U. S. 45, 54.

lands are benefited and how much. But the legislature has the power to determine, by the statute imposing the tax, what lands, which might be benefited by the improvement, are in fact benefited ; and if it does so, its determination is conclusive upon the owners and the courts, and the owners have no right to be heard upon the question whether their lands are benefited or not, but only upon the validity of the assessment, and its apportionment among the different parcels of the class which the legislature has conclusively determined to be benefited.[1] In determining what lands are benefited by the improvement, the legislature may avail itself of such information as it deems sufficient, either through investigations by its committees, or by adopting as its own the estimates or conclusions of others, whether those estimates or conclusions previously had or had not any legal sanction."[2]

In Bell's Gap R'd Co. *v.* Pennsylvania,[3] Mr. Justice Bradley said that the State " may, if it chooses, exempt certain classes of property from any taxation at all, such as churches, libraries and the property of charitable institutions. It may impose different specific taxes upon different trades and professions, and may vary the rates of excise upon various products; it may tax real estate and personal property in a different manner; it

---

[1] Kelly *v.* Pittsburgh, 104 U. S. 78, 81.

[2] Other cases involving assessments for public improvements are Davidson *v.* New Orleans, 96 U. S. 97; Hagar *v.* Reclamation District No. 108, 111 U. S. 701; Lent *v.* Tillson, 140 U. S. 316; Paulsen *v.* Portland, 149 U. S. 30.

[3] 134 U. S. 232, 237. Other leading cases involving taxation are Scholey *v.* Rew, 23 Wall. 331; Kirtland *v.* Hotchkiss, 100 U. S. 491; Barrett *v.* Holmes, 102 U. S. 651; Louisiana *v.* Mayor of New Orleans, 109 U. S. 285; Provident Institution *v.* Jersey City, 113 U. S. 506; Wurts *v.* Hoagland, 114 U. S. 606; Southern Pacific R. R. Co. *v.* California, 118 U. S. 109; Santa Clara Co. *v.* South. Pac. Railroad, 118 U. S. 394; Phila. Fire Association *v.* New York, 119 U. S. 110; Budd *v.* New York, 143 U. S. 517; Aberdeen Bank *v.* Chehalis County, 166 U. S. 440; Savings Society *v.* Multnomah County, 169 U. S. 421; Magoun *v.* Illinois Trust & Savings Bank, 170 U. S. 283.

may tax visible property only, and not tax securities for payment of money ; it may allow deductions for indebtedness, or not allow them. All such regulations, and those of like character, so long as they proceed within reasonable limits and general usage, are within the discretion of the state legislature, or the people of the State in framing their Constitution."

In respect of procedure, civil or criminal, due process of law must depend upon the nature of the proceeding, having regard to the form and nature of the procedure employed, as well as the object of the law. It is only when, under one pretext or another, the State seeks to work spoliation, when it crosses the line which separates regulation from confiscation, when, under the guise of legal procedure, the fundamental rights of the individual are invaded, that relief can be sought under the amendment, and full protection found beneath the strong hand of the federal courts. It may be stated as the general rule that, in all cases, that procedure constitutes due process of law which is reasonably suitable to the nature of the case.[1]

In Lowe *v.* Kansas,[2] the Supreme Court said : " Whether the mode of proceeding, prescribed by this statute, and followed in this case, was due process of law, depends upon the question whether it was in substantial accord with the law and usage in England before the Declaration of Inde-

---

[1] *Ex parte* Wall, 107 U. S. 265, 289. In Pennoyer *v.* Neff, 95 U. S. 714, 733, the Supreme Court, in speaking of due process as applied to legal proceedings, said that it meant " a course of legal proceedings according to those rules and principles which have been established in our systems of jurisprudence for the protection and enforcement of private rights. To give such proceedings any validity, there must be a tribunal competent by its constitution — that is, by the law of its creation — to pass upon the subject-matter of the suit; and, if that involves merely a determination of the personal liability of the defendant, he must be brought within its jurisdiction by service of process within the State, or his voluntary appearance."

[2] 163 U. S. 81, 85.

pendence, and in this country since it became a nation, in similar cases." This is hardly an accurate or safe definition, although it would probably comprise most of the cases arising in procedure. Human institutions are constantly changing and improving. The law is essentially a progressive science; and its structure and the rules of procedure must continue to change as required by new conditions of society.[1] For instance, public policy in regard to crimes is advancing and becoming more and more liberal in all countries. Indeed the public policy of one generation is frequently not the policy of the succeeding generation.[2] Thus, at the time of the Declaration of Independence, death was the penalty in England for stealing a sheep, and one of the earliest statutes enacted by the First Congress imposed the punishment of death for counterfeiting. Neither Congress nor the States would at the present day inflict such a cruel and unusual punishment for such offences. If any such statute were now passed, the legislation would shock mankind and ought to be held unconstitutional; yet it would be in accord with the usage obtaining at the time the Constitution was adopted. Death for horse-stealing might well be inflicted in the West, or in sparsely settled and inadequately policed communities; but would it not be deemed unjustifiably cruel if imposed in New York?

In relation to matters of criminal procedure, the question of what is or is not due process of law is largely left for determination to the judgment of the legislatures and the courts in the individual States. The leading case upon this point is Hurtado *v.* California.[3] The requirements of

---

[1] Holden *v.* Hardy, 169 U. S. 366, 385.

[2] Davies *v.* Davies, L. R. 36 Ch. Div. 359, 364, Kekewich, J.

[3] 110 U. S. 516, discussed *supra.* lecture ii., pp. 63, 64; see also as to criminal procedure *In re* Converse, 137 U. S. 624; Caldwell *v.* Texas, 137 U. S. 692; *Ex*

due process of law, in capital cases, differ materially from those essential in prosecutions for misdemeanors; and, in turn, the latter are based on a different form of procedure from that pursued in civil causes. As the Fourteenth Amendment was not intended to confer upon Congress power to enact a code of municipal law for the States, it does not prevent the States from regulating in all reasonable ways their own systems of police and internal order, and does not confine their legal procedure to strict compliance with the technical rules of the common law.[1]

In all matters of procedure relating to civil causes, the requirements of due process of law are even more difficult to define with precision than when applied to criminal law. Of the many instances found in the reports a few will serve for illustration. One of the earlier decisions, Pennoyer *v.* Neff,[2] established the rule that a personal judgment against a non-resident defendant was invalid in an ordinary civil case where the service of process upon the defendant had been made by publication. It was held that to render the judgment or decree of a court effectual the court must have had jurisdiction of the subject matter or of the parties; and that to enter a money judgment against a non-resident defendant, who had been served only by the publication of process against him, was

---

*parte* Wall, 107 U. S. 265, 289; Barbier *v.* Connolly, 113 U. S. 27, 31; Cross *v.* North Carolina, 132 U. S. 131, 140; *In re* Kemmler, 136 U. S. 436, 448; Holden *v.* Minnesota, 137 U. S. 483; McElvaine *v.* Brush, 142 U. S. 155; Schwab *v* Berggren, 143 U. S. 442; Fielden *v.* Illinois, 143 U. S. 452; Hallinger *v.* Davis, 146 U. S. 314, 322; McNulty *v.* California, 149 U. S. 645, 648: McKane *v.* Durston, 153 U. S. 684; Lambert *v.* Barrett, 157 U. S. 697; Ibid. 159 U. S. 660; Allen *v.* Georgia, 166 U. S. 138; Hodgson *v.* Vermont, 168 U. S. 262, 272.

[1] As to due process of law in contempt proceedings, see *Ex parte* Wall. 107 U. S. 265; Eilenbecker *v.* Plymouth County, 134 U. S. 31; Montana Company *v.* St. Louis Mining &c. Co. 152 U. S. 160, 171; *In re* Debs, Petitioner, 158 U. S. 564; Tinsley *v.* Anderson, 171 U. S. 101.

[2] 95 U. S. 714. Compare York *v.* Texas, 137 U. S. 15.

to proceed without jurisdiction of the party, and, therefore, without due process of law. Of course, this rule does not affect the jurisdiction to proceed *in rem*, as in attachment proceedings. In Wheeler *v.* Jackson,[1] the rule was reiterated, that, where none previously existed, the legislature may prescribe a limitation for the bringing of suits as well as shorten the time within which suits to enforce existing causes of action may be commenced; provided that, in each case, taking all the circumstances into consideration, a reasonable time for the commencement of suit be given by the new law before the bar takes effect. As was said in this case by Mr. Justice Harlan, speaking for the court: " A statute of limitation cannot be said to impair the obligation of a contract, or to deprive one of property without due process of law, unless, in its application to an existing right of action, it unreasonably limits the opportunity to enforce that right by suit." [2]

In Morley *v.* Lake Shore Railway Company [3] a judgment was obtained on a cause of action arising out of contract. Subsequently the legislature of the State of New York passed a statute reducing the rate of interest from seven to six per centum. This act was upheld by the New York Court of Appeals, and their decision affirmed by the Supreme Court of the United States on the ground that the duty to pay interest on this particular judgment (the original contract not having borne interest) arose purely by force of an act of the legislature; and, therefore, the reduction of the rate of interest on the judgment did not impair the obligation of a contract nor deprive the judgment creditor of property without due process of

[1] 137 U. S. 245.
[2] Wheeler *v.* Jackson, 137 U. S. 245, 258; Barrett *v.* Holmes, 102 U. S. 651, 658; Campbell *v.* Holt, 115 U. S. 620; Turner *v.* New York, 168 U. S. 90.
[3] 146 U. S. 162.

law. So, also, statutes validating loans made by a foreign mortgage company,[1] restricting to two the number of new trials to which a party is entitled in a civil action,[2] investing courts with summary powers in certain classes of cases, and especially state statutes authorizing direct and summary methods of procedure in the collection of taxes, have been upheld.[3]

The conclusion at which we must arrive from a consideration of the authorities is that the systems and forms of legal procedure regularly adopted by the States and impartially administered will usually be held by the Supreme Court to be due process of law as far as the Fourteenth Amendment is concerned. Of course, if the legislature provides a system of laws for the government of the courts which secures to the parties the necessary constitutional protection, mere error by the courts in administering the law gives rise to no federal question. When, however, under the pretence of altering or regulating the mode of enforcing the remedy, the statute clearly invades some substantive right,[4] or when a statute harmless on its face is systematically enforced in

---

[1] Gross v. United States Mortgage Co., 108 U. S. 477, 488.

[2] Louisville &c. Railroad Co. v. Woodson, 134 U. S. 614.

[3] McMillen v. Anderson, 95 U. S. 37, 42; Davidson v. New Orleans, 96 U. S. 97, 105; Kelly v. Pittsburgh, 104 U. S. 78; Hagar v. Reclamation District No. 108, 111 U. S. 701; Kentucky Railroad Tax Cases, 115 U. S. 321, 335; Spencer v. Merchant, 125 U. S. 345; Palmer v. McMahon, 133 U. S. 660, 669; Bell's Gap R'd Co. v. Pennsylvania, 134 U. S. 232.

[4] See Thompson v. Utah, 170 U. S. 343, where a statute reducing the number of jurors in criminal cases, not capital, was declared an *ex post facto law* and unconstitutional as applied to felonies committed before the Territory became a State. Compare Thompson v. Missouri, 171 U. S. 380. See criticism of Thompson v. Utah in 32 Am. Law Rev. 633. This criticism seems to me narrow and technical. A perusal of the opinion in its entirety shows the conclusion of Mr. Justice Harlan to be that the word "jury," in the Constitution and the Sixth Amendment, then meant twelve men. That it had come to have that meaning at the time of the adoption of the Constitution cannot be questioned. See discussion, *supra*, pp. 67–70.

violation of fundamental rights, or when a court, trans-
gressing its functions, attempts to render a judgment
without jurisdiction of the subject-matter or notice to the
party, the procedure is not due process of law, and may
be declared void and set aside by the courts under the
jurisdiction conferred by the Fourteenth Amendment.

# LECTURE IV.

## OF THE EQUAL PROTECTION OF THE LAWS.

THE distinctive and characteristic feature of the American system is equality before the law. The first declaration of the American people, upon asserting their independence as a nation, was "that all men are created equal"; and the purpose of the founders of the Union was to establish a government of equality before the law in which privileged classes should not exist — a government of equality of rights, equality of duties and equality of burdens.[1] Our government was the first in the history of the world instituted upon the basis of civil equality and equal law — that "*jus æquum*" for which the Romans longed as embodying true freedom,[2] that *égalité* for which the French have striven so hard and so blindly.[3]

Prior to 1868, there was no provision in the Federal Constitution that specifically secured equal laws and equality before the law. The toleration of slavery undoubtedly prevented the insertion of any reference to

---

[1] "Equality in right, in protection and in burden is the thought which has run through the life of this Nation and its constitutional enactments from the Declaration of Independence to the present hour." Mr. Justice Brewer dissenting in Magoun *v.* Illinois Trust & Savings Bank, 170 U. S. 283, 301.

[2] Wilson's Works (ed. 1896), i. 275.

[3] The French Constitution of 1795 defined equality in these words: "L'égalité consiste en ce que la loi est la même pour tous, soit qu'elle protège, soit qu'elle punisse." It is said that the term "equality before the law" was a translation from the French. At any rate, it is not found in the common law, nor was it used at the time of the adoption of the Constitution. See argument of Charles Sumner in Roberts *v.* Boston, Dec. 4, 1849; Sumner's Works, ii. 327.

equality or liberty. The guaranty to the States of a republican form of government was found to be vague and indefinite, although the Convention of 1787 undoubtedly believed that this provision would constitute a guaranty of individual rights, and be far more efficacious than it proved to be. In proposing the Fourteenth Amendment, its framers pointed out that equality, although "the very spirit and inspiration of our system of government, the absolute foundation upon which it was established," [1] was nowhere adequately secured, and that it had, in many instances, been denied by the States; [2] and they urged the adoption of a measure which would guarantee equality in the future. In order, therefore, to secure this equality before the law, the Reconstruction Committee placed at the end of section 1 a clause providing that no State should "deny to any person within its jurisdiction the equal protection of the laws," [3] and this

---

[1] Cong. Globe, 39th Cong. 1st Session, 2961.

[2] Andrews, Hist. of the United States, ii. 199, 200, 201.

[3] In the Civil Rights Cases, 109 U. S. 3, 11, 13, will be found a very clear exposition of the powers of the Congress in enforcing by legislation the provisions of the Fourteenth Amendment. See also Logan *v.* United States, 144 U. S. 263, 281–295. Consult U. S. Rev. Stat., §§ 1977 *et seq.* The two principal sections are : SEC. 1977. "All persons within the jurisdiction of the United States shall have the same right in every State and Territory to make and enforce contracts, to sue, be parties, give evidence, and to the full and equal benefit of all laws and proceedings for the security of persons and property as is enjoyed by white citizens, and shall be subject to like punishment, pains, penalties, taxes, licenses, and exactions of every kind, and to no other." SEC. 1978. "All citizens of the United States shall have the same right, in every State and Territory, as is enjoyed by white citizens thereof to inherit, purchase, lease, sell, hold, and convey real and personal property." Sections 1977 and 1978 have been applied in the following cases: *In re* Lee Sing, 43 Fed. Rep. 359; Ah Kow *v.* Nunan, 5 Sawy. 552, 562, 563. The language of Mr. Justice Field in the latter case is inspiring. He says: "It is certainly something in which a citizen of the United States may feel a generous pride that the government of his country extends protection to all persons within its jurisdiction; and that every blow aimed at any of them, however humble, come from what quarter it may, is 'caught upon the broad shield of our blessed constitution and our equal laws.'"

has been interpreted to be " a pledge of the protection of equal laws." [1] The provision supplemented and completed the guaranties embodied in the requirement of due process of law; and the framers of the Fourteenth Amendment contemplated that this guaranty of the equal protection of the laws would have the broadest scope.[2] It will probably be found in the future to be the most important and far-reaching of the provisions of this amendment, and to protect where due process of law would be found inadequate fully to conserve our civil and political liberty.

In speaking of our constitutional rights, the words " equality " and " liberty " are sometimes used as if they were synonymous; but this use is quite erroneous. Equality of itself is far from constituting liberty, for it may well exist under the worst of despotisms. " Napoleon distinguished between the two very pointedly when he said to Las Cases at St. Helena that he gave to the Frenchmen all that the circumstances allowed — namely, equality — and that his son, had he succeeded him, would have added liberty. The dictum of Napoleon is mentioned here merely to show that he appreciated the difference in the meaning of the two terms. Equality, of itself, without many other elements, has no intrinsic connection with liberty. All may be equally degraded, equally slavish, or equally tyrannical. Equality is one of the pervading features of Eastern despotism." [3]

[1] Mr. Justice Matthews in Yick Wo v. Hopkins, 118 U. S. 356, 369.

[2] Cong. Globe, 39th Cong. 1st Session, 2764, 2765, 3070 ; app. 217, 219, 253.

[3] Lieber's Civil Liberty and Self-Government, 30. In Missouri v. Lewis, 101 U. S. 22, 31, Mr. Justice Bradley, speaking of this clause, said: "It means that no person or class of persons shall be denied the same protection of the laws which is enjoyed by other persons or other classes in the same place and under like circumstances." In Yick Wo v. Hopkins, 118 U. S. 356, 369, Mr. Justice Matthews said : "These provisions [of the Fourteenth Amendment]

A law may be equal and yet arbitrary and grossly unjust. For example, a law providing for one form of worship and compelling all to attend one church would be equal, but it would be so unjust that it could not possibly stand in any civilized country at the present day. A law confiscating all property of a certain kind might be equal. A law, providing that no class of workmen or of business or professional men should labor more than eight hours per day or demand more than a fixed compensation, would be equal. A law depriving all persons of a certain form of liberty, of freedom of contract, etc., would be equal. Instances might be multiplied. The mere statement of these few examples must suffice to show that an equal law may be an unjust and improper law. Equality is but an attribute of liberty. The true definition of liberty with us is that state of freedom existing under a republican form of government based on just as well as equal laws.[1]

are universal in their application, to all persons within the territorial jurisdiction, without regard to any differences of race, of color, or of nationality ; and the equal protection of the laws is a pledge of the protection of equal laws." In United States *v.* Cruikshank, 92 U. S. 542, 554, Chief Justice Waite said : " The Fourteenth Amendment prohibits a State from denying to any person within its jurisdiction the equal protection of the laws ; but this provision does not, any more than the one which precedes it, and which we have just considered, add anything to the rights which one citizen has under the Constitution against another. The equality of the rights of citizens is a principle of republicanism. Every republican government is in duty bound to protect all its citizens in the enjoyment of this principle, if within its power. That duty was originally assumed by the States; and it still remains there. The only obligation resting upon the United States is to see that the States do not deny the right. This the amendment guarantees, but no more."

[1] Equal laws must not be confounded with diversity of laws, even in the same State. There may be one system in one part of a State and an entirely different system in other parts. Missouri *v.* Lewis, 101 U. S. 22, 31; Hayes *v.* Missouri, 120 U. S. 68. An interesting article on the term "liberty" will be found in 4 Harvard Law Rev. 365. A definition of "liberty" will also be found in The Stockton Laundry Case, 26 Fed. Rep. 611, 614. The definition of Mr. Justice Swayne in the Slaughter-House Cases, 16 Wall. 36, 127, is terse and emphatic: "Liberty is freedom from all restraints but such as are justly imposed by law."

By the Fourteenth Amendment, the principle of equality before the law, a principle so vital and fundamental in American institutions, ceased to be a mere theory or sentiment, or an implied condition, and became incorporated into the organic law as the fundamental right of every individual. Previous to that time, "equality" was an abstract theory; there was no method of enforcing the right. It had force only as a general principle of political action, and practically depended for its observance upon the wisdom and fair-mindedness of the state legislatures. Under the Fourteenth Amendment, that which had previously been recognized only as a principle of natural justice became a part of the Constitution itself; "equality" was made an essential principle of "liberty" and of the "republican form of government" guaranteed to the States, and power was given to the Congress and the federal judiciary to enforce the right. The provision, if properly construed, assures to every person within the jurisdiction of any State, whether he be rich or poor, humble or haughty, citizen or alien, the protection of equal laws, applicable to all alike and impartially administered without favor or discrimination. Thus what was the spirit became the written rule of American state governments; and equality, infused through the mass of our rights and duties, now pervades, unites, invigorates, the whole system.

As has been said in the preceding lectures, although the wrongs of the colored race may have furnished the immediate occasion for the Fourteenth Amendment, it was not intended that the protection of its beneficent provisions should be limited to that race; and, accordingly, protection against unequal laws has been sought and found under the shield of the Fourteenth Amendment by persons of

every race, rank and grade — not only citizens but aliens.
Indeed, in only a few instances, and those for the most
part criminal cases, has this provision of the amendment
been invoked on behalf of the negroes.[1] "The equal
protection of the laws" has been authoritatively declared
to mean that all persons subject to legislation "shall be
treated alike, under like circumstances and conditions,
both in the privileges conferred and in the liabilities
imposed."[2]

The principal cases affecting the colored race may be
briefly mentioned.[3] In Bush *v.* Kentucky[4] the Supreme
Court said : "A denial to citizens of African descent, because of their race, of the right or privilege accorded to
white citizens, of participating as jurors in the administration of justice, is a discrimination against the former inconsistent with the amendment, and within the power of
Congress, by appropriate legislation, to prevent ; that to
compel a colored man to submit to a trial before a jury
drawn from a panel from which is excluded, because of
their color, every man of his race, however well qualified

---

[1] Holden *v.* Hardy, 169 U. S. 366, 383; Williams *v.* Mississippi, 170 U. S. 213.

[2] Hayes *v.* Missouri, 120 U. S. 68, 71, 72 ; see also Barbier *v.* Connolly, 113
U. S. 27, 31, 32 ; Kentucky Railroad Tax Cases, 115 U. S. 321, 337; Phila. Fire
Association *v.* New York, 119 U. S. 110, 120, 121; Missouri Railway Co. *v.* Mackay,
127 U. S. 205, 209; Home Ins. Co. *v.* New York, 134 U. S. 594, 606, 607; Hal-
linger *v.* Davis, 146 U. S. 314, 321; Giozza *v.* Tiernan, 148 U. S. 657, 662; St.
Louis & San Francisco R'y *v.* Mathews, 165 U. S. 1, 25; Gulf, Colorado and
Santa Fé R'y *v.* Ellis, 165 U. S. 150, 155. Compare Railroad Company *v.* Brown,
17 Wall. 445.

[3] United States *v.* Reese, 92 U. S. 214; United States *v.* Cruikshank, 92 U. S.
542; Strauder *v.* West Virginia, 100 U. S. 303; Virginia *v.* Rives, 100 U. S. 313;
*Ex parte* Virginia, 100 U. S. 339 ; Neal *v.* Delaware, 103 U. S. 370; Pace *v.* Alabama, 106 U. S. 583; Bush *v.* Kentucky, 107 U. S. 110; Civil Rights Cases, 109
U. S. 3 ; *Ex parte* Yarbrough, 110 U. S. 651 ; Gibson *v.* Mississippi, 162 U. S.
565 ; Charley Smith *v.* Mississippi, 162 U. S. 592 ; Plessy *v.* Ferguson, 163 U. S.
537 ; People *v.* King, 110 N. Y. 418 ; Ferguson *v.* Gies, 82 Mich. 358 ; Baylies *v.*
Curry, 128 Ill. 287.

[4] 107 U. S. 110, 118.

by education and character to discharge the functions of
jurors, is a denial of the equal protection of the laws; " but
in Pace *v.* Alabama,[1] it was decided that a state statute pun-
ishing adultery or fornication between persons of the white
and black races more severely than where the parties are of
the same color did not constitute inequality or a discrimination, the punishment of each offending party being the
same.    And in Plessy *v.* Ferguson,[2] the Supreme Court
upheld an act of the legislature of Louisiana by which all
railway companies were compelled to provide equal but
separate accommodations for colored passengers, and the
officers of the trains were given power to assign each passenger to the coach or compartment used for the race
to which that passenger belonged.    In delivering the
opinion of the court, Mr. Justice Brown emphasized what
seems to be the crucial test of the validity of an act of a
state legislature under the police power in so far as the
provisions of the Fourteenth Amendment are concerned.
He said : " So far, then, as a conflict with the Fourteenth
Amendment is concerned, the case reduces itself to the
question whether the statute of Louisiana is a reasonable
regulation, and with respect to this there must necessarily
be a large discretion on the part of the legislature.    In
determining the question of reasonableness it is at liberty
to act with reference to the established usages, customs
and traditions of the people, and with a view to the promotion of their comfort, and the preservation of the public peace and good order."    In this case the railroad was
a purely local line, and no question as to the effect of

[1] 106 U. S. 583.

[2] 163 U. S. 537, 550; Louisville &c. Railway Co. *v.* Mississippi, 133 U. S. 587.
Compare Railroad Company *v.* Brown, 17 Wall. 445, where an act of Congress
(12 Stat. 805) provided that no person should be excluded from the cars on
account of color.

such legislation upon the federal control over interstate commerce was raised or decided.[1]

Two principal classes of questions arise under the constitutional requirement of equal laws : the one relates to the power of classification, and the other to the power of taxation.[2] Under one or the other of these two heads most of the cases are to be found.

Many statutes have been sustained as proper classification, which selected particular classes of corporations or particular trades or businesses or kinds of property for taxation or regulation not imposed upon other classes of property.[3] This rule is reasonable and necessary. But

[1] As to the power to maintain separate schools for white and colored children, see Lehew *v.* Brummell, 103 Mo. 546; Chrisman *v.* Brookhaven, 70 Miss. 477. Compare Louisville, &c. R'y Co. *v.* Miss., 133 U. S. 587, and Roberts *v.* The City of Boston, 5 Cush. 198. See also Board of Education *v.* Tinnon, 26 Kans. 1 ; The People *v.* Board of Education, 101 Ill. 308.

[2] In Phila. Fire Association *v.* New York, 119 U. S. 110, 120, 121, Mr. Justice Harlan, in the dissenting opinion, said: " The denial of the equal protection of the laws may occur in various ways. It will most often occur in the enforcement of laws imposing taxes. An individual is denied the equal protection of the laws if his property is subjected by the State to higher taxation than is imposed upon like property of other individuals in the same community."

[3] Munn *v.* Illinois, 94 U. S. 113; Peik *v.* Chicago, etc. Railway Co., 94 U. S. 164; Railroad Co. *v.* Richmond, 96 U. S. 521 ; Barbier *v.* Connolly, 113 U. S. 27; Soon Hing *v.* Crowley, 113 U. S. 703; Wurts *v.* Hoagland, 114 U. S. 606; Bank of Redemption *v.* Boston, 125 U. S. 60; Pembina Mining Co. *v.* Pennsylvania, 125 U. S. 181 ; Dow *v.* Beidelman, 125 U. S. 680; Missouri Railway Co. *v.* Mackey, 127 U. S. 205; Minneapolis &c. Railway Co. *v.* Herrick, 127 U. S. 210; Powell *v.* Pennsylvania, 127 U. S. 678 ; Kidd *v.* Pearson, 128 U. S. 1 ; Minneapolis Railway Co. *v.* Beckwith, 129 U.S. 26 ; Palmer *v.* McMahon, 133 U. S. 660 ; Eilenbecker *v.* Plymouth County, 134 U. S. 31; Home Ins. Co. *v.* New York, 134 U. S. 594; Crowley *v.* Christensen, 137 U. S. 86; Charlotte &c. Railroad *v.* Gibbes, 142 U.S. 386; Budd *v.* New York, 143 U. S. 517 ; New York *v.* Squire, 145 U. S. 175 ; Giozza *v.* Tiernan, 148 U. S. 657 ; Minneapolis & St. Louis Railway *v.* Emmons, 149 U. S. 364; Columbus Southern Railway *v.* Wright, 151 U. S. 470; N. Y. & N. E. Railroad Co. *v.* Bristol, 151 U. S. 556; Montana Company *v.* St. Louis Mining &c. Co., 152 U. S. 160; Marchant *v.* Pennsylvania Railroad, 153 U. S. 380; Brass *v.* Stoeser, 153 U. S. 391; St. L. & San Francisco Railway *v.* Gill, 156 U. S. 649 ; Moore *v.* Missouri, 159 U. S. 673; Lowe *v.* Kansas, 163 U. S. 81; Plessy *v.* Ferguson, 163 U. S. 537; Fallbrook Irrigation District *v.* Bradley, 164 U. S. 112; Covington &c. Turnpike Co. *v.* Sandford, 164 U. S. 578, 597; St. Louis &

classification cannot be arbitrary;[1] it must be just and reasonable; it can never be a cloak or mask for class legislation. And whether or not the classification is warranted or permissible under the Federal Constitution must always be a judicial question for the federal courts finally to determine.[2]

In Gulf, Colorado and Santa Fé Railway *v.* Ellis,[3] the whole subject of classification by the States in its various aspects was reviewed by Mr. Justice Brewer, who said: " Yet it is equally true that such classification cannot be made arbitrarily. The State . . . may not say that all men beyond a certain age shall be alone thus subjected, or all men possessed of a certain wealth. These are distinctions which do not furnish any proper basis for the attempted classification. That must always rest upon some difference which bears a reasonable and just relation to the act in respect to which the classification is proposed, and can never be made arbitrarily and without any such basis. . . . But arbitrary selection can never be justified by calling it classification. The equal protection demanded by the Fourteenth Amendment forbids this. . . . No duty rests more imperatively upon the courts than the

San Francisco R'y *v.* Mathews, 165 U. S. 1; Jones *v.* Brim, 165 U. S. 180; N. Y. N. H. and H. Railroad *v.* New York, 165 U. S. 628; Chicago, Burlington &c. R'd *v.* Chicago, 166 U. S. 226; Merchants' Bank *v.* Pennsylvania, 167 U. S. 461; Holden *v.* Hardy, 169 U. S. 366; Wilson *v.* North Carolina, 169 U. S. 586; Williams *v.* Mississippi, 170 U. S. 213; Magoun *v.* Illinois Trust & Savings Bank, 170 U. S. 283; Tinsley *v.* Anderson, 171 U. S. 101; King *v.* Mullins, 171 U. S. 404. Compare, however, Yick Wo *v.* Hopkins, 118 U. S. 356; Chicago &c. Railway Co. *v.* Minnesota, 134 U. S. 418; Minneapolis Railway Co. *v.* Minnesota, 134 U. S. 467; Gulf, Colorado & Santa Fé R'y *v.* Ellis, 165 U. S. 150; Smyth *v.* Ames, 169 U. S. 466; Schollenberger *v.* Pennsylvania, 171 U. S. 1; Collins *v.* New Hampshire, 171 U. S. 30.

[1] As Hamilton said, The Continentalist, Hamilton's Works, i. 270, "The genius of liberty reprobates everything arbitrary or discretionary in taxation."

[2] Smyth *v.* Ames, 169 U. S. 466, 526.

[3] 165 U. S. 150, 155, 159, 160, 165; see also The Railroad Tax Cases, 13 Fed. Rep. 722, 773, 782; The State *v.* Loomis, 115 Mo. 307.

enforcement of those constitutional provisions intended to secure that equality of rights which is the foundation of free government. . . . It is apparent that the mere fact of classification is not sufficient to relieve a statute from the reach of the equality clause of the Fourteenth Amendment, and that in all cases it must appear not only that a classification has been made, but also that it is one based upon some reasonable ground — some difference which bears a just and proper relation to the attempted classification — and is not a mere arbitrary selection." [1]

In holding the Anti-Trust law of Texas unconstitutional, Swayne, D. J. [2] said : " This subject of equality before the law is a fundamental principle of English and American liberty, which not only has been held sacred in all latterday constitutions, state and federal, but the principle has been guarded by the courts with jealous watchfulness, to see that the citizen may have guaranteed to him this inestimable privilege and condition. . . . This statute under discussion is clearly class legislation, discriminating against some and favoring others. It is not that character of legislation which, in carrying out a public purpose, is limited in its application, and, within the sphere of its operation, affects alike all persons similarly situated. It may affect, and does affect, individuals of the same class in an opposite way. It favors some individuals of a certain class, and denounces other individuals of the same class. This statute exempts no class. On the contrary, it seeks to exempt certain classes of property, which is carrying the doctrine beyond any case to which we have had access. All property in the State is entitled to equal

---

[1] Bell's Gap R'd Co. *v.* Pennsylvania, 134 U. S. 232 ; Adams Express Company *v.* Ohio, 165 U. S. 194, 228; Western Union Telegraph Co. *v.* Indiana, 165 U. S. 304, 309.

[2] *In re* Grice, 79 Fed. Rep. 627, 645, 646.

protection, and no special property is entitled to, or ought to receive, any special favors. Discrimination may be as potent against the citizen, in the direction of his property, as if aimed directly against himself personally."

In The State *v.* Loomis,[1] recognized as one of the leading cases, the Supreme Court of Missouri, by Black, J., said : " Classification for legislative purposes must have some reasonable basis upon which to stand. It must be evident that differences which would serve for a classification for some purposes furnish no reason whatever for a classification for legislative purposes. The differences which will support class legislation must be such as in the nature of things furnish a reasonable basis for separate laws and regulations."

Among cases of proper classification will be found Hayes *v.* Missouri,[2] in which it was held that a state statute providing that, in capital cases in cities having a population of over one hundred thousand inhabitants, the State was to be allowed fifteen peremptory challenges to jurors, while elsewhere in the State it was allowed only eight, did not deny to a person accused of murder in a city containing over one hundred thousand inhabitants the equal protection of the laws enjoined by the Fourteenth Amendment ; and that it was not error to refuse to limit the number of peremptory challenges of the State to eight. The classification as well as the regulation of municipal corporations is within the almost unlimited power of the legislatures.[3]

---

[1] 115 Mo. 307, 314.        [2] 120 U. S. 68.

[3] Kelly *v.* Pittsburgh, 104 U. S. 78 ; Forsyth *v.* Hammond, 166 U. S. 506. In Williams *v.* Eggleston, 170 U. S. 304, 310, Mr. Justice Brewer says: " The regulation of municipal corporations is a matter peculiarly within the domain of state control ; that the State is not compelled by the Federal Constitution to grant to all its municipal corporations the same territorial extent, or the same duties and powers. A municipal corporation is, so far as its purely municipal relations are concerned, simply an agency of the State for

In Missouri Railway Co. *v.* Mackey,[1] it was said that a statute of Kansas abolishing the fellow-servant doctrine as applied to railway accidents, did not deny to railroads the equal protection of the laws. The same ruling has been made in reference to statutes requiring railways to erect and maintain fences and cattle guards, and making them liable for double damages for failure to do so.[2] So also a statute has been upheld which made railway companies liable for fires resulting from escaping cinders irrespective of the general rule of negligence.[3]

The more important cases arise under statutes levying taxes. The Supreme Court has declared that the Fourteenth Amendment was not intended to compel the States to conform to an iron rule of equal taxation.[4] Indeed, in one of the early cases, the extreme statement was made that "the Federal Constitution imposes no restraints on the States" in regard to unequal taxation. If this lan-

conducting the affairs of government, and as such it is subject to the control of the legislature. That body may place one part of the State under one municipal organization and another part of the State under another organization of an entirely different character. These are matters of a purely local nature, in respect to which the Federal Constitution does not limit the power of the State."

[1] 127 U. S. 205, 209. This case also points out clearly that there is no constitutional objection to legislation that is merely special in its character. "The greater part of all legislation is special, either in the objects sought to be attained by it, or in the extent of its application."

[2] Missouri Pacific Railway Co. *v.* Humes, 115 U. S. 512 ; Minneapolis Railway Co. *v.* Beckwith, 129 U. S. 26; Minneapolis & St. Louis Railway *v.* Emmons, 149 U. S. 364.

[3] St. Louis & San Francisco R'y *v.* Mathews, 165 U. S. 1.

[4] Bell's Gap R'd Co. *v.* Pennsylvania, 134 U. S. 232, 237; Giozza *v.* Tiernan, 148 U. S. 657, 662. "Perfect equality and perfect uniformity of taxation as regards individuals or corporations, or the different classes of property subject to taxation, is a dream unrealized. It may be admitted that the system which most nearly attains this is the best. But the most complete system which can be devised, must, when we consider the immense variety of subjects which it necessarily embraces, be imperfect." State Railroad Tax Cases, 92 U. S. 575, 612.

[5] Davidson *v.* New Orleans, 96 U. S. 97, 105.

guage means that the amendment does not prohibit legitimate classification, and that it does not require all kinds of property to be taxed at the same rate, the statement is correct. Certain kinds of property and certain classes of persons can be singled out for taxation, even though this may result in exempting other property and other classes from any tax burden. But the statement is too broad, and is misleading. Unequal taxes may not be imposed upon property of the same kind, in the same condition and used for the same purpose. "Equality is of the very essence of the taxing power itself."[1] The Fourteenth Amendment does impose a practical and effective restraint against such taxes. It requires that the power of taxation, so great and so liable to abuse, shall be exercised impartially and by equal laws, and that taxes shall be imposed proportionately upon all persons and corporations properly within the same class, owning like property or exercising like rights under substantially similar conditions. In other words, as Mr. Justice Matthews said in the Kentucky Railroad Tax cases:[2] "The rule of equality, in respect to the subject, only requires the same means and methods to be applied impartially to all the constituents of each class, so that the law shall operate equally and uniformly upon all persons in similar circumstances." Or as Chief Justice Fuller said in Giozza *v.* Tiernan:[3] "It is enough that there is no discrimination in favor of one as against another of the same class."

The extent of the power of the States was stated by Mr. Justice Lamar in Pacific Express Company *v.* Seibert[4] as follows: "This court has repeatedly laid down

---

[1] In Railroad & Telephone Co's *v.* Board of Equalizers, 85 Fed. Rep. 302, 317, Clark, D. J. said, 317: "An unequal and unjust exaction is no longer a tax, but confiscation."

[2] 115 U. S 321, 337.     148 U. S. 657, 662.     [4] 142 U. S. 339, 351

the doctrine that diversity of taxation, both with respect to the amount imposed and the various species of property selected either for bearing its burdens or from being exempt from them, is not inconsistent with a perfect uniformity and equality of taxation in the proper sense of those terms; and that a system which imposes the same tax upon every species of property, irrespective of its nature or condition or class, will be destructive of the principle of uniformity and equality in taxation and of a just adaptation of property to its burdens." And in Bell's Gap R'd Co. *v.* Pennsylvania,[1] Mr. Justice Bradley said : " The provision in the Fourteenth Amendment, that no State shall deny to any person within its jurisdiction the equal protection of the laws, was not intended to prevent a State from adjusting its system of taxation in all proper and reasonable ways. . . . But clear and hostile discriminations against particular persons and classes, especially such as are of an unusual character, unknown to the practice of our governments, might be obnoxious to the constitutional prohibition. It would, however, be impracticable and unwise to attempt to lay down any general rule or definition on the subject, that would include all cases. They must be decided as they arise." [2]

---

[1] 134 U. S. 232, 237.

[2] In the following cases the equality clause was discussed with reference to taxation : Albany City Nat. Bank *v.* Maher, 9 Fed. Rep. 884, 885 ; Louisville & N. R. Co. *v.* Railroad Commission of Tennessee, 19 Fed. Rep. 679, 693; Northern Pac. R. Co. *v.* Walker, 47 Fed. Rep. 681, 686 ; State Railroad Tax Cases, 92 U. S. 575, 612; Kelly *v.* Pittsburgh, 104 U. S. 78 ; Hagar *v.* Reclamation District No. 108, 111 U. S. 701, 705; Kentucky Railroad Tax Cases, 115 U. S. 321, 337; Santa Clara Co. *v.* South. Pac. Railroad, 118 U. S. 394; Spencer *v.* Merchant, 125 U. S. 345; Paulsen *v.* Portland, 149 U. S. 30; Fallbrook Irrigation District *v.* Bradley, 164 U. S. 112; Aberdeen Bank *v.* Chehalis County, 166 U. S. 440, 454; Savings Society *v.* Multnomah County, 169 U. S. 421; Magoun *v.* Illinois Trust & Savings Bank, 170 U. S. 283; Dundee Mortgage, etc., Co. *v.* School-Dist. No. 1, 19 Fed. Rep. 359; Gillette *v.* City of Denver, 21

We saw in the second lecture of this course that corporations are protected by the Fourteenth Amendment. In almost every State today there is observable a determination and a tendency to impose upon corporations much more than their fair share of the burdens of taxation. This is now done sometimes under the pretence of classification,[1] and sometimes as a franchise or license fee. That these taxes are becoming grossly unjust and oppressive cannot be denied. Relief will undoubtedly be found in time, as relief was found from the rule supposed to have been sanctioned by Munn *v.* Illinois. But until a limit is declared to discrimination and inequality in the taxation of corporations, the vested interests represented by corporate enterprises must submit to taxes more or less unjust and at times confiscatory.

In the case of San Bernardino Co. *v.* Southern Pacific Railroad,[2] Mr. Justice Field, in referring to taxes unjustly discriminating against corporations, expressed his regret that the Supreme Court did not deem it necessary to decide the point there presented, and said : " At the present day nearly all great enterprises are conducted by corporations. Hardly an industry can be named that is not in

Fed. Rep. 822; Dundee Mortgage Trust Investment Co. *v.* Parrish, 24 Fed. Rep. 197; Fraser *v.* M'Conway & Torley Co., 82 Fed. Rep. 257. The following are some of the decisions in the state courts recognizing the requirement of equality in the levying of taxes: Stuart *v.* Palmer, 74 N. Y. 183, 189; People *v.* Equitable Trust Co., 96 N. Y. 387, 395; Hammett *v.* Philadelphia, 65 Pa. St. 146, 153; Washington Avenue, 69 Pa. St. 352, 363; Ruan Street, 132 Pa. St. 257, 277, 279; Davis *v.* City of Litchfield, 145 Ill. 313, 327; Knowlton *v.* Supervisors of Rock County, 9 Wis. 410, 421–423; Woodbridge *v.* The City of Detroit, 8 Mich. 274, 301; The People *v.* Salem, 20 Mich. 452, 474, 475; Lexington *v.* McQuillan's Heirs, 9 Dana (Ky.), 513, 517; State *v.* Express Co., 60 N. H. 219, 236, 252, 253, 263; State *v.* Township Committee of Readington, 36 N. J. L. 66, 70; Exchange Bank of Columbus *v.* Hines, 3 Ohio St. 1, 15; Mayor *v.* Dargan, 45 Ala. 310, 320.

[1] Adams Express Company *v.* Ohio, 165 U. S. 194 and 166 U. S. 185; Adams Express Company *v.* Kentucky, 166 U. S. 171.

[2] 118 U. S. 417, 422.

some way promoted by them, and a vast portion of the wealth of the country is in their hands. It is, therefore, of the greatest interest to them whether their property is subject to the same rules of assessment and taxation as like property of natural persons, or whether elements which affect the valuation of property are to be omitted from consideration when it is owned by them, and considered when it is owned by natural persons; and thus the valuation of property be made to vary, not according to its condition or use, but according to its ownership. The question is not whether the State may not claim for grants of privileges and franchises a fixed sum per year, or a percentage of earnings of a corporation — that is not controverted — but whether it may prescribe rules for the valuation of property for taxation which will vary according as it is held by individuals or by corporations. The question is of transcendent importance, and it will come here and continue to come until it is authoritatively decided in harmony with the great constitutional amendment which insures to every person, whatever his position or association, the equal protection of the laws; and that necessarily implies freedom from the imposition of unequal burdens under the same conditions." This was said in May, 1886, but the point has not been squarely decided to this day. The question arose in Northern Pacific Railroad Co. *v.* Walker,[1] argued be-

---

[1] 47 Fed. Rep. 681, 685, 686. That national banks can be classified by themselves for purposes of taxation but cannot be taxed higher than other capital of the same class, see Boyer *v.* Boyer, 113 U. S. 689, 701: " Upon such facts, and in view of the revenue laws of the State, it seems difficult to avoid the conclusion that, in respect of county taxation of national bank shares, there has been, and is, such a discrimination, in favor of other moneyed capital against capital invested in such shares, as is not consistent with the legislation of Congress. The exemptions in favor of other moneyed capital appear to be of such a substantial character in amount as to take the present case out of the operation of the rule that it is not absolute equality that is contemplated

fore United States Judges Caldwell and Thomas, of the Eighth Circuit. In that case lands belonging to railroad companies were exempted simply because owned by such companies, presenting the converse of a tax law discriminating against railroads. It was held that property of the same kind and in the same condition, and used for the same purpose, cannot be divided into different classes for purposes of taxation and taxed by a different rule, because it belongs to different owners, whether natural persons or corporations.

In the Illinois Inheritance Tax cases, just decided,[1] the Supreme Court has held that a progressive inheritance tax was not in conflict with the Fourteenth Amendment, and that inheritances may be classified solely according to amount, and each class taxed at a different rate. The tax imposed by the Illinois statute was not in itself unreasonable; the maximum was six per cent on estates of over fifty thousand dollars, being the equivalent of about one year's income.[2] If the maximum rate could be stopped there, no one would complain of graduated taxation, but the rate which is reasonable today may be

by the act of Congress; a rule which rests upon the ground that exact uniformity or equality of taxation cannot in the nature of things be expected or attained under any system. But as substantial equality is attainable, and is required by the supreme law of the land, in respect of State taxation of national bank shares, when the inequality is so palpable as to show that the discrimination against capital invested in such shares is serious, the courts have no discretion but to interfere." See also the following cases: Mercantile Bank v. New York, 121 U. S. 138; Davenport Bank v. Davenport, 123 U. S. 83; Bank of Redemption v. Boston, 125 U. S. 60; Palmer v. McMahon, 133 U. S. 660; Aberdeen Bank v. Chehalis County, 166 U. S. 440; Merchants' Bank v. Pennsylvania, 167 U. S. 461; Young v. Wempe, 46 Fed. Rep. 354.

[1] Magoun v. Illinois Trust & Savings Bank, 170 U. S. 283; but see State v. Ferris, 53 Ohio St. 314; State v. Gorman, 40 Minn. 232; State v. Mann, 76 Wis. 469; Curry v. Spencer, 61 N. H. 624; State v. Hamlin, 86 Me. 495; Gelsthorpe v. Furnell, 51 Pac. Rep. 267; *In re* House Bill No. 122, 48 Pac. Rep. 535; and dissenting opinion of Lathrop, J., in Minot v. Winthrop, 162 Mass. 113, 129.

[2] Magoun v. Illinois Trust & Savings Bank, 170 U. S. 283, 285.

confiscatory to-morrow. Last year the New York legislature passed a statute imposing a progressive inheritance tax rising to a maximum of fifteen per cent. Governor Black vetoed the bill on grounds of broad public policy and high statesmanship. A few years ago an act was introduced in the Illinois legislature limiting to $500,000 the amount any person could inherit even from a parent, and forfeiting or escheating the surplus to the State, but the attempt then failed. Or was it only postponed? The effect of the New York measure, although vetoed, was to drive millions of capital out of the State. Many men of wealth, justly apprehensive of taxation so unequal and unfair as to amount to confiscation, changed their residences.

If the best interests of a State are to be consulted, the legislature will always levy equal and uniform taxes. Confidence is the greatest strength of any State, as it is the best capital of any business man. Security from socialistic and arbitrary taxation is the most essential of all elements in a strong and stable government. It is true that one can escape from arbitrary state taxation by going into some more conservative State; but surely the necessity for this extreme step ought to be avoided. There is, however, a still more serious danger. The Federal Congress may constitutionally impose an inheritance tax, for such a tax is clearly an excise or duty.[1] Congress has power to reach out and tax all inheritances; and, by exempting estates or inheritances of twenty thousand dollars in value, the great burden of federal taxation could be thrown on the richer States of the North. From unfair, unequal, destructive federal legislation there is no refuge except expatriation. Such a policy would drive capital to Canada. The Fourteenth Amendment

[1] Scholey *v.* Rew, 23 Wall. 331, 346.

has failed, at least for the present, to prevent graduated state inheritance taxes. It remains to be determined whether the requirement of section 8 of Article I. of the Constitution that "all duties, imposts and excises" laid and collected by Congress "shall be uniform throughout the United States," will protect the people from progressive federal inheritance taxes.[1] Congress has no power to regulate inheritances; it could not prescribe the proportion that should go to the widow and the children; it could not escheat in default of heirs; it could not ordain the division in cases of intestacy. This subject is wholly within the exclusive province of the States. The power of Congress, therefore, is circumscribed; it can only tax inheritances; it cannot regulate them. In this distinction, perhaps, we may find protection from federal progressive inheritance taxes.

It is important to bear in mind that while the Supreme Court has declined to nullify under the Fourteenth Amendment a state law imposing a progressive inheritance tax, there is no intimation that progressive taxation upon property or individuals or corporations would have been sustained. On the contrary, in the dissenting opinion, Mr. Justice Brewer said: "It seems to be conceded that if this were a tax upon property such increase in the rate of taxation could not be sustained."[2]

Recognizing, as we must, that, under this decision, the Fourteenth Amendment does not prohibit the particular form of arbitrary and unequal taxation involved in progressive inheritance taxes, there still remains the question of public policy to be argued in the forum of public

[1] See discussion in Dos Passos' Inheritance Tax Law, 46–50.

[2] Magoun *v.* Illinois Trust & Savings Bank, 170 U. S. 283, 302 ; see also *In re* Yot Sang, 75 Fed. Rep. 983, 985.

opinion; there still remains the appeal to the ultimate tribunal of the public judgment and the more enlarged theatre of public discussion.[1] If the arbitrary power does exist, it is the duty of the bar to strive to prevent the general adoption by the States of this policy, which tends so strongly towards socialism and spoliation. The tendency to impose such taxes must be checked.[2] The country will not sanction progressive taxation if public opinion be properly directed and enlightened, for the American people seldom go wrong if they thoroughly understand the tendency and the scope of objectionable measures. Constitutions are written in vain and built on shifting sands if public opinion be not just and honest, if there be no prevalent sense of right and justice, if the spirit of the people be not sound and honest and conservative.[3] Character, after all, really governs the world in "the working of that immutable law of justice, which rules the destinies

---

[1] Yick Wo *v.* Hopkins, 118 U. S. 356, 370; Davidson *v.* New Orleans, 96 U. S. 97, 104.

[2] In this connection Mr. Justice Miller's famous language in Loan Association *v.* Topeka, 20 Wall. 655, 662, is well worth quoting: "It must be conceded that there are such rights in every free government beyond the control of the State. A government which recognized no such rights, which held the lives, the liberty, and the property of its citizens subject at all times to the absolute disposition and unlimited control of even the most democratic depository of power, is after all but a despotism. It is true it is a despotism of the many, of the majority, if you choose to call it so, but it is none the less a despotism. It may well be doubted if a man is to hold all that he is accustomed to call his own, all in which he has placed his happiness, and the security of which is essential to that happiness, under the unlimited dominion of others, whether it is not wiser that this power should be exercised by one man than by many."

"The theory of our governments, state and national, is opposed to the deposit of unlimited power anywhere. The executive, the legislative, and the judicial branches of these governments are all of limited and defined powers."

"There are limitations on such power which grow out of the essential nature of all free governments. Implied reservations of individual rights, without which the social compact could not exist, and which are respected by all governments entitled to the name."

[3] De Tocqueville's Democracy in America, i. 413.

of nations, to their peace or their misery, to their shame or to their glory." [1]  As Judge Story said : "Republics are created by the virtue, public spirit, and intelligence of the citizens." [2]  Let the bar instruct public opinion, and the people will see to it that progressive taxation secures no footing in our States.

Although many writers and philosophers of the school of Rousseau have written in favor of progressive or graduated taxation, in order, as some frankly avow, to level property and thus force a redistribution of wealth, yet thoughtful, practical and broad-minded statesmen and political economists have repeatedly shown that the progressive or graduated tax is the most arbitrary form of taxation, vicious in principle and dangerous in tendency.

The rule of our past has been proportional taxation — namely, the taxation of all property of the same class on the same rate of computation.  Where the principle of proportional or equal taxation is abandoned, no definite rule remains.  As Mr. Lecky has said in his "Democracy and Liberty" : [3] "At what point the higher scale is to begin, or to what degree it is to be raised, depends wholly on the policy of governments and the balance of parties.  The ascending scale may at first be very moderate, but it may at any time, when fresh taxes are required, be made more severe till it reaches or approaches the point of confiscation.  No fixed line or amount of graduation can be maintained upon principle, or with any chance of finality. . . . Graduated taxation is certain to be contagious, and it is certain not to rest within the limits that its originators desired."  Even those who favor progressive taxes on

[1] Nicoll's Political Life of our Time, i. 22, 252; ii. 204.

[2] Story on the Const. 5 ed. ii. 658.  See also Thorpe's Const. Hist. of the U. S. i. 7.

[3] i. 286 *et seq.*

inheritances frankly warn us to be cautious in advocating
or attempting any general application of the principle,
and confess that the objections to progression in this
country may be insuperable if we give heed to the dangers
it threatens.   Many historians and writers show the true
nature and tendency of progressive taxation.   It cannot be
other than arbitrary; that is to say, there is no rule or
principle yet discovered by which to control or prevent
the severest rate, or, indeed, spoliation.   Great dangers
lurk in progressive taxation; it contains the germs of
confiscation.[1]

[1] David A. Wells in North Am. Rev. cxxx. 238-239; Bastable on Public
Finance, 292-294, 555; Leroy-Beaulieu, Traité d'Economie Politique (1896), iv.
748-767; Leroy-Beaulieu, Science des Finances, i. 139, 140; Beauregard, Elé-
ments d'Economie Politique, 313; Stourm, Dictionnaire d'Economie Politique,
ii. 21.   In McCulloch on Taxation, published in London in 1845, and for fifty
years the standard treatise in England on the subject, the author says (pp.
141 *et seq.*): "It is argued that, in order fairly to proportion the tax to the
ability of the contributors, such a graduated scale of duty should be adopted
as should press lightly on the smaller class of properties and incomes, and
increase according as they become larger and more able to bear taxation.
We take leave, however, to protest against this proposal, which is not more
seductive than it is unjust and dangerous. . . . If it either pass entirely over
some classes, or press on some less heavily than on others, it is unjustly imposed.   Government, in such a case, has plainly stepped out of its proper
province, and has assessed the tax, not for the legitimate purpose of appro-
priating a certain proportion of the revenues of its subjects to the public
exigencies, but that it might at the same time regulate the incomes of the
contributors; that is, that it might depress one class and elevate another.
The toleration of such a principle would necessarily lead to every species of
abuse.   That equal taxes on property or income will be more severely felt by
the poorer than by the richer classes is undeniable; but the same is true of
every imposition which does not subvert the subsisting relations among the
different orders of society. . . . Let it not be supposed that the principle of
graduation may be carried a certain extent, and then stopped. . . . In such
matters the maxim of *obsta principiis* should be firmly adhered to by every
prudent and honest statesman.   Graduation is not an evil to be paltered
with.   Adopt it and you will effectually paralyze industry and check accu-
mulation; at the same time that every man who has any property will hasten,
by carrying it out of the country, to protect it from confiscation.   The savages
described by Montesquieu, who to get at the fruit cut down the tree, are
about as good financiers as the advocates of this sort of taxes.   Wherever
they are introduced security is at an end.   Even if taxes on income were

There can be no doubt that the rate of taxation upon selected subjects or classes is in the discretion of the legislature. The rate may be excessive or unjust, but the courts cannot interfere. " The power to tax involves the power to destroy." [1]  But, if legislatures are compelled to impose equal taxes on all, we have, in a country like ours where property is generally distributed, a sufficient protection and safeguard against abuse by the majority. Grant, however, that the legislatures are free to impose progressive taxes, and the security of property is gone. Concede the principle of progression, and there is no limit to the injustice a legislature may commit upon the minority.

The commencement of this dangerous form of taxation will be found in the inheritance tax laws of various States. The theory upon which these taxes are based is that the right to bequeath or inherit is entirely statutory — a privilege granted by the legislature — and that, therefore, any conditions, however arbitrary, can be imposed.[2] This view is erroneous. In the Illinois Inheritance Tax cases [3] the Supreme Court declared that, even " if the power of devise or of inheritance be a privilege, it must be conferred or regulated by equal laws." The right of succession, as

otherwise the most unexceptionable, the adoption of the principle of graduation would make them about the very worst that could be devised. The moment you abandon, in the framing of such taxes, the cardinal principle of exacting from all individuals the same proportion of their income or of their property, you are at sea without rudder or compass, and there is no amount of injustice and folly you may not commit."

[1] M'Culloch *v.* Maryland, 4 Wheat. 316, 431.

[2] Matter of Embury, 19 App. Div. 214, 218. Dos Passos' Inheritance Tax Law, 31, cites many authorities to show that the theory of inheritance tax laws is that they are not taxes on property but excises or imposts exacted by the State upon the right of succession. See the language of Mr. Justice Brown in United States *v.* Perkins, 163 U. S. 625, 628. Also State *v.* Dalrymple, 70 Maryland, 294, 299; Wallace *v.* Myers, 38 Fed. Rep. 184, 185; Magoun *v.* Illinois Trust & Savings Bank, 170 U. S. 283, 288.

[3] 170 U. S. 283, 292.

long as it exists, as long as it is granted to anybody, rich or poor, must be recognized as a property right of pecuniary value and must be granted impartially and by general laws : it cannot be granted to those of moderate means and denied wholly or partially to those of larger means. The acts of grace of a State are not like the gifts of a private person, or of an irresponsible despotic sovereign who bestows according to his fancy. They are solemn laws which must affect impartially and equally all persons within their purview. The power of a State to prescribe rules for the devolution of property does not eliminate or diminish the necessity for equal laws. Those who legislate must be made to appreciate, as Locke said in his Civil Government, that laws are "not to be varied in particular cases, but to have one rule for the rich and poor, for the favorite at court and the countryman at the plough."[1] Judge Cooley said: "To forbid to an individual or a class the right to the acquisition or enjoyment of property in such manner as should be permitted to the community at large, would be to deprive them of *liberty* in particulars of primary importance to their ' pursuit of happiness.'"[2] The right of succession, whatever its origin and character, is a property right of immense value, and while unrevoked, all, rich or poor, are entitled to enjoy it impartially under "the equal protection of the laws." Special privileges should not, in any State of the Union, be granted under any pretense or any form of class legislation.[3]

[1] Locke, Civil Government, sec. 142.
[2] Cooley, Const. Lim.,* 393.
[3] The Norwich Gas Light Company *v.* The Norwich City Gas Company, 25 Conn. 19, 39. The language of Cooley, J., in deciding that the State of Michigan had no right to authorize a township to execute and issue bonds for the construction of a purely private railroad to be built and run through the town, in The People *v.* Salem, 20 Mich. 452, 486, well expresses the danger of unequal

The principles of classification do not inhibit a State from placing the property of decedents, or rights of succession thereto, in a distinct class for purposes of taxation. Having drawn a line between transfers of property *inter vivos* and successions after death, the State may subject the latter to further classification in respect of successors. Thus, aliens may be singled out for special burdens, or excluded altogether; distinctions may be drawn between relatives and strangers, and relatives may be classified according to their degrees of kinship to the decedent.[1] All these classes are definable with regard to relative differences and existing distinctions. They are not arbi-

and class legislation. " But the discrimination by the State between different classes of occupations, and the favoring of one at the expense of the rest, whether that one be farming or banking, merchandising or milling, printing or railroading, is not legitimate legislation, and is an invasion of that equality of right and privilege which is a maxim in State government. When the door is once opened to it, there is no line at which we can stop and say with confidence that thus far we may go with safety and propriety, but no further. Every honest employment is honorable; it is beneficial to the public; it deserves encouragement. The more successful we can make it, the more does it generally subserve the public good. But it is not the business of the State to make discriminations in favor of one class against another, or in favor of one employment agaiust another. The State can have no favorites. Its business is to protect the industry of all, and to give all the benefit of equal laws. It cannot compel an unwilling minority to submit to taxation in order that it may keep upon its feet any business that cannot stand alone. Moreover, it is not a weak interest only that can give plausible reasons for public aid: when the State once enters upon the business of subsidies, we shall not fail to discover that the strong and powerful interests are those most likely to control legislation, and that the weaker will be taxed to enhance the profits of the stronger."

[1] Mager *v.* Grima, 8 How. 490, 493–4. Chief Justice Taney, delivering the opinion of the court, said in this case : " Every state or nation may unquestionably refuse to allow an alien to take either real or personal property, situated within its limits, either as heir or legatee, and may, if it thinks proper, direct that property so descending or bequeathed shall belong to the state. In many of the States of this Union at this day, real property devised to an alien is liable to escheat. And if a State may deny the privilege altogether, it follows that, when it grants it, it may annex to the grant any conditions which it supposes to be required by its interests or policy." See United States *v.* Fox, 94 U. S. 315, where a devise of real estate, situated in New York, to the United States was held void under the local law. Also United States *v.* Perkins, 163 U. S. 625.

trary, and different rates may be imposed upon property passing to each class without necessarily denying to successors the equal protection of the laws. If the classification rests upon an intelligible and reasonable foundation, it will be upheld provided all in each class selected are equally taxed or equally exempted.

The State may reasonably regulate the right of devise and bequest just as it may regulate the transfer or the holding of real or personal property, but the power to regulate cannot involve the power to escheat or confiscate property. The State may designate heirs in case of intestacy, grant full testamentary power, exclude aliens, confer rights of curtesy and dower, forbid perpetuities, safeguard creditors, declare want of capacity in infants or insane persons, and otherwise regulate the holding or disposition of property according to its policy; but this general power of the State to regulate does not include the power to convert such property to public use upon the death of the owner, without compensation and in disregard of the claims of child or widow.[1] Frequent sanction by legislative enactment of the right of inheritance or testamentary disposition is entirely consistent with the claim that these rights are natural or fundamental rights which, under our system, the States are bound to recognize in one form or another. The State may regulate successions to property just as it may declare that aliens shall not hold property within its borders, and may prescribe the manner, the form, the method of transfers *inter vivos*. Yet no one would take the position that this power of regulation — for example, as to the conveyance of land or the exclusion of aliens or corporations — would enable the State to pass a law prohibiting all sales and dispositions of real prop-

[1] Minot *v.* Winthrop, 162 Mass. 113, 117.

erty, or unreasonably and arbitrarily limiting the use of property.  If a State should attempt to impose arbitrary regulations previously unknown, the power would have to be denied.  A deed may have to be under seal, with certain formalities, accompanied by the payment of a stamp tax or duty and other reasonable requirements; all this is regulation.  But to limit the use of property unreasonably and arbitrarily, or to restrain transfers even to resident citizens, would be quite a different thing.  It would be confiscation or spoliation, not regulation.  It would be depriving a man of property without due process of law; and it would not be legitimate legislation.

The consideration of this general question of legislative power over successions presents two different aspects, which should be briefly noticed : the one as to the right of inheritance; the other, as to the power of a testator to devise or bequeath his property.

The right of inheritance, although regulated by statute for hundreds of years, is not the creation of statute law.  It existed among the Anglo-Saxons, and prevailed in England long before the Conquest.  It was recognized and perpetuated in the great charters of English liberty.  By legal historians it is treated as " our common law of inheritance." [1]  It was a customary right prior to any statute of which we have record.  " The general consent of the most enlightened nations has, from the earliest historical period, recognized a natural right in children to inherit the property of their parents." [2]  In the latest authoritative history of English law, by Pollock and Maitland, the authors say that, " in calling to our aid a law of intestate succession, we are not invoking a modern force,"

---

[1] Pollock & Maitland's Hist. Eng. Law, ii. 257.
[2] United States *v.* Perkins, 163 U. S. 625, 628.

and that " the time when no such law existed is in strictest sense a prehistoric time."[1] This right of inheritance was established in every one of the thirteen original States at the time the government was founded. It had existed in the colonies and for centuries before in England, and has always been exercised and enjoyed by our race. It was recognized as a right by the Romans in the Twelve Tables. It was a right with the Egyptians. We find it everywhere in the Mosaic law, and a distinguished writer holds it to be the general direction of Providence.[2] As Chancellor Kent said, " nature and policy have equally concurred to introduce and maintain this primary rule of inheritance in the laws and usages of all civilized nations." [3] The right of children to inherit in the case of intestacy is recognized in every State, and always has been.

The power to devise or bequeath property at will developed as a limitation upon the right of inheritance, and in order to prevent escheat for want of heirs, and as the progress of society or the policy of a country demanded more and more absolute powers of ownership. However evidenced — whether in statutes or in the old customs and the practice of *post obit* gifts — the power has been recognized from time immemorial, as an incident of the right of property — as a natural right; and in the United States it has been considered a common-law right. It originated in custom long before the period of Norman rule in England. It was practised for centuries before the battle of Hastings, both in Normandy and in England; it was deemed a disgrace to die intestate, for that implied death without absolution; the priest always witnessed the *post obit* gift. Blackstone said that " in England, this power of

---

[1] Hist. of English Law, ii. 237, 248, 257.
[2] Kent, Com., ii. 326; iv. 376.
[3] Com. iv. 376.

bequeathing is coeval with the first rudiments of the law : for we have no traces or memorials of any time when it did not exist." [1]    There is not a civilized — if, indeed, there be a barbarous — state in the world to-day, that does not recognize the rights of inheritance and of testamentary disposition.    The dying Indian can dispose of what he has accumulated.    The savage, all over the world, instinctively considers it a natural right at death to dispose of his property.    It is a right exercised everywhere, subject only to the limitation which we all recognize and concede — that the government may step in on grounds of public policy and ordain that natural heirs shall not be disinherited, or that property shall not pass to aliens, or to foreign corporations, or to such corporations as it deems should not be allowed to hold or accumulate property. The State in making such regulations derives its power not from the idea that the property escheats and belongs of right to it on the death of the decedent, nor from any notion that the ownership is in the State, but from that *suprema lex* which justifies every society in reasonably protecting itself according to its public policy — a power it may exercise as to the property of the living as well as of the dead.

Under our system of constitutional government, no legislature has the arbitrary and absolute power to deny all right of inheritance or all power of testamentary disposition.    Nor have any of the cases held that there was any such despotic power, although expressions to that effect, *obiter* and speculative, are to be found.    These expressions depend upon erroneous assumptions, and were made without investigation.    No State ever attempted to exercise such a power, nor did the British Parliament in

---

[1] Bl. Com., ii 491.

its most despotic period ; and no court in this country has ever decided that any such arbitrary power existed, for no such point was involved. There is, it is true, no authority adjudging that inheritance and testamentary disposition are natural and fundamental rights which the legislatures cannot deny. The reason is obvious; no State ever attempted to deny the right. To quote the language of Mr. Justice Patterson one hundred years ago :[1] " Every person ought to contribute his proportion for public purposes and public exigencies ; but no one can be called upon to surrender or sacrifice his whole property, real and personal, for the good of the community, without receiving a recompense in value. . . . The English history does not furnish an instance of the kind; the Parliament, with all their boasted omnipotence, never committed such an outrage on private property; and if they had, it would have served only to display the dangerous nature of unlimited authority; it would have been an exercise of power and not of right. Such an act would be a monster in legislation, and shock all mankind."

Another important branch of this question of taxation and equal laws is as to exemptions from taxation. The power of the state legislatures to grant reasonable exemptions to individuals has been declared, and also to grant exemption to corporations which serve to a greater or less extent some public purpose. Reasonable exemptions have been upheld in some cases on the ground that the expense of collection would exceed the amount collected, and in other cases as relieving the very poor and needy from the burdens of government. Desty, in his work on " Taxation,"[2] said that the only justification for such exemptions is the public policy which seeks " to en-

[1] Van Horne's Lessee *v.* Dorrance, 2 Dall. 304, 310.       [2] i. 633.

able the poor man not yet a pauper to escape becoming a public burden." As one of the leading cases states the rule: "Exemption from taxation should be based only on a well-grounded public policy, by which all share in the benefits." [1] Exemption from taxation is but a form of class legislation, and it is open to the worst abuses. Its legality is capable of being tested by the standard of reasonableness; in substance, it involves placing the exempted in a specially favored class. Although the power to exempt has been said to be of legislative discretion, yet its exercise cannot, of course, be arbitrary. The legislature may define classes of property or individuals that actually exist, but it cannot create them; it cannot classify individuals as such merely according to their wealth; it cannot classify the same property or subjects simply according to value for taxation at different rates. An exception must be reasonable and impartial, and be granted to all similarly situated. The exemption must tend to subserve some public purpose. Within the decisions of the court in analogous cases, an exemption " cannot be sustained when special, partial and arbitrary." [2]

A tax law which contains arbitrary exemptions cannot be termed equal in any sense. All exemptions necessarily tend to increase the taxes to be levied on the non-exempted. If all property owners could be allowed an exemption from ordinary taxes of property worth five or ten or twenty thousand dollars, it would free from taxation the greater part of the taxable property of every State,

---

[1] State *v.* Indianapolis, 69 Ind. 375, 378; National Bank *v.* Iola, 9 Kan. 689, 702; Exchange Bank *v.* Hines, 3 Ohio St. 1, 13, 14; City of New Orleans *v.* Fourchy, 30 La. Ann. 910, 913; People *v.* McCreery, 34 Cal. 432, 437.

[2] Caldwell *v.* Texas, 137 U. S. 692, 698; Cooley, Taxation, 2 ed. 215; Orr *v.* Baker, 4 Ind. 86, 88; State *v.* Indianapolis, 69 Ind. 375, 377.

and of necessity impose a much heavier burden on the non-exempted. A very high and unjust rate must then be imposed on those not equally favored with exemption.

It is sometimes suggested that there is no inequality or discrimination if the same exemption be granted to each person, rich or poor. This is sheer sophistry. Such an argument would sustain an act, for example, which exempted from a property tax farms or other property, of the value of twenty or fifty or one hundred thousand dollars, and imposed all the burdens of government and taxation upon those who owned more valuable property, because the exemption was allowed to all and consequently was equal. The result would be that the whole burden of the taxes at confiscatory rates would have to be imposed upon the few rich. Perhaps it sounds plausible to argue that there is no discrimination, no inequality, if the same exemption be allowed to all alike; but there should be no difficulty in exploding so fallacious a proposition. Such a tax law is but a pretense of equality; it lacks the essence of legitimate legislation. If exemptions can be sustained on any such ground, when the true intention, motive and purpose of the legislature are obviously to exempt the majority of voters and property owners, and to enable the law-makers to single out the few rich for the benefit of the many — if exemptions can thus be granted and all property owners of moderate means relieved of taxation and the whole burden of government thrown on the few rich, then there is no real security for property and the pledge of the protection of equal laws is empty and delusive. We should be as much at the mercy of legislatures and would suffer as bitterly therefrom as France suffered from her National Assembly when, during the Revolution, it practically taxed at one hundred per cent. and thus confiscated, what they were pleased to call the "superfluous."

There is a scheme of public policy inspiring these forms of tax legislation, a motive prompting these exemptions and this beginning of progressive taxation. Certain writers and philosophers, as well as the socialists, are not at all satisfied with the distribution of wealth as they find it in the world to-day. They would remodel society, level fortunes, limit acquisitions, redistribute wealth. They argue that this should be commenced by limiting inheritances or testamentary dispositions or by taxing the large fortunes so as to force redistribution. Chancellor Kent refuted these writers in his Commentaries, and showed that human society would be in a most unnatural and miserable condition if it had been instituted or could be reorganized upon the basis of such speculations, and that, as long as society is constituted as it is, the right of acquisition and of property ought to be sacredly protected. In one of his eloquent passages he said : " the legislature has no right to limit the extent of the acquisition of property, as was suggested by some of the regulations in ancient Crete, Lacedæmon, and Athens ; and has also been recommended in some modern utopian speculations. A state of equality as to property is impossible to be maintained, for it is against the laws of our nature ; and if it could be reduced to practice, it would place the human race in a state of tasteless enjoyment and stupid inactivity, which would degrade the mind and destroy the happiness of social life." [1]

The history of every country has proved that no better device could be imagined for checking industrial progress than any such policy of veiled confis-

---

[1] Kent's Com. 14 ed., ii. 319, 327, 328.

cation tending toward state ownership which excessive exemptions involve. As Nicholson admonishes us in his work on " Historical Progress and Socialism " : [1] " It would be to introduce a creeping paralysis ; and, when the time was considered ripe for taking over the land and capital, the land would be a wilderness, and the capital old iron."

Nor is redistribution of wealth or equalization of property a legitimate consideration of public policy in any form of tax laws. Twenty-three years ago, in the famous Seed case, Mr. Justice Brewer, speaking from the bench of the Supreme Court of Kansas [2] said, in language so applicable to the present discussion : " Such taxation would be simply an attempt on the part of the State to equalize the property of its citizens. . . . The mere mention of these questions suggests the dangers which would follow the adoption of this as a rule of public conduct."

I regret that it is impossible to discuss this subject of taxation at greater length. No more can be done than to suggest lines of thought and study.

In considering these problems of taxation, we must bear in mind that the science of government and the principles of taxation are intimately connected and interwoven. The highest attribute of the sovereignty of governments is the taxing power ; when we discuss it we enter the realm of practical statesmanship and of the higher politics of which the object is the happiness of mankind. The power to tax is not only the strongest and most pervading of all powers of government, but is the most liable to abuse. In exercising it, legislatures should be controlled by considerations of politics in the grandest and highest signification

---

[1] 1894, p. 32.
[2] The State *v.* Osawkee Township, 14 Kans. 418, 422, 427.

of the term. In the service of politics thus presented, they should apply the great principles of government which rest upon solid foundations of truth, justice and equality. The true statesman and patriot must recognize that there can be no stability or progress where there is no security or confidence, and that these can never exist under a government which imposes unequal taxes.

Expediency or prejudice may hereafter prompt attempts at progressive taxes, or tax laws exempting those of moderate means; but we shall pay a fearful price if we introduce any such principle into our legislation. Equality of burden, by making every man according to his means a contributor to the expenses of the State, is one of the most wholesome things in our civil institutions. It is the contributing citizen who is the watchful citizen. The people would care little what expenditures were made by the legislature if the entire amount could be levied upon twenty wealthy men in the State. The best assurance of watchful care and interest and vigilance in our institutions — the best assurance of honesty, integrity and economy in public expenditure — is in a wide distribution of the burdens of taxation. The man who pays watches; and the smaller his means, the more closely and vigilantly does he observe public expenditure.

If progressive or unequal taxes are permitted, the time cannot be distant when the majority of the voters will confiscate private property under the cloak or pretense of taxation and the worst follies and crimes of history be repeated. Our supreme danger is in the tyranny of majorities where one class or section of the country will vote taxes for the others to pay. The bar can never be called upon to perform a duty of more vital and comprehensive

interest to the nation and the States — to the future
security of American institutions — than that of preventing the adoption throughout the country of so dangerous
a policy as that embodied in progressive taxation or
exemptions.

In the requirement of equality of taxation — that is, of
impartial imposition for public purposes by equal laws —
we have a principle which is safe for the people and safe
for the government, state or national. Let each citizen
contribute his share up to the full measure of the requirements, the necessities, the emergencies of the State, even if
it shall take all; but let those legislating feel the practical
and just check and restraint which must result from the
rule that all must be taxed impartially and equally according to their means. If the power to tax thus exercised
leads to destruction, the destruction will be submitted to
because equal and not of selected individuals. The State
should not discriminate against the few rich in favor of
the many of moderate means; it should not sacrifice or
spoliate the property of one — the lowliest or the richest
— for the benefit of others.

The observance of the principle of equality in the past
has built up a great and prosperous nation. Security of
property rights and confidence in the impartial administration of the laws have been the true source of a prosper-
ity which is the wonder and the envy of the world. The
principle of equality has given us stability and immense
effective force. Whatever temporary local interest or prejudice or blindness may be, the people will inevitably realize that the disregard of the principle of equality is in
conflict with their own vital and permanent welfare and
cannot be tolerated if we are to remain a free people under
the rule of constitutional guaranties restraining all arbi-

trary and despotic exercise of the powers of government. To quote Burke's language, we must appreciate that, " in this sense, the restraints on men, as well as their liberties, are to be reckoned among their rights." [1]

[1] Burke's Works, "Reflections on the Revolution in France," Little, Brown & Co's. Am. ed., iii. 310.

# LECTURE V.

IT is impossible to examine the decisions of the Supreme Court of the United States upon questions arising under the Fourteenth Amendment without being impressed with the necessity of closely observing and conforming to the system of practice which the court has built up in its long history. The rules of practice are of such importance and affect so directly and vitally the result of litigation in that court that they may almost be said to be of the very substance of the remedies there administered. The strictest attention to this procedure is essential to the proper presentation of a case for review. A failure to observe the rules may not only cause delay and disadvantage, but often may altogether defeat the aggrieved party or deprive him of an adequate remedy by postponing an adjudication on the merits until too late to be of any practical benefit.

If we consider the cases during the last five years, covering twenty-one volumes, from 150 to 170 United States Reports, we may appreciate how essential it is to understand and follow the rules of practice. In these twenty-one volumes there are decisions in one hundred and fifty-six cases where the appeals or writs of error were dismissed. Ninety-eight of these cases were dismissed on points of practice. Fifty-six were dismissed for lack of requisite jurisdictional facts; and in ten of these cases the jurisdictional defects were of such a nature as to make the question really one of practice. The remaining two cases were dismissed on grounds involving both jurisdiction and practice. In fact, a majority of the cases fail because of ignorance or carelessness on the part of those preparing the records or conducting the proceedings in the courts of original jurisdiction. It has been stated as an established fact that fifty-three per cent of the cases decided by all the courts of review in the United States turn upon questions of procedure which in no way go to the merits of the case.[1]

In order to secure the benefit of the provisions of the Fourteenth Amendment, it is essential to have an exact technical knowledge of the machinery of the tribunals which administer and expound the Constitution. It is not too much to say that an intimate acquaintance with the various regulations and distinctions of practice is of as much importance as knowledge of the principles of constitutional law. The remarks of Mr. Stephen in relation to the science of pleading may well be applied to the system of practice which regulates the proceedings of the Supreme Court. He said: "The system known by the name of pleadings is of remote antiquity in its origin, and has been gradually moulded into its present form by the wisdom of the successive ages. Its great and extensive importance in legal practice has long recommended it to the early and assiduous attention of every professional student. Nor is this its only claim to notice, for where properly understood and appreciated it appears to be an instrument so well adapted to the ends of distributive justice, so simple and striking in its fundamental principles, so ingenious and elaborate in its details, as fairly to be entitled to the character of a fine juridical

[1] 53 Alb. L. J. 321, 322 ; 1 Rice, Evidence, preface, 5.

invention." [1]  These words are equally true of the logical
and consistent decisions by which the Supreme Court has
defined and administered its jurisdiction.  In this lecture
I shall attempt to state the points of practice ordinarily
presented in litigation in cases arising under the Fourteenth Amendment; and so far as practicable, I shall use
the exact language of the leading decisions.

The original jurisdiction of the Supreme Court is quite
limited, and is at the present time of comparatively little
practical importance to us.  Constitutional questions such
as have been considered in these lectures are brought to
that court in its appellate capacity.  Causes come to the
Supreme Court for review from two sources: from the
state courts and from the inferior federal courts.

The jurisdiction of the Supreme Court to review the
judgments or decrees of state courts is regulated by section 709 of the Revised Statutes of the United States.
This section reads as follows, eliminating provisions not
relating to the present subject:

" SEC. 709.  A final judgment or decree in any suit in the highest court of a State, in which a decision in the suit could be had,
. . . where is drawn in question the validity of a statute of, or an
authority exercised under, any State, on the ground of their being
repugnant to the Constitution, treaties, or laws of the United States,
and the decision is in favor of their validity; or where any title,
right, privilege, or immunity is claimed under the Constitution, or any
treaty or statute of, or commission held or authority exercised under,
the United States, and the decision is against the title, right, privilege,
or immunity specially set up or claimed, by either party, under such
Constitution, treaty, statute, commission, or authority, may be re-
examined and reversed or affirmed in the Supreme Court upon a writ
of error.  The writ shall have the same effect as if the judgment or
decree complained of had been rendered or passed in a court of the
United States. . . . The Supreme Court may reverse, modify, or
affirm the judgment or decree of the state court, and may, at their

1 Stephen, Pleading, 2.

discretion, award execution, or remand the same to the court from which it was removed by the writ."

The questions arising under this section may be grouped under four heads, namely: (1) as to the highest state court; (2) as to what constitutes a final judgment or decree; (3) as to when and how the federal question is properly presented; and (4) as to the method of review by writ of error.

1. **As to the highest state court.** — It will be observed that the language of the statute does not limit the issuing of the writ of error to the highest court of a State, but that the writ may issue to the highest court "in which a decision in the suit could be had." Accordingly where, under the local practice and procedure, no appeal lies to the highest court of the State, the writ may issue from the Supreme Court to one of the inferior state courts.[1] The amount involved may be small and preclude appellate jurisdiction of the highest court of the State; but, as is important to bear in mind, no matter how small the invasion of a constitutional right, the privilege of appeal to the supreme judicial tribunal of the country is open and available, even from the judgment of a justice of the peace.[2] When the highest court of a State has dismissed an action for want of jurisdiction, or has declined to issue a writ of error or to allow an appeal,[3] it has been held that the writ should run to the intermediate court or the court of original jurisdiction as the case may be.[4]

[1] Downham v. Alexandria, 9 Wall. 659.

[2] Downham v. Alexandria, 9 Wall. 659; Miller v. Joseph, 17 Wall. 655.

[3] Bigelow v. Forrest, 9 Wall. 339, 347; Gregory v. McVeigh, 23 Wall. 294. The refusal to grant the appeal must appear. "We are not to assume that an appeal would not have been granted if applied for. The record must show its refusal." Fisher v. Perkins, 122 U. S. 522, 527; Clark v. Pennsylvania, 128 U. S. 395.

[4] Stanley v. Schwalby, 162 U. S. 255, 269; Great Western Telegraph Co. v. Burnham, 162 U. S. 339, 342, citing McComb, Ex'r, v. Commissioners, etc., 91 U. S. 1; Bacon v. Texas, 163 U. S. 207, 215.

Where the highest court of a State reverses the judgment of an inferior court and remands the case for further proceedings, and the inferior court then proceeds to render final judgment, an appeal cannot be taken from this latter judgment to the Supreme Court, but the case must first be carried again to the highest court in the State, and an appeal taken from that court to the Supreme Court, although the highest court of the State may not re-examine the case upon the merits at all.[1]

The writ of error from the Supreme Court can only issue to the court where the record is found, and it has, therefore, been ruled that where, by the practice prevailing in the state courts, the record itself has been returned with the appellate court's decision to the court of original jurisdiction, the writ should run to the latter court. Under such circumstances, the state appellate court would have no record to return in compliance with the writ; nor, perhaps, would that court have power to execute the mandate from the Supreme Court in case of a reversal of its ruling. It must be admitted that the decisions exhibit some lack of uniformity upon this point.[2]

2. **As to what constitutes a final judgment or decree.** — A final judgment or decree is one which leaves nothing judicially to be determined between the parties in the trial court.[3]

[1] McComb, Ex'r, *v.* Commissioners, etc., 91 U. S. 1; Rice *v.* Sanger, 144 U. S. 197; Union Mutual Life Ins. Co. *v.* Kirchoff, 160 U. S. 374, 378; Great Western Telegraph Co. *v.* Burnham, 162 U. S. 339, 342, 345.

[2] Gelston *v.* Hoyt, 3 Wheat. 546; Atherton *v.* Fowler, 91 U. S. 143, 146; Polleys *v.* Black River Co., 113 U. S. 81; McClellan *v.* Chipman, 164 U. S. 347; N. Y., N. H. and H. Railroad *v.* New York, 165 U. S. 628.

[3] Bostwick *v.* Brinkerhoff, 106 U. S. 3; Grant *v.* Phœnix Ins. Co., 106 U. S. 429; St. L., I. M. & S. R. R. Co. *v.* Southern Ex. Co., 108 U. S. 24; *Ex parte* Norton, 108 U. S. 237; Winthrop Iron Co. *v.* Meeker, 109 U. S. 180; Mower *v.* Fletcher, 114 U. S. 127; Lewisburg Bank *v.* Sheffey, 140 U. S. 445, 452. After petition for removal has been properly made in the state court and denied, the petitioner does not waive any rights by continuing to contest the suit in the state court, and may afterward review the error that may have been committed

It must terminate the controversy between all necessary parties upon the merits,[1] and finally dispose of the subject matter of the litigation. The principal test is that the judgment is final, if, in case of an affirmance, the court below would have nothing to do but to execute the judgment it had already rendered. It is, however, not necessary that the result below be evidenced by a technical judgment. It is sufficient if it be a final determination in some form of judicial proceeding.[2]

The term " decree " is used with reference to suits in equity. It is sometimes very difficult to determine whether a decree has the character of finality for purposes of appeal. No such difficulty exists in the case of a judgment at law. Probably no question of equity practice has been the subject of more frequent discussion in the Supreme Court than the finality of decrees. It has usually arisen upon appeals taken from decrees claimed to be interlocutory, but it has occasionally happened that the power of the court to set aside such a decree at a subsequent term has been the subject of dispute. The cases are not altogether harmonious. It is clear that a decree is final, notwithstanding a reference to a master to execute the decree by a sale of property or otherwise, as in the case of the foreclosure of a mortgage.[3] If the decree of foreclosure and sale leave the amount due upon the debt to be determined, or the property,

in the Supreme Court. Powers *v.* Chesapeake & Ohio Railway, 169 U. S. 92, 102. Orders remanding causes to state courts or denying motions to remand are not final judgments. Joy *v.* Adelbert College, 146 U. S. 355, 357 ; Bender *v.* Pennsylvania Company, 148 U. S. 502. See also Luxton *v.* North River Bridge Co., 147 U. S. 337 ; Texas & Pacific Railway Co. *v.* Gentry, 163 U. S. 353, 363.

[1] Pacific R. R. *v.* Ketchum, 101 U. S. 289 ; Dainese *v.* Kendall, 119 U. S. 53; Meagher *v.* Minnesota Thresher M'f'g Co., 145 U. S. 608, 610 ; Hohorst *v.* Hamburg-American Packet Co., 148 U. S. 262, 264; Bank of Rondout *v.* Smith, 156 U. S. 330, 335; The Three Friends, 166 U. S. 1.

[2] Memphis *v.* Brown, 94 U. S. 715; Davies *v.* Corbin, 112 U. S. 36.

[3] Ray *v.* Law, 3 Cranch. 179; Bronson *v.* Railroad Company, 2 Black, 524; Green *v.* Fisk, 103 U. S. 518; Lewisburg Bank *v.* Sheffey, 140 U. S. 445.

which is to be sold, to be ascertained and defined, it is not final.[1] A like result follows if it merely determine the validity of the mortgage, and, without ordering a sale, direct the case to stand continued for further decree upon the coming in of the master's report.[2] It is equally well settled that a decree in admiralty determining the question of liability for a collision or other tort, or in equity establishing the validity of a patent and referring the case to a master to compute and report the damages, is merely interlocutory.[3] The general rule is that, if the court make a decree fixing the rights and liabilities of the parties, and thereupon refer the case to a master for a ministerial purpose only, and no further proceedings in court are contemplated, the decree is final; but, if it refer the case to him as a subordinate court and for a judicial purpose, as to state an account between the parties upon which a further decree is to be entered, the decree is not final.[4] So, a decree is not final which directs a perpetual injunction and orders an accounting with a view to a decree for damages.[5] But even when an account is ordered taken, if such accounting be not asked for in the bill, and be directed simply in execution of the decree, and such decree be final as to all matters within the pleadings, the decree will nevertheless be regarded as final.[6]

[1] Railroad Company *v.* Swasey, 23 Wall. 405; Grant *v.* Phœnix Ins. Co., 106 U. S. 429; Louisiana Bank *v.* Whitney, 121 U. S. 284; Parsons *v.* Robinson, 122 U. S. 112; Lodge *v.* Twell, 135 U. S. 232.

[2] Railroad Company *v.* Swasey, 23 Wall. 405; Parsons *v.* Robinson, 122 U. S. 112.

[3] The Palmyra, 10 Wheat. 502; Chace *v.* Vasquez, 11 Wheat. 429; Montgomery *v.* Anderson, 21 How. 386; Humiston *v.* Stainthorp, 2 Wall. 106; Thomson *v.* Dean, 7 Wall. 342.

[4] Lodge *v.* Twell, 135 U. S. 232, 235.

[5] Keystone Iron Co. *v.* Martin, 132 U. S. 91, 93; Winters *v.* Ethell, 132 U. S. 207, 210.

[6] Whiting *v.* The Bank of the United States, 13 Pet. 6; Michoud *v.* Girod, 4 How. 503; Forgay *v.* Conrad, 6 How. 201.

The rule is practically universal that, when the case is remanded by the appellate court to the court below for further judicial proceedings in conformity with the opinion of the appellate court, the judgment or decree of the appellate court is not final. Until such proceedings are had, the rights of the parties cannot be said to be fixed in any final sense so as to give the Supreme Court jurisdiction of an appeal.[1] The rule is so strict that, where the judgment of the highest court of a State reversed the judgment of an inferior court overruling a demurrer, on the ground that the demurrer was well taken, and remanded the cause for further proceedings, it was held not to be a final judgment, and the same was held where the judgment of the highest state court affirmed an order overruling a demurrer, with leave to answer over.[2]

3. **As to raising the federal question.** — By section 709 the jurisdiction of the Supreme Court to review the decisions of the state courts is circumscribed. There can be a reexamination by the Supreme Court only where the decision of the state court is in favor of the state statute or authority, or where the decision is against the right, title, privilege or immunity under the Federal Constitution specially set up or claimed by either party. In one of the cases the Supreme Court said: "The federal question may have

[1] Brown v. Baxter, 146 U. S. 619; Union Mutual Life Ins. Co. v. Kirchoff, 160 U. S. 374; Hollander v. Fechheimer, 162 U. S. 326, 328.

[2] Brown v. The Union Bank of Florida, 4 How. 465; Tracy v. Holcomb, 24 How. 426; Moore v. Robbins, 18 Wall. 588; McComb, Ex'r, v. Commissioners, etc., 91 U. S. 1; Davis v. Crouch, 94 U. S. 514; Meagher v. Minnesota Thresher M'f'g Co., 145 U. S. 608, 610; Werner v. Charleston, 151 U. S. 360; Great Western Telegraph Co. v. Burnham, 162 U. S. 339, 341. As to the finality of decrees for costs, see Elastic Fabrics Co. v. Smith, 100 U. S. 110; City Bank of Fort Worth v. Hunter, 152 U. S. 512, 516; DuBois v. Kirk, 158 U. S. 58; Citizens' Bank v. Cannon, 164 U. S. 319. An appeal cannot be taken from a decree for costs alone; but where the appeal is taken on other grounds, the court may consider whether costs were properly awarded.

been erroneously decided. It may be quite apparent to this court that a wrong construction has been given to the federal law, but if the right claimed under it by plaintiff in error has been conceded to him, this court cannot entertain jurisdiction of the case, so very careful is the statute, both of 1789 and of 1867, to narrow, to limit, and define the jurisdiction which this court exercises over the judgments of the state courts."[1] The object of the section was not to give a right of review wherever the validity of a state statute was drawn in question, but to prevent the courts of the several States from impairing the benefit of the Constitution by denying constitutional rights.[2] When the construction or decision of the state court is favorable to the constitutional right, the same reason or necessity does not exist for a review by the Supreme Court. Yet it is to be regretted that this appellate jurisdiction should thus be limited in cases involving federal questions, for, although it is of course true that the state courts are equally bound to administer and obey the Federal Constitution,[3] it is desirable that there should be uniformity of decision under provisions of the Constitution. State courts have held statutes to be in conflict with the Fourteenth Amendment in cases which, if they had been appealable by the State itself to the Supreme Court, would have resulted in a different decision in that court.[4] It has happened that state courts have held statutes to conflict with the Fourteenth Amendment, and that subsequently in other cases presenting the same point, the

---

[1] Murdock *v.* City of Memphis, 20 Wall. 590, 626.

[2] United States *v.* Lynch, 137 U. S. 280; Missouri *v.* Andriano, 138 U. S. 496; Belden *v.* Chase, 150 U. S. 674.

[3] Robb *v.* Connolly, 111 U. S. 624, 637; Cook *v.* Hart, 146 U. S. 183, 195.

[4] State *v.* Mann, 76 Wis. 469; Curry *v.* Spencer, 61 N. H. 624. Compare with Magoun *v.* Illinois Trust & Savings Bank, 170 U. S. 283.

Supreme Court has arrived practically at a contrary conclusion. In other cases, the state courts have upheld the state statute in question or denied the federal right merely to enable the case to be appealed. Many instances might be cited to emphasize this point, and to show the desirability of permitting the State to appeal to the Supreme Court and thus secure an authoritative decision by the only court that can finally determine such questions.

The validity of a state statute is said to be drawn in question within the meaning of section 709 whenever the power to enact it, as its terms read, or are made to read by construction, is fairly open to denial.[1] The validity is not drawn in question every time rights claimed under a statute are controverted, nor is the validity of an authority drawn in question every time an act done by such authority is disputed.[2] Something more than the bare assertion of an authority under a State is essential to the jurisdiction of the Supreme Court. The case must directly and necessarily involve a judicial inquiry into, and determination of, the validity or extent of the alleged authority under the limitations of the Federal Constitution. In many cases the question of the existence of an authority is so closely connected with the question of its validity that the court will not undertake to separate them, and in such cases the question of jurisdiction will not be considered apart from the question upon the merits.[3] Where, however, the single question is not as to the validity but as to the existence of an authority, there is no jurisdic-

---

[1] Balt. & Pot. Railroad v. Hopkins, 130 U. S. 210 ; Miller v. Cornwall Railroad Company, 168 U. S. 131, 133.

[2] Ferry v. King County, 141 U. S. 668, 673; South Carolina v. Seymour, 153 U. S. 353, 360.

[3] Millingar v. Hartupee, 6 Wall. 258, 261, 262.

tion of the writ of error.[1] The word "authority" in the statute stands upon the same footing with "treaty" and "statute";[2] and it was undoubtedly intended to reach the action of executive officers.

The most important point in practice is the proper method of raising the federal question so as to come within the scope of the language of section 709, which requires that the validity of a statute be drawn in question or that the title, right, privilege or immunity be "specially set up or claimed."

A real and not a fictitious question is essential to the jurisdiction.[3] The bare averment of a federal question is not sufficient.[4] The claim of a right under the Constitution must not be wholly without foundation. Otherwise a federal question might be set up in almost any case, and the jurisdiction of the Supreme Court invoked simply for the purpose of delay. The Supreme Court has said that the word "specially" in this statute is the equivalent of "unmistakably"[5] and "duly." The only safe course is to draw the validity of the statute in question, or set up and claim the right under the Fourteenth Amendment in the first pleading filed.[6] The allegation of the federal question should be drawn explicitly and distinctly, in order that there shall be no possible ambiguity, and that the Supreme Court can see from the pleading that the very

---

[1] Norton *v.* Shelby County, 118 U. S. 425, 440; Baldwin *v.* Kansas, 129 U. S. 52, 57; Leeper *v.* Texas, 139 U. S. 462, 467.

[2] Balt. & Pot. Railroad *v.* Hopkins, 130 U. S. 210, 224.

[3] Hamblin *v.* Western Land Company, 147 U. S. 531.

[4] New Orleans *v.* N. O. Water Works Co., 142 U. S. 79; Kaukauna Co. *v.* Green Bay &c. Canal, 142 U. S. 254.

[5] Oxley Stave Company *v.* Butler County, 166 U. S. 648, 655.

[6] Kipley *v.* Illinois, 170 U. S. 182, 187. See California Bank *v.* Kennedy, 167 U. S. 362, 365, where the federal question was raised in the answer, in the grounds of the motion for a new trial and in the specifications of error in the state supreme court.

constitutional point sought to be reviewed was actually presented.[1] The jurisdiction to re-examine the final judgment of a state court cannot arise from inference.[2] It must be made to appear on the face of the record so distinctly and positively as to place it beyond question that the party bringing the case to the Supreme Court from a state court intended to assert and did specially set up or claim the federal right at the proper time and in the proper way.[3] It matters not that the enforcement of the statute must have operated to deprive the plaintiff in error of a constitutional right. If no such claim was specifically and properly made below, the Supreme Court can afford no relief.[4] It was long ago held that, where it was objected in the state courts that an act of the State was unconstitutional and void, the objection only raised the question whether the state legislature had the power under the state constitution to pass the act, and did not present any point under the Constitution of the United States.[5]

The federal question must be raised before the entry of final judgment in the state court;[6] it cannot be raised for the first time in the petition to the Supreme Court for the writ of error, for the petition forms no part of the record upon which action is taken in that court;[7] and it is equally

[1] Sayward *v.* Denny, 158 U. S. 180; Winona & St. Peter Land Co. *v.* Minnesota, 159 U. S. 526; compare Winona & St. Peter Land Co. *v.* Minnesota, 159 U. S. 540 ; Oxley Stave Company *v.* Butler County, 166 U. S. 648, 655.

[2] Powell *v.* Brunswick County, 150 U. S. 433, 439; Louisville & Nashville R'd *v.* Louisville, 166 U. S. 709.

[3] Oxley Stave Company *v.* Butler County, 166 U. S. 648 ; Levy *v.* Superior Court of San Francisco, 167 U. S. 175.

[4] Miller *v.* Cornwall Railroad Company, 168 U. S. 131; Kipley *v.* Illinois, 170 U. S. 182, 186.

[5] Ibid. Compare Spencer *v.* Merchant, 125 U. S. 345.

[6] Simmerman *v.* Nebraska, 116 U. S. 54; Morrison *v.* Watson, 154 U. S. 111, 115; Fowler *v.* Lamson, 164 U. S. 252, 255.

[7] Manning *v.* French, 133 U. S. 186; Butler *v.* Gage, 138 U. S. 52; Leeper *v.* Texas, 139 U. S. 462; California Powder Works *v.* Davis, 151 U. S. 389; Miller *v.* Texas, 153 U. S. 535.

unavailing to set up the constitutional right for the first time in the assignment of errors in the Supreme Court.[1]  Nor will it answer to raise the question for the first time upon a petition for a rehearing in the highest state court,[2] or to present the point in the briefs or arguments of counsel.[3] The certificate of the state court as to the fact that the federal question was duly raised, while always regarded with respect by the Supreme Court, cannot confer jurisdiction upon it to re-examine the judgment below, unless the statute was duly drawn in question, or the federal right was specially set up or claimed, at the proper time and in the proper way.[4]  Such certificate cannot cure the omission in the record of due proof of the raising of the federal question;[5] but it may, nevertheless, be used to make more certain and specific what may be too general and indefinite in the record, or to render clear what may be ambiguous.[6]  Wherever by statute or settled practice in a State the opinion of its highest court is a part of the record, the Supreme Court may examine that opinion for the purpose of ascertaining the grounds of the judgment.[7]

[1] Missouri Pacific Railway *v.* Fitzgerald, 160 U. S. 556, 575; Fowler *v.* Lamson, 164 U. S. 252.

[2] Texas &c. R'y Co. *v.* Southern Pacific Co., 137 U. S. 48; Caldwell *v.* Texas, 137 U. S. 692; Butler *v.* Gage, 138 U. S. 52, 56; Leeper *v.* Texas, 139 U. S. 462, 468; Bushnell *v.* Crooke Mining Co., 148 U. S. 682, 689; Loeber *v.* Schroeder, 149 U. S. 580; Duncan *v.* Missouri, 152 U. S. 377, 383; Sayward *v.* Denny, 158 U. S. 180 ; Pim *v.* St. Louis, 165 U. S. 273; Miller *v.* Cornwall Railroad Company, 168 U. S. 131; see also Fowler *v.* Lamson, 164 U. S. 252; Wade *v.* Lawder, 165 U. S. 624.

[3] Zadig *v.* Baldwin, 166 U. S. 485.  See Castillo *v.* McConnico, 168 U. S. 674.

[4] Railroad Co. *v.* Rock, 4 Wall. 177, 180; Parmelee *v.* Lawrence, 11 Wall. 36, 39; Brown *v.* Atwell, 92 U. S. 327, 330; Felix *v.* Scharnweber, 125 U. S. 54; Johnson *v.* Risk, 137 U. S. 300; Roby *v.* Colehour, 146 U. S. 153; Powell *v.* Brunswick County, 150 U. S. 433; Newport Light Co. *v.* Newport, 151 U. S. 527; Dibble *v.* Bellingham Bay Land Company, 163 U. S. 63.

[5] Powell *v.* Brunswick County, 150 U. S. 433, 439.

[6] Parmelee *v.* Lawrence, 11 Wall. 36.

[7] N. O. Waterworks *v.* La. Sugar Co., 125 U. S. 18 ; Kreiger *v.* Shelby Railroad Co., 125 U. S. 39, 44; Egan *v.* Hart, 165 U. S. 188, 189.

Under the eighth rule of the Supreme Court all opinions are required to be returned with the record.

Although the only safe practice, as already intimated, is to set up or claim the federal right or draw the validity of the statute in question in the very first pleading, the Supreme Court has permitted a looser rule ; and, if the right be unmistakably set up or claimed before final judgment in the state court, it will be deemed to have been properly raised. Thus, in a very important condemnation proceeding in Illinois, the federal right was not claimed at the trial, and was set up for the first time upon the motion to set aside the verdict, and the Supreme Court entertained jurisdiction.[1] In that case the point was also distinctly made in the assignment of errors in the state appellate court, and thus became matter of record in that court. But if the claim be not made in the trial court, and, by the law and practice of the State, could not be considered by the state appellate court ; or if it be not claimed in any form before judgment in the highest court of the State, it is too late to attempt to assert it in the Supreme Court.[2] The question thus often becomes one of the practice in the particular State.

There are many proceedings where no answer or other pleading is required to be filed by the party whose interests are affected, such as condemnation proceedings, assessments for local improvements, etc. In criminal pro-

---

[1] Chicago, Burlington &c. R'd v. Chicago, 166 U. S. 226. And see N. Y. & N. E. Railroad Co. v. Bristol, 151 U. S. 556, 560, 566, where the federal question does not appear to have been specially raised until after the hearing in the trial court, when it was placed upon the record by means of an amendment to the "reasons on appeal."

[2] Spies v. Illinois, 123 U. S. 131, 181; Brooks v. Missouri, 124 U. S. 394; Chappell v. Bradshaw, 128 U. S. 132, 134; Brown v. Massachusetts, 144 U. S. 573; Schuyler National Bank v. Bolling, 150 U. S. 85; Miller v. Texas, 153 U. S. 535; Morrison v. Watson, 154 U. S. 111, 115; Louisville & Nashville R'd v. Louisville, 166 U. S. 709.

ceedings ordinarily the only plea is guilty or not guilty; and it is difficult in such cases to determine how and when to draw in question the validity of the statute or to specially set up or claim the constitutional right. Much will depend upon the local practice. It is seldom that some plea cannot be put upon the record to evidence the claim of the federal right. If the point can be made by a demurrer to an indictment, that course may be the simplest and quickest; but the question may be one of mixed law and fact; and, in such a case, either at the time of pleading or at the time of trial, some way can always be found of making the point unmistakably on the record. I recall a case, occurring lately, where a defendant entered a plea of not guilty, and, on the trial, contended that the state statute was in conflict with the Federal Constitution. The court so ruled. Thereupon, the State, as authorized under the local practice, appealed to the highest court of the State, where the act was held constitutional and the judgment reversed, with instructions to enter a judgment of conviction. As the State had appealed, it was not practicable for the defendant to procure a bill of exceptions or to make any assignment of errors in the appellate court. When the case came to be prepared for argument in the Supreme Court of the United States, it did not anywhere appear that the federal question had been formally set up or claimed, although it was the only question in the case. Fortunately, in the instance I have in mind, the opinion and the certificate of the state court and certain findings of the jury on the original trial were found sufficient to satisfy the Supreme Court that the federal question was really in the case and had been sufficiently raised; but the point was quite close and caused much doubt and anxious study as to whether a hearing on the merits would be allowed.

The federal question must not only be actually presented for decision by the state court, but it must be decided adversely to the party claiming the constitutional right, or necessarily involved in the judgment pronounced, and the decision of the point must be necessary to the determination of the cause.[1] Where, however, the court below could not have reached its conclusion without deciding adversely to a claim under the Constitution or federal laws, that is sufficient to give the Supreme Court jurisdiction. In cases where a federal right is claimed and denied, it frequently happens that there is also another sufficient ground for the decision below, not involving a federal question. If it appear that the state court in fact based its decision on the ground not involving a federal question, or if it does not appear upon which ground the decision of the state court was based, but it may have been based on a sufficient ground not involving a federal question, then the Supreme Court will not take jurisdiction.[2] But if the independent ground is not a good and valid one, sufficient of itself to sustain the judgment, the Supreme Court will take jurisdiction because, when put to inference as to what points the state court decided, it will not assume that the state court proceeded on

---

[1] Murdock v. Memphis, 20 Wall. 590; Cook County v. Calumet & Chicago Canal Co. 138 U. S. 635; Miller's Executors v. Swann, 150 U. S. 132; Eustis v. Bolles, 150 U. S. 361; California Powder Works v. Davis, 151 U. S. 389, 393; Snell v. Chicago, 152 U. S. 191, 196; Harrison v. Morton, 171 U. S. 38.

[2] Hale v. Akers, 132 U. S. 554, 565; Hopkins v. McLure, 133 U. S. 380, 386; Beatty v. Benton, 135 U. S. 244, 253; Johnson v. Risk, 137 U. S. 300, 306; Beaupré v. Noyes, 138 U. S. 397, 402; Walter A. Wood Co. v. Skinner, 139 U. S. 293, 297; Henderson Bridge Co. v. Henderson City, 141 U. S. 679, 688; O'Neil v. Vermont, 144 U. S. 323, 336; Sherman v. Grinnell, id. 198, 202; Haley v. Breeze, id. 130, 132; Eustis v. Bolles, 150 U. S. 361; California Powder Works v. Davis, 151 U. S. 389, 393; N. Y. & N. E. Railroad Co. v. Woodruff, 153 U. S. 689; Gillis v. Stinchfield, 159 U. S. 658; Rutland Railroad v. Cent. Vt. Railroad, 159 U. S. 630; Chemical Bank v. City Bank of Portage, 160 U. S. 646, 653; Seneca Nation v. Christy, 162 U. S. 283, 289; Dibble v. Bellingham Bay Land Co., 163 U. S. 63.

untenable grounds.[1]  In this class of cases, therefore, the Supreme Court sometimes has to pass upon purely local questions of state law in order to determine whether it has jurisdiction.[2]

4. **As to the method of review by writ of error.** — It is important to bear in mind that Congress by section 709 has provided that the final judgment of the highest court of the State in cases of which the Supreme Court may take cognizance shall be examined only upon writ of error. This is a well-known process of common law origin, and it brings up nothing for examination but the questions of law arising upon the record.   The findings of fact of the jury or of the state court are conclusive upon the Supreme Court, which only inquires whether the court below prescribed any rule of law in disregard of the protection of the constitutional provision.   Even if the Supreme Court were of opinion, in view of the evidence, that the jury or court erred on the question of fact, the final judgment of the state court cannot be reversed upon any such ground.[3]

After some expressions of doubt, it has been authoritatively determined by the Supreme Court that the writ of error under section 709 cannot be used even in chancery cases to review rulings of the highest courts of a State upon questions of fact.[4]  The writ is confined to

---

[1] Klinger v. State of Missouri, 13 Wall. 257; Johnson v. Risk, 137 U. S. 300.

[2] The practice of the Supreme Court in cases where it lacked jurisdiction was not consistent in former years, the judgments below being affirmed in some cases, while in others the writs of error were dismissed.   It was finally held in Eustis v. Bolles, 150 U. S. 361, 370, that the logical course was to dismiss the writ of error.

[3] Lehnen v. Dickson, 148 U. S. 71; Dower v. Richards, 151 U. S. 658; Carr v. Fife, 156 U. S. 494; Central Pacific Railroad v. California, 162 U. S. 91; Carter v. Ruddy, 166 U. S. 493.

[4] Harrison v. Perea, 168 U. S. 311; Young v. Amy, 171 U. S. 179; compare Egan v. Hart, 165 U. S. 188.   It was broadly stated by Mr. Justice Miller in

its province of bringing up for examination decisions upon questions of law. It is, therefore, absolutely essential that no question of fact involving the federal point appear undetermined upon the face of the record, and that each such question should be so found as distinctly to present that point. Otherwise, the writ may fail for lack of a sufficient finding or decision upon the facts to justify an examination of the ruling of the state court in point of law. The Supreme Court has gone to a considerable length in holding the findings below conclusive, and some of the decisions raise a doubt as to whether the supervisory power created by section 709 is not deprived of its intended efficacy by the presumption indulged in favor of the determination of the state court upon questions of fact, and, as a necessary result, upon questions of mixed law and fact. It is, however, a wise policy which leaves to state tribunals the decision of questions of fact according to the modes of trial sanctioned by the constitution and laws of each State, and the suitor can rarely be deprived of a review of a ruling involving a substantial claim under the Federal Constitution, if the rules of practice be carefully observed. A seeming qualification of the rule is that, where the question decided by the state court is not merely of the weight or

River Bridge Co. *v.* Kansas Pac. Ry. Co., 92 U. S. 315, 317, that "in chancery cases, or in any other class of cases where all the evidence becomes part of the record in the highest court of the State, the same record being brought here, this court can review the decision of that court on both the law and the fact so far as may be necessary to determine the validity of the right set up under the act of Congress." This dictum may well be doubted in view of the well known office of the writ of error, and the Court, by Mr. Justice Gray, carefully abstained from approving it in Dower *v.* Richards, 151 U. S. 658, 671. The authorities cited in the latter case seem to negative the rule laid down as above by Mr. Justice Miller. And it was finally held in Egan *v.* Hart, 165 U. S. 188, 189, that on writ of error to a state court in an equity case the Supreme Court was concluded by the findings of fact below.

sufficiency of the evidence to prove a fact, but of the competency or legal effect of the evidence as bearing upon a question of federal law, the decision may be reviewed by the Supreme Court.[1] Such a review is, after all, only an exercise of the power of the court upon a writ of error according to the common law, and is sometimes essential to make really effective the jurisdiction conferred by section 709.

The writ of error to the state court must be allowed either by a justice of the Supreme Court or by the chief or presiding judge of the state court.[2] A writ of error is not allowed as of right.[3] The practice upon the issue of the writ is quite technical. The Christian names of the parties should be given in full,[4] and the writ of error will be fatally defective if it lacks the test required by law.[5] If the judgment or decree be joint, all the parties against whom it is rendered must unite in the writ of error unless there be summons and severance or its equivalent.[6] Applications for the allowance of a writ of error cannot be made to the Supreme Court itself unless one of the justices has endorsed on the application a request that counsel proceed in that way.[7] The Supreme Court has decided that it will not issue a writ

---

[1] Mackay *v.* Dillon, 4 How., 421, 447; Dower *v.* Richards, 151 U. S. 658, 667. The latter case contains an exhaustive discussion of the method and limitations of review in the Supreme Court by Mr. Justice GRAY.

[2] The case of Havnor *v.* New York, 170 U. S. 408, was dismissed because the writ had been allowed by an Associate Judge of the New York Court of Appeals instead of by the Chief Judge. See Northwestern Union Packet Co. *v.* Home Insurance Co., 154 U. S. 588.

[3] Spies *v.* Illinois, 123 U. S. 131; *In re* Kemmler, 136 U. S. 436, 438.

[4] United States *v.* Schoverling, 146 U. S. 76; Miller *v.* Texas, 153 U. S. 535; Godbe *v.* Tootle, 154 U. S. 576.

[5] Moulder *v.* Forrest, 154 U. S. 567; Germain *v.* Mason, 154 U. S. 587.

[6] Shannon *v.* Cavazos, 131 U. S. Appx. lxxi; Downing *v.* McCartney, 131 U. S. Appx. xcviii; Hardee *v.* Wilson, 146 U. S. 179; Sipperley *v.* Smith, 155 U. S. 86.

[7] *In re* Ingalls, 139 U. S. 548; *In re* Robertson, Petitioner, 156 U. S. 183.

of error if it is apparent upon the face of the record that the issue of the writ could only result in the affirmance of the judgment. This was held in Spies *v.* Illinois,[1] involving the trial of the Chicago anarchists, and in the Kemmler case,[2] involving the constitutionality of the New York statute providing for execution by electricity. The Supreme Court will not correct errors in the record of the state court. All that it can do is to require omissions to be supplied by certiorari.[3] An application to correct or amend the record should be made when the record is prepared. With the transcript of the record, there must be an assignment of errors and a prayer for reversal, with a citation to the adverse party as required by section 997 of the Revised Statutes.[4]

The defendant in error need not wait until the case is reached in its regular order upon the calendar of the Supreme Court, but may at once make a motion to dismiss. If it appear on such motion that the federal question was not duly raised below and does not properly appear in the record, the court will dismiss the writ with costs for want of jurisdiction. If the defendant's case on the merits be strong, and there be a doubt whether the constitutional point was properly raised, then it is always advisable to move to dismiss or affirm.[5] If there be color for the motion to dismiss, and the court decides against dismissal, it will nevertheless examine the case and affirm if satisfied that the decision below is correct.[6] Thus, where the state

---

1 123 U. S. 131.   2 136 U. S. 436.

3 Goodenough Horse-Shoe Manuf. Co. *v.* Rhode Island Horse-Shoe Co., 154 U. S. 635.

4 Rowe *v.* Phelps, 152 U. S. 87; Tripp *v.* Santa Rosa Street Railroad, 144 U. S. 126.

5 Supreme Court Rule 6, subdivision 5.

6 Roby *v.* Colehour, 146 U. S. 153, 160; N. Y. & N. E. Railroad Co. *v.* Bristol, 151 U. S. 556; Douglas *v.* Wallace, 161 U. S. 346.

court did not appear to have expressly passed on the federal question, although it was raised on the record, it was held that there was color under the rules of the Supreme Court for the motion to dismiss, and the judgment was affirmed on the merits.[1] In another case, the federal question was not raised in the trial court, but was raised for the first time in the highest court of the State, and it was held that this fact gave color to a motion to dismiss for want of jurisdiction.[2] In still another case, no federal question appeared anywhere in the record, except that two days after the rendition of final judgment by the highest court in the State the judgment was amended so as to show that the federal question had really been presented by counsel and argued and decided adversely. It was held that there was color for the motion to dismiss, but the court denied that motion and affirmed the judgment on the merits.[3] Where there is no federal question presented for decision, the proper course is to move to dismiss the writ of error.[4] A form of the motion to dismiss will be found in the last case upon the point — Richardson *v.* Louisville and Nashville Railroad Company, decided at the present term of the Supreme Court.[5] Where there is color for the motion to dismiss for want of jurisdiction, the court inquires whether the questions on which jurisdiction depends are such as, in the language of rule six, "not to need further argument." If they do require extended argument, the motion to dismiss will be denied, and the question of jurisdiction

---

[1] Bell's Gap R'd Co. *v.* Pennsylvania, 134 U. S. 232.

[2] Sugg *v.* Thornton, 132 U. S. 524.

[3] East Tenn., &c. Railway *v.* Frazier, 139 U. S. 288; see also Sire *v.* Ellithorpe Air Brake Co., 137 U. S. 579.

[4] Eustis *v.* Bolles, 150 U. S. 361; Rutland Railroad *v.* Cent. Vt. Railroad, 159 U. S. 630 ; Gillis *v.* Stinchfield, 159 U. S. 658 ; Seneca Nation *v.* Christy, 162 U. S. 283.

[5] 169 U. S. 128.

considered upon the argument of the whole case. On a motion to dismiss or affirm, only so much of the record need be printed as will enable the Supreme Court to act understandingly without reference to the transcript.[1] This practice frequently saves very great expense in printing.

The writ of error to a state court is governed by the same rules of practice and decision in the Supreme Court as when used to review the judgment of an inferior federal court.[2] Thus, a judgment will not be affirmed upon a ground not taken at the trial unless it is made clear beyond doubt that this cannot prejudice the rights of the plaintiff in error.[3] And the judgment will not be reversed where the error complained of works no injury to the party against whom it was made; but this must also be perfectly clear.[4]

A writ of error from the Supreme Court to state, circuit or district courts must be sued out, and an appeal direct from the circuit court to the Supreme Court must be taken within two years after the entry of the judgment or decree.[5] To the circuit court of appeals the time is six months,[6] except in prize,[7] claim[8] and appraisal cases,[9] and in the appeals allowed from certain interlocutory orders.[10] From the circuit court of appeals to the Supreme Court the time is one year.[11] There is no

---

[1] Carey *v.* Houston & Texas Central Railway, 150 U. S. 170.

[2] Rev. St. § 1003.

[3] Peck *v.* Heurich, 167 U. S. 624, 629.

[4] Deery *v.* Cray, 5 Wall. 795, 807; Smiths *v.* Shoemaker, 17 Wall. 630, 639; Moores *v.* National Bank, 104 U. S. 625, 630; Gilmer *v.* Higley, 110 U. S. 47, 50; Vicksburg & Meridian Railroad *v.* O'Brien, 119 U. S. 99, 103; Mexia *v.* Oliver, 148 U. S. 664, 673; Boston & Albany Railroad *v.* O'Reilly, 158 U. S. 334, 337.

[5] Rev. St. § 1008.    [6] 26 Stat. 829, § 11.    [7] Rev. St. § 1009.

[8] Rev. St. § 708.    [9] 26 Stat. 138, § 15.    [10] *Id.* 828, § 7.

[11] *Id.* 828, § 6.

time limited within which a writ of habeas corpus must be issued. The nature of the remedy prevents this. Probably a writ of certiorari from the Supreme Court to the circuit court of appeals to review the judgment of the latter court must, by analogy, be issued within the same time limited for an appeal or a writ of error.[1] The point has not yet been determined by the Supreme Court.

**As to writs of error to or appeals from the United States circuit courts.** — The jurisdiction of the Supreme Court on writ of error or appeal direct from the circuit court is broader than on error to the highest court of a State, and frequently the same record coming from a United States circuit court and from a state court upon exactly the same facts may present different questions. In the first place, the review of the decision of the circuit court by the Supreme Court is not only by writ of error, but by appeal, as the case is in law or equity; and, on an appeal in equity, the facts may be reviewed, which is not the rule where the court is reviewing the decree of the highest court of a State.[2] In cases involving the construction or application of the United States Constitution, the decision of the circuit court may be reviewed without reference to whether the decision was in favor of or against the federal right or the validity of the state statute, while on writ of error to a state court this class of cases can only be reviewed when the decision sustains the validity of the state statute or is against the federal right.[3] The same may be said in respect of treaties. A writ of error or

---

[1] Harris v. Barber, 129 U. S. 366; Amer. Const. Co. v. Jacksonville Railway, 148 U. S. 372, 387; People v. Hill, 53 N. Y. 547, 549; People v. City, 77 N. Y. 605; People v. Police Comrs., 24 Hun, 284; Smith v. Superior Court, 97 Cal. 348; Hyslop v. Finch, 99 Ill. 171, 179; Crittenden v. Reilly, 97 Mich. 637; Young's Petition, 9 Pa. St. 215; The State v. Milwaukee County, 58 Wis. 4.

[2] *Supra*, 159, 160.  [3] *Supra*, 150, 151.

appeal from the United States circuit court to the Supreme Court will review the decision below in all cases where the validity or construction of a treaty is drawn in question. On writ of error to the state court, however, the decision can only be reviewed when it is against the right, title, or privilege claimed under the treaty.

There is a very important distinction between the rule of decision applied by the Supreme Court to cases coming from the federal courts and to those coming from a state court. In the former class of cases, the Supreme Court has jurisdiction to try the whole question and to examine and decide not only as to the conformity of the state statute to the requirements of the Federal Constitution, but in addition whether it be a violation of the state constitution, and whether the provisions of the act itself have been complied with.[1] The Supreme Court in such cases will follow and be guided by the decisions in the highest state court;[2] but, in the absence of such decisions, will itself construe the state statute in connection with the state constitution, and will likewise pass upon the merits.[3] This has been most clearly shown by Mr. Justice Gray, as follows:[4] "The distinction, as to the authority of this court, between writs of error to a court of the United States and writs of error to the highest court of a State, is well illustrated by two of the earliest cases relating to municipal bonds, in both of which the opinion was

---

[1] Laclede Gas Light Company *v.* Murphy, 170 U. S. 78, 100.

[2] Long Island Water Supply Co. *v.* Brooklyn, 166 U. S. 685; Merchants' Bank *v.* Pennsylvania, 167 U. S. 461. A different rule applies when the question is whether a statute does in fact impair the obligation of contracts. Water Power Co. *v.* Water Commissioners, 168 U. S. 349, 371. See also Yick Wo *v.* Hopkins, 118 U. S. 356, 366.

[3] Fallbrook Irrigation District *v.* Bradley, 164 U. S. 112.

[4] Central Land Company *v.* Laidley, 159 U. S. 103, 111; compare Mobile & Ohio R'd *v.* Tennessee, 153 U. S. 486.

delivered by Mr. Justice Swayne, and in each of which the question presented was whether the constitution of the State of Iowa permitted the legislature to authorize municipal corporations to issue bonds in aid of the construction of a railroad. The Supreme Court of the State, by decisions made before the bonds in question were issued, had held that it did; but, by decisions made after they had been issued, held that it did not. A judgment of the District Court of the United States for the District of Iowa, following the later decisions of the state court, was reviewed on the merits and reversed by this court for misconstruction of the constitution of Iowa.[1] But a writ of error to review one of those decisions of the Supreme Court of Iowa was dismissed for want of jurisdiction, because, admitting the constitution of the State to be a law of the State, within the meaning of the provision of the Constitution of the United States forbidding a State to pass any law impairing the obligation of contracts, the only question was of its construction by the state court." [2]

The circumstances alluded to by Mr. Justice Gray present the anomaly of a decision of the highest court of Iowa directly in conflict with a final decision of the Supreme Court of the United States upon the same subject. This divergence is wholly due to the different rules of decision applying in cases brought from the supreme court of a State and in cases brought from a court of the United States. In the case referred to it cannot be doubted that, if an appeal from the decision of the supreme court of Iowa had been entertained by the Supreme Court of the United States, the decision of the state court

[1] Gelpcke *v.* City of Dubuque, 1 Wall. 175, 206.
[2] Railroad Company *v.* McClure, 10 Wall. 511, 515

upon the true construction of the constitution of Iowa would have been regarded as conclusive.

The jurisdiction of the United States circuit courts is twofold: what is termed original jurisdiction, and jurisdiction by removal. The latter class includes those cases removed under the Removal Acts of Congress. An action may be begun in the United States circuit court whenever there are the necessary diversity of citizenship and the jurisdictional amount, or when the case itself arises under the Constitution or laws of the United States. If from the questions involved it appears that some title, right, privilege, or immunity on which the recovery depends will be defeated by one construction of the Constitution, or sustained by the opposite construction, then the case is said to be one arising under the Constitution or laws of the United States.[1] Here it may be well to remind you that, for the purposes of suing and being sued in the federal courts, a corporation is deemed to be a citizen of the State under whose laws it was created,[2] and that the federal courts have jurisdiction of all suits by or against a corporation incorporated by Congress, as arising under a law of the United States.[3] If the case does not depend upon diversity of citizenship, but upon the constitutional right, then it must appear affirmatively from the plaintiff's statement of his own case that the suit arises under the Constitution. The fact that the only point in controversy between the parties involves a federal question or that the only anticipated defense is under the Constitution cannot

[1] Starin *v.* New York, 115 U. S. 248, 257; Germania Insurance Co. *v.* Wisconsin, 119 U. S. 473; Cooke *v.* Avery, 147 U. S. 375; Pratt *v.* Paris Gas Light & Coke Company, 168 U. S. 255, 259.

[2] United States *v.* Northwestern Express Co., 164 U. S. 686, 689.

[3] Northern Pacific Railroad *v.* Amato, 144 U. S. 465; Union Pacific Railway *v.* Harris, 158 U. S. 326.

confer jurisdiction. It is the settled law of the Supreme Court that the federal question must be a necessary basis of the plaintiff's own case and appear from his own showing, and that a suggestion of one party that the other will or may set up a claim under the Constitution or laws of the United States does not make the suit one arising under that Constitution or those laws.[1] So, also, when a case is removed, if the removal be not based upon diversity of citizenship. It may be that the defendant desiring to remove has no defense whatever to the plaintiff's claim except the federal right, and that no other question will be litigated on the trial. Nevertheless, if the federal question be no part of the plaintiff's case, the removal cannot be had, and the defendant must specially set up or claim the federal right in the state court, litigate it there, and reach the Supreme Court finally through writ of error to the highest court of the State.[2] This may involve years of delay. Attempts have been made to set up the federal question in the petition for removal or in the defendant's answer, but the rule required by the peculiar wording of the statute is rigid — the suit cannot be removed as one arising under the Constitution, laws, or treaties of the United States, unless it so appears by the plaintiff's statement of his own claim; and if it does not so appear, the want cannot be supplied by any statement in the petition for removal or in the subsequent pleadings.[3] Nor is the

---

[1] Colorado Central Mining Co. *v.* Turck, 150 U. S. 138, 142; Tennessee *v.* Union and Planters' Bank, 152 U. S. 454, 464; Oregon Short Line &c. R'y *v.* Skottowe, 162 U. S. 490, 493; Press Publishing Company *v.* Monroe, 164 U. S. 105, 110; Muse *v.* Arlington Hotel Company, 168 U. S. 430, 435; Galveston &c. Railway *v.* Texas, 170 U. S. 226, 235.

[2] Chappell *v.* Waterworth, 155 U. S. 102, 107; Postal Telegraph Cable Co. *v.* Alabama, 155 U. S. 482, 487; Mattingly *v.* N. W. Virginia Railroad, 158 U. S. 53, 56.

[3] Hanford *v.* Davies, 163 U. S. 273.

mere allegation of the existence of a federal question sufficient. There must be a real substantive question on which the case may be made to turn. Jurisdiction cannot be inferred argumentatively from the averments in the pleadings. The presumption is that a cause is without the jurisdiction of the circuit court unless the contrary affirmatively appears.[1] The essential facts averred must show clearly and distinctly that the suit is one of which the circuit court is entitled to take cognizance.

Under the present practice, most of the cases tried in the United States district and circuit courts may be carried to the circuit courts of appeals established by the Evarts Act of 1891. If, however, the suit arises under the Constitution, laws or treaties of the United States, the appeal is taken direct from the circuit or district court to the Supreme Court without passing through an intermediate appellate court, and that appeal gives to the Supreme Court jurisdiction of the entire case and of all questions involved in it.[2] In these cases, the federal question must

---

[1] St. Joseph & Grand Island R'd v. Steele, 167 U. S. 659; Hanford v. Davies, 163 U. S. 273, 279; where the court said: "These principles have been applied in cases where the jurisdiction of the Circuit Court was invoked upon the ground of diverse citizenship. But they are equally applicable where its original jurisdiction of a suit between citizens of the same State is invoked upon the ground that the suit is one arising under the Constitution or laws of the United States. We are not required to say that it is essential to the maintenance of the jurisdiction of the Circuit Court of such a suit that the pleadings should refer, in words, to the particular clause of the Constitution relied on to sustain the claim of immunity in question, but only that the essential facts averred must show, not by inference or argumentatively, but clearly and distinctly, that the suit is one of which the Circuit Court is entitled to take cognizance."

[2] Nishimura Ekiu v. United States, 142 U. S. 651; Horner v. United States. No. 2., 143 U. S. 570, 576; United States v. Jahn, 155 U. S. 109, 112, 113; Chappell v. United States, 160 U. S. 499, 509; Press Publishing Company v. Monroe, 164 U. S. 105, 111; Scott v. Donald, 165 U. S. 58, 73; Penn Mutual Life Insurance Co. v. Austin, 168 U. S. 685, 695.

clearly appear upon the record, as in writs of error to a state court under section 709.[1]

The practitioner frequently finds that the case involves not only a federal question, but other questions upon the general merits of the controversy aside from constitutional points; and there is often great embarrassment in determining what course to follow — whether to appeal direct on the constitutional question to the Supreme Court or to take the case to the circuit court of appeals, with the chance that that court may certify the constitutional question up, or that the Supreme Court itself may subsequently take it under advisement by writ of certiorari. The defeated party cannot, as of right, have the benefit of an appeal to both courts. If the case clearly arises under the Constitution, the proper practice is to go directly from the circuit or district court to the Supreme Court; but this course should not be adopted in doubtful cases. The safer practice is to appeal to the circuit court of appeals and then ask that court to certify the federal question to the Supreme Court and to suspend decision upon the merits until the federal question has been determined. It must be observed, however, that this practice might involve the loss of the right to go to the Supreme Court upon the federal question, for the circuit court of appeals might decline to certify the question and the Supreme Court itself might subsequently decline to issue the writ of certiorari.[2] The practice of taking the whole case up to the circuit court of appeals, when in doubt, and then asking that court to certify the federal question is based upon a

---

[1] Ansbro *v.* United States, 159 U. S. 695, 697; Cornell *v.* Green, 163 U. S. 75, 78; Muse *v.* Arlington Hotel Company, 168 U. S. 430, 435.

[2] McLish *v.* Roff, 141 U. S. 661; United States *v.* Jahn, 155 U. S. 109; Ansbro *v.* United States, 159 U. S. 695; Van Wagenen *v.* Sewall, 160 U. S. 369; Chappell *v.* United States, 160 U. S. 499; Cornell *v.* Green, 163 U. S. 75; Robinson *v.* Caldwell, 165 U. S. 359.

decision of the Supreme Court which laid down the following rules as to the practice in case the jurisdiction of the circuit court is in issue, namely :

" (1) If the jurisdiction of the Circuit Court is in issue and decided in favor of the defendant, as that disposes of the case, the plaintiff should have the question certified and take his appeal or writ of error directly to this court; (2) If the question of jurisdiction is in issue, and the jurisdiction sustained, and then judgment or decree is rendered in favor of the defendant on the merits, the plaintiff, who has maintained the jurisdiction, must appeal to the Circuit Court of Appeals, where, if the question of jurisdiction arises, the Circuit Court of Appeals may certify it; (3) If the question of jurisdiction is in issue, and the jurisdiction sustained, and judgment on the merits is rendered in favor of the plaintiff, then the defendant can elect either to have the question certified and come directly to this court, or to carry the whole case to the Circuit Court of Appeals, and the question of jurisdiction can be certified by that court; (4) If in the case last supposed the plaintiff has ground of complaint in respect of the judgment he has recovered, he may also carry the case to the Circuit Court of Appeals on the merits, and this he may do by way of cross-appeal or writ of error if the defendant has taken the case there, or independently, if the defendant has carried the case to this court on the question of jurisdiction alone, and, in this instance, the Circuit Court of Appeals will suspend a decision upon the merits until the question of jurisdiction has been determined ; (5) The same observations are applicable where a plaintiff objects to the jurisdiction and is, or both parties are, dissatisfied with the judgment on the merits." [1]

[1] Fuller, C. J., in United States *v.* Jahn, 155 U. S. 109, 114, 115.

Where the circuit court of appeals is willing to certify to the Supreme Court under the Evarts Act of 1891, the questions certified must be distinct points or propositions of law so stated that they can be answered independently of other questions of law in the case. The Supreme Court will decline to pass upon the merits of the whole controversy when attempted to be presented under the form of such a certificate.[1]

In addition to the necessity for purposes of jurisdiction of putting a clear statement of the federal question upon the record in cases originally brought in, or removed to the circuit court, it is also necessary that the plaintiff's statement of his own case should show that the federal question is involved, in order to preserve the right to an appeal direct to the Supreme Court.[2] Where the statement of claim or declaration shows that jurisdiction is based upon diverse citizenship and it does not appear that jurisdiction is or can be asserted on any other ground, the appeal or writ of error from the judgment of the circuit court must be taken to the circuit court of appeals, and the decision of that court is final. The inquiry as to the real basis of jurisdiction is referred to the time and method of the commencement of the suit, although subsequent proceedings may bring to light a federal question, which, if properly set up in the beginning, would have sustained the original jurisdiction of the circuit court independently of the diverse citizenship of the parties.[3] The federal

---

[1] Graver *v.* Faurot, 162 U. S. 435; United States *v.* Rider, 163 U. S. 132 ; Warner *v.* New Orleans, 167 U. S. 467 ; United States *v.* Union Pacific Railway, 168 U. S. 505 ; McHenry *v.* Alford, 168 U. S. 651.

[2] Colorado Central Mining Co. *v.* Turck, 150 U. S. 138; Borgmeyer, Administrator, *v.* Idler, 159 U. S. 408.

[3] "In Colorado Central Mining Co. *v.* Turck, 150 U. S. 138, we held that when the original jurisdiction of a Circuit Court of the United States is invoked upon the ground that the determination of the suit depends upon some ques-

question should therefore always be averred in addition to the diversity of citizenship. This assures a double hold upon the jurisdiction of the court, and leaves the way open for a review of its decision by the Supreme Court.

Under the Evarts Act of 1891, the Supreme Court may also review the final judgment of a circuit court of appeals by writ of certiorari, which brings up all the proceedings in the inferior court and is in the nature of a writ of error, but which is only granted in the discretion of the court.[1]

**Remedy by injunction.** — A suit in equity, with the remedy of injunction, often affords the most prompt and satisfactory relief where property rights are involved. Such a

tion of a Federal nature, it must appear, at the outset, from the pleadings, that the suit is one of that character, of which the Circuit Court could properly take cognizance at the time its jurisdiction is invoked; and that when the jurisdiction of a Circuit Court is invoked solely on the ground of diverse citizenship, the judgment of the Circuit Court of Appeals is final, although another ground for jurisdiction in the Circuit Court may be developed in the course of subsequent proceedings in the case." Fuller, C. J., in Borgmeyer, Administrator, v. Idler, 159 U. S. 408, 412, 413. It was accordingly held that, where the statement of claim or declaration showed that jurisdiction was based on diverse citizenship and it did not appear that jurisdiction could be asserted on any other ground, the appeal or writ of error must be taken to the circuit court of appeals and that the judgment of the latter court was final. This authority indicates the necessity, in cases where it may be desired to appeal to the Supreme Court, of resting the jurisdiction of the circuit court upon some federal question which will permit such an appeal. Diverse citizenship alone will not accomplish this result, although sufficient grounds may exist at the time of bringing the suit and may subsequently appear upon the record.

[1] Harris v. Barber, 129 U. S. 366, 369 ; Amer. Const. Co. v. Jacksonville Railway, 148 U. S. 372 ; *In re* Debs, Petitioner, 158 U. S. 564; 159 U. S. 251; *In re* Chetwood, Petitioner, 165 U. S. 443. No time within which the writ must be applied for is fixed either in the act or in the rules. The Supreme Court may declare that it will not issue the writ in case of a delay for more than two years, following the analogy of the limit of appeal where appeal or writ of error will lie. The Supreme Court will only issue the writ of *certiorari* in cases of gravity, Lau Ow Bew, Petitioner, 141 U. S. 583; The Three Friends, 166 U. S. 1, 49. The power may be exercised at any time while the case is pending ; or the transcript of the record in the circuit court is in the court of appeals, even though a mandate has gone down, The Conqueror, 166 U. S. 110, 113; Forsyth v. Hammond, 166 U. S. 506, 511. On such a writ of *certiorari* the entire case is brought before the Supreme Court, Panama Railroad v. Napier Shipping Co., 166 U. S. 280.

remedy cannot be resorted to where personal liberty alone is affected. There must be some injury to property coupled with facts bringing the case within one of the recognized grounds of equitable jurisdiction, and showing that there is no plain, adequate and complete remedy at law. The courts have repeatedly held that an arrest upon a charge of having committed a crime cannot be restrained, but this rule is subject to the limitation that, if such arrest interferes with the property rights of the aggrieved party, there may be circumstances justifying the interposition of a court of equity.

The cases which most frequently arise are under laws imposing taxes. The federal courts will not interfere, simply upon the ground that a tax law is unconstitutional.[1] It should appear that there is clearly no adequate remedy at law, such as the payment of the tax under protest and a suit to recover it.[2] Special circumstances must attend the threatened injury, distinguishing it from a common trespass and bringing the case under some recognized head of equity jurisdiction. Before the aid of a court of equity can be invoked, it must appear that the enforcement of the tax would lead to a multiplicity of suits, or produce irreparable injury, or, where the property is real estate, would throw a cloud upon the title of the complainant, or that there is an element of fraud or breach of trust, or some other ground of equitable jurisdiction.[3] If any portion of the tax is admitted or, upon the bill, can be seen to be due, that portion must be paid or tendered.[4]

---

[1] Shelton *v.* Platt, 139 U. S. 591; Allen *v.* Pullman's Palace Car Co., 139 U. S. 658.

[2] Ogden City *v.* Armstrong, 168 U. S. 224.

[3] State Railroad Tax Cases, 92 U. S. 575; Pacific Express Company *v.* Seibert, 142 U. S. 339; Pollock *v.* Farmers' Loan & Trust Co., 157 U. S. 429 ; Burlington Gas Co. *v.* Burlington &c. R'y, 165 U. S. 370.

[4] Albuquerque Bank *v.* Perea, 147 U. S. 87 ; Northern Pacific Railroad *v.* Clark, 153 U. S. 252.

In considering cases seeking to enjoin the collection of a tax, we must bear in mind that, if this jurisdiction were generally exercised, the very existence of the state or federal government might be placed in jeopardy and the collection of all taxes indefinitely postponed. Indeed, the collection of necessary funds for carrying on the national and state governments might be absolutely in the power of a hostile judiciary, if suits in equity to restrain the collection of taxes were generally permitted.

The Eleventh Amendment provides that the judicial power of the United States shall not be construed to extend to any suit in law or equity commenced or prosecuted against one of the United States by citizens of another State or by citizens or subjects of any foreign state. It is, therefore, essential that it should appear that any suit in equity is not against an officer of the State in his official capacity, to compel him to do or refrain from doing any act as such officer, but that the ground of the application is that the defendant is acting without authority of law, or, what is the same thing, under the pretense of a void statute, or threatening to do an act which, being without authority of law, cannot constitute official action, and therefore is but a trespass. When state officers are seeking to enforce a statute which deprives the individual or corporation of property without due process of law, and there is no plain, adequate and complete remedy at law, an injunction may issue against such officers, upon the theory that the individual is restrained from a trespass acting under pretended authority of a void law. The final conclusion of numerous cases in the Supreme Court is that where a suit is against defendants who claim to act as officers of the State, and who, under color of an unconstitutional statute, permit acts of wrong and injury to the

property of the plaintiff, and the proceeding is brought
to recover money or property in their hands unlawfully
taken by them on behalf of the State, or for compensation
for damages, or to restrain threatened illegal action, such
a suit is not, within the meaning of the Eleventh Amendment, an action against the State, but against individual
trespassers.[1]

**Habeas corpus.** — In cases involving personal liberty under
the Fourteenth Amendment, the regular practice is for the
accused, if convicted, to take his appeal to the highest
court of the State and then, if the conviction be affirmed,
sue out the writ of error from the Supreme Court of the
United States. If this were the only remedy, it would
expose the people in many instances to the danger of
arbitrary action on the part of the States and imprisonment might be endured for years before relief could be
secured. There is, therefore, an additional remedy by the
writ of *habeas corpus*, which may be issued by the Supreme
Court itself or by any United States circuit or district
court for the purpose of an inquiry into the cause of
restraint of liberty whenever a person is in custody in
violation of the Constitution of the United States. But it
cannot be used to perform the office of a writ of error or
an appeal.[2] It can only be used when the action sought
to be reviewed is a nullity.[3]

The practice upon *habeas corpus* is regulated by sections
751 *et seq.* of the Revised Statutes. While the circuit and
district courts of the United States have a discretion to

---

[1] Osborn *v.* U. S. Bank, 9 Wheat. 738; Tuchman *v.* Welch, 42 Fed. Rep.
548; *In re* Tyler, Petitioner, 149 U. S. 164; Scott *v.* Donald, 165 U. S. 58.

[2] Tinsley *v.* Anderson, 171 U. S. 101.

[3] *In re* Swan, Petitioner, 150 U. S. 637; *In re* Schneider, Petitioner (No. 2),
148 U. S. 162; *In re* Tyler, Petitioner, 149 U. S. 164; Andrews *v.* Swartz, 156
U. S. 272; *In re* Lennon, 166 U. S. 548.

issue the writ of *habeas corpus* in the case of any person in custody in alleged violation of the Constitution, laws, or treaties of the United States, the settled and proper procedure is that the courts will not exercise that jurisdiction by the discharge of a prisoner unless in cases of peculiar urgency.[1] Instead of discharging the prisoner, they will ordinarily leave him to be dealt with by the courts of the State ; and, even after a final determination of the case by the state courts, the federal courts generally leave the petitioner to his remedy by writ of error from the Supreme Court to the highest state court. The federal courts recognize that it is an exceedingly delicate jurisdiction by which a person under an indictment in a state court and subject to its laws may, by the decision of a single judge of a federal court upon a writ of *habeas corpus*, be taken out of the custody of the officers of the State and finally discharged therefrom, and thus a trial by the state court of an indictment found under the laws of that State be finally prevented. The federal courts always bear in mind, in the exercise of this discretion, that the public good requires that the relations existing under our system of government between the federal judicial tribunals and those of the States should not be disturbed by unnecessary conflict between courts equally bound to guard and protect the rights secured by the Constitution of the United States.[2] Exceptional cases, however, arise which justify the exercise of this discretion by the federal courts. In peculiar and urgent cases, where the act under which the prisoner is held is clearly unconstitutional and the

---

[1] *Ex parte* Royall, 117 U. S. 241; Cook *v.* Hart, 146 U. S. 183, 194; New York *v.* Eno, 155 U. S. 89 ; *In re* Chapman, Petitioner, 156 U. S. 211; Whitten *v.* Tomlinson, 160 U. S. 231; Baker *v.* Grice, 169 U. S. 284; Tinsley *v.* Anderson, 171 U. S. 101.

[2] Robb *v.* Connolly, 111 U. S. 624, 637 ; Cook *v.* Hart, 146 U. S. 183, 195.

circumstances involve hardship and arbitrary action, the writ of *habeas corpus* will be issued by the federal court and the prisoner discharged.

Upon the hearing of such a writ, the inquiry is not as to the guilt or innocence of the prisoner, but as to whether the statute under which he has been indicted and arrested is clearly unconstitutional and should be treated as void. The court committing him would then really have no jurisdiction.[1] In the latest case considered by the Supreme Court of the United States where the writ of *habeas corpus* had been granted and the prisoner discharged before his trial in the state court, the order was unanimously reversed; but Mr. Justice Peckham said : " If this application had been made subsequently to a trial of the petitioner in the state court and his conviction upon such trial under a holding by that court that the law was constitutional, and where an appeal from such judgment of conviction merely imposing a fine could not be had, excepting upon the condition of the defendant's imprisonment until the hearing and decision of the appeal, a different question would be presented and one which is not decided in this case, and upon which we do not now express any opinion." [2]

Indeed, the protection of the Fourteenth Amendment would be of very little value if a person could be deprived of his liberty pending the long delay of an appeal from a judgment of conviction. He might be imprisoned for years before, in the regular course of procedure, he could secure a hearing on the constitutional point under a writ of error from the Supreme Court to the highest state court. While the better practice undoubtedly is, ex-

---

[1] Andrews *v.* Schwartz, 156 U. S. 272, 276.
[2] Baker *v.* Grice, 169 U. S. 284, 294.

cept in peculiar and urgent cases, to raise the constitutional point distinctly in the state courts and await the result of the trial and the appeal, it will probably be declared by the Supreme Court as the true rule that immediately after a trial, if there be no way to stay the execution of the sentence upon an appeal or writ of error in the state courts, and the prisoner must therefore submit to imprisonment, he is entitled at once to apply to the federal courts to prevent imprisonment and deprivation of liberty and to be released from custody, provided he can show that the proceedings are in violation of his rights under the Federal Constitution. No other rule can adequately protect the people in the inestimable right of personal liberty.[1]

---

[1] As to final judgments in *habeas corpus* proceedings, see Clarke *v.* McDade, 165 U. S. 168, 172. Appeal does not lie from order of circuit judge at chambers refusing to issue writ. Carper *v.* Fitzgerald, 121 U. S. 87; Lambert *v.* Barrett, 157 U. S. 697; s. c. 159 U. S. 660. As to practice in contempt proceedings, see *In re* Debs, Petitioner, 158 U. S. 564.

# CONSTITUTION OF THE UNITED STATES.

We the People of the United States, in Order to form a more perfect Union, establish Justice, ensure domestic Tranquillity, provide for the common defence, promote the general Welfare, and secure the Blessings of Liberty to ourselves and our Posterity, do ordain and establish this Constitution for the United States of America.[1]

## ARTICLE. I.

Section. 1. All legislative Powers herein granted shall be vested in a Congress of the United States, which shall consist of a Senate and House of Representatives.[2]

Section. 2. The House of Representatives shall be composed of Members chosen every second Year by the People of the several States, and the Electors in each State shall have the Qualifications requisite for Electors of the most numerous Branch of the State Legislature.[3]

No Person shall be a Representative who shall not have attained to the Age of twenty five Years, and been seven Years a Citizen of the United States, and who shall not, when elected, be an Inhabitant of that State in which he shall be chosen.

[Representatives and direct Taxes shall be apportioned among

---

[1] Chisholm v. Georgia, 2 Dall. 419, 465, 470, 474; Martin v. Hunter's Lessee, 1 Wheat. 304, 324; M'Culloch v. Maryland, 4 Wheat. 316, 403; Cohens v. Virginia, 6 Wheat. 264, 380, 417; Buckner v. Finley, 2 Pet. 586, 590; Barron v. Baltimore, 7 Pet. 243, 247; Rhode Island v. Massachusetts, 12 Pet. 657, 730; Dodge v. Woolsey, 18 How. 331, 356; Dred Scott v. Sandford, 19 How. 393, 410; Lane Co. v. Oregon, 7 Wall. 71, 76; Texas v. White id. 700, 725; Legal Tender Cases, 12 Wall. 457, 554; Minor v. Happersett, 21 Wall. 162, 166; In re Ross, 140 U. S. 453, 464.

[2] Hayburn's Case, 2 Dall. 409, 410; United States v. Ferreira, 13 How. 40, 48; United States v. Todd, id. 52; Gordon v. United States, 117 U. S. 697, 702, 705; Kilbourn v. Thompson, 103 U. S. 168, 192; Field v. Clark, 143 U. S. 649, 681.

[3] Ex parte Yarbrough, 110 U. S. 651, 663; In re Green, 134 U. S. 377, 379.

the several States which may be included within this Union, according to their respective Numbers, which shall be determined by adding to the whole Number of free Persons, including those bound to Service for a Term of Years, and excluding Indians not taxed, three fifths of all other Persons.[1]] The actual Enumeration shall be made within three Years after the first Meeting of the Congress of the United States, and within every subsequent Term of ten Years, in such Manner as they shall by Law direct. The Number of Representatives shall not exceed one for every thirty Thousand, but each State shall have at Least one Representative; and until such enumeration shall be made, the State of New Hampshire shall be entitled to chuse three, Massachusetts eight, Rhode Island and Providence Plantations one, Connecticut five, New-York six, New Jersey four, Pennsylvania eight, Delaware one, Maryland six, Virginia ten, North Carolina five, South Carolina five, and Georgia three.

When vacancies happen in the Representation from any State, the Executive Authority thereof shall issue Writs of Election to fill such Vacancies.

The House of Representatives shall chuse their Speaker and other Officers; and shall have the sole Power of Impeachment. SECTION. 3. The Senate of the United States shall be composed of two Senators from each State, chosen by the Legislature thereof, for six Years; and each Senator shall have one Vote.

Immediately after they shall be assembled in Consequence of the first Election, they shall be divided as equally as may be into three Classes. The Seats of the Senators of the first Class shall be vacated at the Expiration of the second Year, of the second Class at the Expiration of the fourth Year, and of the third Class at the Expiration of the sixth Year, so that one third may be chosen every second Year; and if Vacancies happen by Resignation, or otherwise, during the Recess of the Legislature of any State, the Executive thereof may make temporary Appointments until the next Meeting of the Legislature, which shall then fill such Vacancies.

[1] Clause in brackets amended by 14th Amend., § 2, *post*. Hylton v. United States, 3 Dall. 171, 172; Dodge v. Woolsey, 18 How. 331, 351; Pac. Ins. Co. v. Soule, 7 Wall. 433, 443; Veazie Bank v. Fenno, 8 Wall. 533, 540; Scholey v. Rew, 23 Wall. 331, 347; Springer v. United States, 102 U. S. 586, 595; Pollock v. F. L. & T. Co., 157 U. S. 429, 558; 158 U. S. 601, 618.

No Person shall be a Senator who shall not have attained to the Age of thirty Years, and been nine Years a Citizen of the United States, and who shall not, when elected, be an Inhabitant of that State for which he shall be chosen.

The Vice President of the United States shall be President of the Senate, but shall have no Vote, unless they be equally divided.

The Senate shall chuse their other Officers, and also a President pro tempore, in the Absence of the Vice President, or when he shall exercise the Office of President of the United States.

The Senate shall have the sole Power to try all Impeachments. When sitting for that Purpose, they shall be on Oath or Affirmation. When the President of the United States is tried, the Chief Justice shall preside: And no Person shall be convicted without the Concurrence of two thirds of the Members present.

Judgment in Cases of Impeachment shall not extend further than to removal from Office, and disqualification to hold and enjoy any Office of honor, Trust or Profit under the United States: but the Party convicted shall nevertheless be liable and subject to Indictment, Trial, Judgment and Punishment, according to Law.

SECTION. 4. The Times, Places and Manner of holding Elections for Senators and Representatives, shall be prescribed in each State by the Legislature thereof; but the Congress may at any time by Law make or alter such Regulations, except as to the Places of chusing Senators.[1]

The Congress shall assemble at least once in every Year, and such Meeting shall be on the first Monday in December, unless they shall by Law appoint a different Day.

SECTION. 5. Each House shall be the Judge of the Elections, Returns and Qualifications of its own Members, and a Majority of each shall constitute a Quorum to do Business; but a smaller Number may adjourn from day to day, and may be authorized to compel the Attendance of absent Members, in such Manner, and under such Penalties as each House may provide.[2]

---

[1] *Ex parte* Siebold, 100 U. S. 371, 383; *Ex parte* Clarke, *id.* 399, 403; *Ex parte* Yarbrough, 110 U. S. 651, 660; *In re* Coy, 127 U. S. 731, 752.

[2] United States *v.* Ballin, 144 U. S. 1, 4.

Each House may determine the Rules of its Proceedings, punish its Members for disorderly Behaviour, and, with the Concurrence of two thirds, expel a Member.[1]

Each House shall keep a Journal of its Proceedings, and from time to time publish the same, excepting such Parts as may in their Judgment require Secrecy; and the Yeas and Nays of the Members of either House on any question shall, at the Desire of one fifth of those Present, be entered on the Journal.[2]

Neither House, during the Session of Congress, shall, without the Consent of the other, adjourn for more than three days, nor to any other Place than that in which the two Houses shall be sitting.

SECTION. 6. The Senators and Representatives shall receive a Compensation for their Services, to be ascertained by Law, and paid out of the Treasury of the United States. They shall in all Cases, except Treason, Felony and Breach of the Peace, be privileged from Arrest during their Attendance at the Session of their respective Houses, and in going to and returning from the same; and for any Speech or Debate in either House, they shall not be questioned in any other Place.[3]

No Senator or Representative shall, during the Time for which he was elected, be appointed to any civil Office under the Authority of the United States which shall have been created, or the Emoluments whereof shall have been encreased during such time; and no Person holding any Office under the United States, shall be a Member of either House during his Continuance in Office.

SECTION. 7. All Bills for raising Revenue shall originate in the House of Representatives; but the Senate may propose or concur with Amendments as on other Bills.

Every Bill which shall have passed the House of Representatives and the Senate shall, before it becomes a Law, be presented to the President of the United States; If he approve he shall sign it, but if not he shall return it, with his Objections to that House in which it shall have originated, who shall

---

[1] Anderson v. Dunn, 6 Wheat. 204, 225; Kilbourn v. Thompson, 103 U. S. 168, 189; In re Chapman, 166 U. S. 661, 668.

[2] Field v. Clark, 143 U. S. 649, 670; United States v. Ballin, 144 U. S. 1, 3.

[3] Coxe v. M'Clenachan, 3 Dall. 478.

enter the Objections at large on their Journal, and proceed to reconsider it. If after such Reconsideration two thirds of that House shall agree to pass the Bill, it shall be sent, together with the Objections, to the other House, by which it shall likewise be reconsidered, and if approved by two thirds of that House, it shall become a Law. But in all such Cases the Votes of both Houses shall be determined by yeas and Nays, and the Names of the Persons voting for and against the Bill shall be entered on the Journal of each House respectively. If any Bill shall not be returned by the President within ten Days (Sundays excepted) after it shall have been presented to him, the Same shall be a Law, in like Manner as if he had signed it, unless the Congress by their Adjournment prevent its Return, in which Case it shall not be a Law.[1]

Every Order, Resolution or Vote to which the Concurrence of the Senate and House of Representatives may be necessary (except on a question of Adjournment) shall be presented to the President of the United States ; and before the Same shall take Effect, shall be approved by him, or being disapproved by him, shall be repassed by two thirds of the Senate and House of Representatives, according to the Rules and Limitations prescribed in the Case of a Bill.

SECTION. 8. The Congress shall have Power To lay and collect Taxes, Duties, Imposts and Excises,[2] to pay the Debts[3] and provide for the common Defence and general Welfare of the United States; but all Duties, Imposts and Excises shall be uniform throughout the United States ;[4]

To borrow Money on the credit of the United States ;[5]

---

[1] Gardner v. Collector, 6 Wall. 499, 504; Field v. Clark, 143 U. S. 649, 667.

[2] United States v. Rice, 4 Wheat. 246, 253; Murray's Lessee v. Hoboken Co., 18 How. 272, 281; Lane Co. v. Oregon, 7 Wall. 71, 79; Collector v. Day, 11 Wall. 113, 126; Springer v. United States, 102 U. S. 586, 593.

[3] Legal Tender Case, 110 U. S. 421, 439.

[4] Hylton v. United States, 3 Dall. 171, 176; M'Culloch v. Maryland, 4 Wheat. 316, 425; Lougborough v. Blake, 5 Wheat. 317, 318; Gibbons v. Ogden, 9 Wheat. 1, 201; Dobbins v. Commissioners, 16 Pet. 435, 448; Passenger Cases, 7 How. 283, 405; Gilman v. Sheboygan, 2 Black, 510, 516; United States v. Singer, 15 Wall. 111, 121; Township v. Talcott, 19 Wall. 666, 675; Head Money Cases, 112 U. S. 580, 594; Pollock v. F. L. & T. Co., 157 U. S. 429, 555; 158 U. S. 601, 617.

[5] Weston v. Charleston, 2 Pet. 449, 465; Bank v. New York, 2 Black, 620, 629; Van Allen v. Assessors, 3 Wall. 573, 581; Banks v. Mayor, 7 Wall. 16, 23;

To regulate Commerce with foreign Nations, and among the several States, and with the Indian Tribes ; [1]

Bank *v.* Supervisors, *id.* 26, 29; Hepburn *v.* Griswold, 8 Wall. 603, 607; Legal Tender Case, 110 U. S. 421, 437.

[1] Gibbons *v.* Ogden, 9 Wheat. 1, 189; Brown *v.* Maryland, 12 Wheat. 419, 445; Willson *v.* Black Bird Creek Co., 2 Pet. 245, 250; New York *v.* Miln, 11 Pet. 102, 131; United States *v.* Coombs, 12 Pet. 72, 78; Groves *v.* Slaughter, 15 Pet. 449, 504; License Cases, 5 How. 504, 574; Passenger Cases, 7 How. 283, 393; Nathan *v.* Louisiana, 8 How. 73, 80; Mager *v.* Grima, *id.* 490, 493; United States *v.* Marigold, 9 How. 560, 566; Cooley *v.* Board, 12 How. 299, 315; Genesee Chief *v.* Fitzhugh, *id.* 443, 451; Veazie *v.* Moor, 14 How. 568, 571; Smith *v.* State, 18 How. 71, 74; State *v.* Wheeling &c. Bridge Co., 13 How. 518, 561; 18 How. 421, 431; Allen *v.* Newberry, 21 How. 244, 245; Sinnot *v.* Davenport, 22 How. 227, 239; Conway *v.* Taylor's Executor, 1 Black, 603, 633; Steamship Co. *v.* Joliffe, 2 Wall. 450, 459; United States *v.* Holliday, 3 Wall. 407, 416; Gilman *v.* Philadelphia, *id.* 713, 724; License Tax Cases, 5 Wall. 462, 470; Pervear *v.* Commonwealth, *id.* 475, 478; Steamship Co. *v.* Portwardens, 6 Wall. 31, 32; Crandall *v.* State, *id.* 35, 41; Woodruff *v.* Parham, 8 Wall. 123, 138; Hinson *v.* Lott, *id.* 148, 150; United States *v.* Dewitt, 9 Wall. 41, 43; Downham *v.* Alexandria, 10 Wall. 173, 175; The Daniel Ball, *id.* 557, 563; Ward *v.* Maryland, 12 Wall. 418, 427; *Ex parte* McNiel, 13 Wall. 236, 238; State Freight Tax, 15 Wall. 232, 271; Railroad Company *v.* Fuller, 17 Wall. 560, 567; Railroad Company *v.* Maryland, 21 Wall. 456, 469; Welton *v.* State, 91 U. S. 275, 279; Henderson *v.* Mayor, 92 U. S. 259, 270; Chy Lung *v.* Freeman, *id.* 275, 280; Sherlock *v.* Alling, 93 U. S. 99, 102; United States *v.* 43 Gals. Whiskey, *id.* 188, 193; Munn *v.* Illinois, 94 U. S. 113, 135; Foster *v.* Master, *id.* 246, 247; Railroad Co. *v.* Husen, 95 U. S. 465, 468; Hall *v.* De Cuir, *id.* 485, 487; Pensacola Tel. Co. *v.* W. etc. Tel. Co., 96 U. S. 1, 8; Beer Co. *v.* Mass., 97 U. S. 25, 32; Guy *v.* Baltimore, 100 U. S. 434, 437; Tiernan *v.* Rinker, 102 U. S. 123, 125; County *v.* Kimball, *id.* 691, 696; Webber *v.* Virginia, 103 U. S. 344, 347; Telegraph Co. *v.* Texas, 105 U. S. 460, 464; Packet Co. *v.* Catlettsburg, *id.* 559, 561; Turner *v.* Maryland, 107 U. S. 38, 48; People *v.* Compagnie, *id.* 59, 60; Escanaba Co. *v.* Chicago, *id.* 678, 682; Transportation Co. *v.* Parkersburg, *id.* 691, 700; Miller *v.* Mayor, 109 U. S. 385, 393; Moran *v.* New Orleans, 112 U. S. 69, 71; Head Money Cases, *id.* 580, 591; Gloucester Ferry *v.* Penn., 114 U. S. 196, 203; Brown *v.* Houston, *id.* 622, 630; Walling *v.* Michigan, 116 U. S. 446, 454; Coe *v.* Errol, *id.* 517, 524; Pickard *v.* Pullman Car Co., 117 U. S. 34, 44; Spraigue *v.* Thompson, 118 U. S. 90, 94; Morgan *v.* Louisiana, *id.* 455, 463; Wabash, &c. R'y Co. *v.* Illinois, *id.* 557, 563; Huse *v.* Glover, 119 U. S. 543, 547; Robbins *v.* Taxing District, 120 U. S. 489, 492; Fargo *v.* Michigan, 121 U. S. 230, 237; Ouachita Packet Co. *v.* Aiken, *id.* 444, 446; Phila. S. S. Co. *v.* Penn., 122 U. S. 326, 335; W. U. Tel. Co. *v.* Pendleton, *id.* 347, 356; Smith *v.* Alabama, 124 U. S. 465, 473; Willamette, &c. Co. *v.* Hatch, 125 U. S. 1, 7; Pembina Mining Co. *v.* Penn., *id.* 181, 184; Bowman *v.* Chicago, &c. R'y Co., *id.* 465, 476; Ratterman *v.* W. U. Tel. Co., 127 U. S. 411, 423; Leloup *v.* Port of Mobile, *id.* 640, 644; Kidd *v.* Pearson, 128 U. S. 1, 20; Kimmish *v.* Ball, 129 U. S. 217, 220; W. U. Tel. Co. *v.* Alabama, 132 U. S. 472, 473; Louisville &c. R'y Co. *v.* Mississippi, 133 U. S. 587, 589; Leisy *v.* Hardin, 135 U. S. 100, 108; Lyng *v.* Michigan, *id.* 161, 166; Cherokee Nation *v.* Kan. R'y Co., *id.* 641, 657; McCall *v.* California, 136 U. S. 104, 107; Minnesota *v.* Barber, *id.* 313, 319; Brimmer *v.* Rebman, 138 U. S. 78, 81; *In re* Rahrer, 140 U. S. 545, 555; Pullman's Car Co. *v.* Penn., 141 U. S. 18, 21; Crutcher *v.* Ken-

To establish an uniform Rule of Naturalization,[1] and uniform Laws on the subject of Bankruptcies throughout the United States;[2]

To coin Money, regulate the Value thereof, and of foreign Coin, and fix the Standard of Weights and Measures;[3]

To provide for the Punishment of counterfeiting the Securities and current Coin of the United States;[4]

To establish Post Offices and post Roads;[5]

To promote the Progress of Science and useful Arts, by securing for limited Times to Authors and Inventors the exclusive Right to their respective Writings[6] and Discoveries;[7]

tucky, *id.* 47, 56; Maine *v.* G. T. R'y Co., 142 U. S. 217, 228; L. V. R'd *v.* Penn., 145 U. S. 192, 200; Harman *v.* Chicago, 147 U. S. 396, 404; Brennan *v.* Titusville, 153 U. S. 289, 297; Postal Tel. C. Co. *v.* Charleston, *id.* 692, 694; Covington &c. Co. *v.* Kentucky, 154 U. S. 204, 209; Interstate Comm. *v.* Brimson, *id.* 447, 470; Plumley *v.* Mass., 155 U. S. 461, 464; Hooper *v.* California, *id.* 648, 653; Emert *v.* Missouri, 156 U. S. 296, 306; *In re* Debs, 158 U. S. 564, 579; Geer *v.* Conn., 161 U. S. 519, 530; W. U. Tel. Co. *v.* James, 162 U. S. 650, 653; Ill. C. R'd *v.* Illinois, 163 U. S. 142, 153; Hennington *v.* Georgia, *id.* 299, 307; Scott *v.* Donald, 165 U. S. 58, 90; Adams Ex. Co. *v.* Ohio, *id.* 194, 219; N. Y., N. H. & H. R'd *v.* New York, *id.* 628, 630; C. M. &c. R'y *v.* Solan, 169 U. S. 133, 136; Thomas *v.* Gay, *id.* 264, 274; R. &c. R'd *v.* Tobacco Co., *id.* 311, 313; Smyth *v.* Ames, *id.* 466, 519; M., K. & T. R'y *v.* Haber, *id.* 613, 622; Rhodes *v.* Iowa, 170 U. S. 412, 414; Schollenberger *v.* Penn., 171 U. S. 1, 6; Collins *v.* N. H., *id.* 30, 33; Patapsco Guano Co. *v.* North Carolina, *id.* 345, 354.

[1] Campbell *v.* Gordon, 6 Cranch, 176, 182; Chirac *v.* Chirac, 2 Wheat. 259, 269; Dred Scott *v.* Sandford, 19 How. 393, 417; The Chinese Exclusion Case, 130 U. S. 581, 604; United States *v.* Wong Kim Ark, 169 U. S. 649, 652.

[2] Sturges *v.* Crowninshield, 4 Wheat. 122, 192; M'Millan *v.* M'Neill, *id.* 209; Bank *v.* Smith, 6 Wheat. 131, 134; Ogden *v.* Saunders, 12 Wheat. 213, 273, 314; Boyle *v.* Zacharie, 6 Pet. 348; *id.* 635, 643; Beers *v.* Haughton, 9 Pet. 329, 359; Suydam *v.* Broadnax, 14 Pet. 67, 75; Cook *v.* Moffat, 5 How. 295, 307; Bank *v.* Horn, 17 How. 157, 161; Green *v.* Creighton, 23 How. 90, 106; Baldwin *v.* Hale, 1 Wall. 223, 228; Baldwin *v.* Bank, *id.* 234, 239; Gilman *v.* Lockwood, 4 Wall. 409, 410; Cole *v.* Cunningham, 133 U. S. 107, 116; Butler *v.* Goreley, 146 U. S. 303, 313.

[3] Briscoe *v.* Bank, 11 Pet. 257, 316; Fox *v.* Ohio, 5 How. 410, 433; United States *v.* Marigold, 9 How. 560, 567; Bronson *v.* Rodes, 7 Wall. 229, 251; Butler *v.* Horwitz, *id.* 258, 260; Hepburn *v.* Griswold, 8 Wall. 603, 606; Legal Tender Cases, 12 Wall. 457, 544; Legal Tender Case, 110 U. S. 421, 437.

[4] Fox *v.* Ohio, 5 How. 410, 433; United States *v.* Marigold, 9 How. 560, 567.

[5] M'Culloch *v.* Maryland, 4 Wheat. 316, 417; Searight *v.* Stokes, 3 How. 151, 166; Penn. *v.* Wheeling &c. Co., 18 How. 421, 431; *Ex parte* Jackson, 96 U. S. 727, 732; *In re* Debs, 158 U. S. 564, 579.

[6] Wheaton *v.* Peters, 8 Pet. 591, 660; Trade-Mark Cases, 100 U. S. 82, 93; Banks *v.* Manchester, 128 U. S. 244, 251.

[7] Evans *v.* Eaton, 3 Wheat. 454, 513; Grant *v.* Raymond, 6 Pet. 218, 241; Wilson *v.* Rousseau, 4 How. 646, 674; Patterson *v.* Kentucky, 97 U. S. 501, 503; Lithographic Co. *v.* Sarony, 111 U. S. 53, 56.

To constitute Tribunals inferior to the supreme Court;

To define and punish Piracies and Felonies committed on the high Seas, and Offences against the Law of Nations;[1]

To declare War, grant Letters of Marque and Reprisal, and make Rules concerning Captures on Land and Water;[2]

To raise and support Armies, but no Appropriation of Money to that Use shall be for a longer Term than two Years;

To provide and maintain a Navy;

To make Rules for the Government and Regulation of the land and naval Forces;[3]

To provide for calling forth the Militia to execute the Laws of the Union, suppress Insurrections and repel Invasions;

To provide for organizing, arming, and disciplining, the Militia, and for governing such Part of them as may be employed in the Service of the United States, reserving to the States respectively, the Appointment of the Officers, and the Authority of training the Militia according to the discipline prescribed by Congress;[4]

To exercise exclusive Legislation in all Cases whatsoever, over such District (not exceeding ten Miles square) as may, by Cession of particular States, and the Acceptance of Congress, become the Seat of the Government of the United States,[5] and to exercise like Authority over all Places purchased by the Consent of the Legislature of the State in which the Same shall be, for the Erection of Forts, Magazines, Arsenals, dock-Yards, and other needful Buildings;[6] — And

To make all Laws which shall be necessary and proper for

[1] United States *v.* Palmer, 3 Wheat. 610, 630; United States *v.* Klintock, 5 Wheat. 144, 149; United States *v.* Smith, *id.* 153, 157; United States *v.* Pirates, *id.* 184, 192; United States *v.* Holmes, *id.* 412, 417; United States *v.* Arjona, 120 U. S. 479, 483.

[2] Prize Cases, 2 Black, 635, 665; *Ex parte* Milligan, 4 Wall. 2, 139; Miller *v.* United States, 11 Wall. 268, 305.

[3] Dynes *v.* Hoover, 20 How. 65, 78; United States *v.* Hall, 98 U. S. 343, 350; Johnson *v.* Sayre, 158 U. S. 109, 114.

[4] Houston *v.* Moore, 5 Wheat. 1, 12; Martin *v.* Mott, 12 Wheat. 19, 28; Luther *v.* Borden, 7 How. 1, 43; Presser *v.* Illinois, 116 U. S. 252, 260.

[5] Cohens *v.* Virginia, 6 Wheat. 264, 425; Stoutenbergh *v.* Hennick, 129 U. S. 141, 147; Shoemaker *v.* United States, 147 U. S. 282, 298.

[6] Pollard's Lessee *v.* Hagan, 3 How. 212, 223; Fort L. R. R. Co. *v.* Lowe, 114 U. S. 525, 528; Van Brocklin *v.* Tennessee, 117 U. S. 151, 159; Chappell *v.* United States, 160 U. S. 499, 509.

carrying into Execution the foregoing Powers, and all other Powers vested by this Constitution in the Government of the United States, or in any Department or Officer thereof.[1]

SECTION. 9.[2] The Migration or Importation of such Persons as any of the States now existing shall think proper to admit, shall not be prohibited by the Congress prior to the Year one thousand eight hundred and eight, but a Tax or duty may be imposed on such Importation, not exceeding ten dollars for each Person.[3]

The Privilege of the Writ of Habeas Corpus shall not be suspended, unless when in Cases of Rebellion or Invasion the public Safety may require it.[4]

No Bill of Attainder or ex post facto Law shall be passed.

No Capitation, or other direct, Tax shall be laid, unless in Proportion to the Census or Enumeration hereinbefore directed to be taken.[5]

No Tax or Duty shall be laid on Articles exported from any State.[6]

No Preference shall be given by any Regulation of Commerce or Revenue to the Ports of one State over those of another: nor shall Vessels bound to, or from, one State, be obliged to enter, clear, or pay Duties in another.[7]

No Money shall be drawn from the Treasury, but in Consequence of Appropriations made by Law; and a regular Statement and Account of the Receipts and Expenditures of all public Money shall be published from time to time.[8]

---

[1] M'Culloch *v.* Maryland, 4 Wheat. 316, 411; Wayman *v.* Southard, 10 Wheat. 1, 21; U. S. Bank *v.* Halstead, *id.* 51, 53; Ableman *v.* Booth, 21 How. 506, 521; Tennessee *v.* Davis, 100 U. S. 257, 262; Legal Tender Case, 110 U. S. 421, 440; Luxton *v.* N. R. Bridge Co., 153 U. S. 525, 529.

[2] Barron *v.* Baltimore, 7 Pet. 243, 248.

[3] Passenger Cases, 7 How. 283, 452; Dred Scott *v.* Sandford, 19 How. 393, 411.

[4] *Ex parte* Bollman, 4 Cranch, 75, 94; *Ex parte* Milligan, 4 Wall. 2, 114; *Ex parte* Yerger, 8 Wall. 85, 95.

[5] Turpin *v.* Burgess, 117 U. S. 504.

[6] Hylton *v.* United States, 3 Dall. 171, 172; **Dodge** *v.* Woolsey, 18 How. 331, 351; Pac. Ins. Co. *v.* Soule, 7 Wall. 433, 443; Veazie Bank *v.* Fenno, 8 Wall. 533, 540; Scholey *v.* Rew, 23 Wall. 331, 347; Pollock *v.* F. L. & T. Co., 157 U. S. 429, 558; 158 U. S. 601, 618.

[7] License Cases, 5 How. 504, 594; Passenger Cases, 7 How. 283, 405; Cooley *v.* Board, 12 How. 299, 314; State *v.* Wheeling &c. Bridge Co., 18 How. 421, 433; Pittsburg &c. Coal Co. *v.* Louisiana, 156 U. S. 590, 600.

[8] Brashear *v.* Mason, 6 How. 92, 100; Knote *v.* United States, 95 U. S. 149, 154.

No Title of Nobility shall be granted by the United States: And no Person holding any Office of Profit or Trust under them, shall, without the Consent of the Congress, accept of any present, Emolument, Office, or Title, of any kind whatever, from any King, Prince, or foreign State.

SECTION. 10.[1] No State shall enter into any Treaty, Alliance, or Confederation; grant Letters of Marque and Reprisal; coin Money; emit Bills of Credit;[2] make any Thing but gold and silver Coin a Tender in Payment of Debts; pass any Bill of Attainder,[3] ex post facto Law,[4] or Law impairing the Obligation of Contracts,[5] or grant any Title of Nobility.

[1] Barron *v.* Baltimore, 7 Pet. 243, 248; Dodge *v.* Woolsey, 18 How. 331, 349.

[2] Craig *v.* Missouri, 4 Pet. 410, 431; Briscoe *v.* Bank, 11 Pet. 257, 312; Darrington *v.* Bank, 13 How. 12, 14; Virginia Coupon Cases, 114 U. S. 269, 283.

[3] Cummings *v.* Missouri, 4 Wall. 277, 318; *Ex parte* Garland, *id.* 333, 377; Drehman *v.* Stifle, 8 Wall. 595, 601.

[4] Calder *v.* Bull, 3 Dall. 386, 390; Fletcher *v.* Peck, 6 Cranch, 87, 138; Satterlee *v.* Matthewson, 2 Pet. 380, 413; Watson *v.* Mercer, 8 Pet. 88, 110; B. & S. R'd Co. *v.* Nesbit, 10 How. 395, 401; Carpenter *v.* Penn., 17 How. 456, 462; Locke *v.* New Orleans, 4 Wall. 172, 173; Cummings *v.* Missouri, *id.* 277, 325; Drehman *v.* Stifle, 8 Wall. 595, 601; Gut *v.* State, 9 Wall. 35, 37; Kring *v.* Missouri, 107 U. S. 221, 223; *In re* Sawyer, 124 U. S. 200, 219; Medley, Petitioner, 134 U. S. 160, 170; Hawker *v.* New York, 170 U. S. 189, 190.

[5] Fletcher *v.* Peck, 6 Cranch, 87, 136; Sturges *v.* Crowninshield, 4 Wheat. 122, 197; Dartmouth College *v.* Woodward, *id.* 518, 627; Green *v.* Biddle, 8 Wheat. 1, 90; Ogden *v.* Saunders, 12 Wheat. 213, 254; Satterlee *v.* Matthewson, 2 Pet. 380, 412; Bank *v.* Billings, 4 Pet. 514, 560; Lessee *v.* Moore, 7 Pet. 469, 549; Watson *v.* Mercer, 8 Pet. 88, 110; Mumma *v.* Potomac Co., *id.* 281, 286; Charles River Bridge *v.* Warren Bridge, 11 Pet. 420, 539; Bronson *v.* Kinzie, 1 How. 311, 315; McCracken *v.* Hayward, 2 How. 608, 612; Gordon *v.* Appeal Tax Court, 3 How. 133, 149; Bank *v.* Sharp, 6 How. 301, 318; Bridge Company *v.* Dix, *id.* 507, 530; Mills *v.* St. Clair Co., 8 How. 569, 584; Butler *v.* Penn., 10 How. 402, 415; East Hartford *v.* Hartford Bridge Co., *id.* 511, 532; League *v.* De Young, 11 How. 185, 203; The Richmond, &c. R'd Co. *v.* The Louisa R'd Co., 13 How. 71, 81; Bank *v.* Knoop, 16 How. 369, 385; Ohio L. I. & T. Co. *v.* Debolt, *id.* 416, 428; Aspinwall *v.* Commissioners, 22 How. 364, 376; Rector *v.* County, 24 How. 300, 302; Bank *v.* Skelly, 1 Black, 436, 443; Sherman *v.* Smith, *id.* 587, 591; The Binghamton Bridge, 3 Wall. 51, 71; McGee *v.* Mathis, 4 Wall. 143, 156; Von Hoffman *v.* City, *id.* 535, 549; Hepburn *v.* Griswold, 8 Wall. 603, 623; Railroad Company *v.* McClure, 10 Wall. 511, 515; Knox *v.* Exchange Bank, 12 Wall. 379, 383; Legal Tender Cases, *id.* 457, 547; Curtis *v.* Whitney, 13 Wall. 68, 70; Pennsylvania College Cases, *id.* 190, 212; State Tax on Foreign-held Bonds, 15 Wall. 300, 320; Miller *v.* The State, *id.* 478, 492; Walker *v.* Whitehead, 16 Wall. 314, 317; North Missouri R'd *v.* Maguire, 20 Wall. 46, 60; New Jersey *v.* Yard, 95 U. S. 104, 111; Farrington *v.* Tennessee, *id.* 679, 682; Murray *v.* Charleston, 96 U. S. 432, 443; Edwards *v.* Kearzey, *id.* 595, 598; Sinking-Fund Cases, 99 U. S. 700, 718; R'd Co. *v.* Tennessee, 101 U. S. 337, 339; R'y Co. *v.* Philadelphia, *id.* 528, 532; Stone *v.* Mississippi, *id.* 814, 816;

No State shall, without the Consent of the Congress, lay any Imposts or Duties on Imports or Exports, except what may be absolutely necessary for executing it's inspection Laws: and the net Produce of all Duties and Imposts, laid by any State on Imports or Exports, shall be for the Use of the Treasury of the United States; and all such Laws shall be subject to the Revision and Controul of the Congress.[1]

No State shall, without the Consent of Congress, lay any Duty of Tonnage,[2] keep Troops, or Ships of War in time of Peace, enter into any Agreement or Compact with another State,[3] or with a foreign Power, or engage in War, unless actually invaded, or in such imminent Danger as will not admit of delay.

Louisiana *v.* New Orleans, 102 U. S. 203, 206; Hall *v.* Wisconsin, 103 U. S. 5, 8; Wolff *v.* New Orleans, *id.* 358, 365; Koshkonong *v.* Burton, 104 U. S. 668, 674; Greenwood *v.* Freight Co., 105 U. S. 13, 19; Wiggins Ferry Co. *v.* St. Louis, 107 U. S. 365, 370; Louisiana *v.* Jumel, *id.* 711, 719; Antoni *v.* Greenhow, *id.* 769, 774; Louisville &c. R. R. Co. *v.* Palmes, 109 U. S. 244, 256; Louisiana *v.* Mayor, *id.* 285, 287; Virginia Coupon Cases, 114 U. S. 269, 297; Effinger *v.* Kenney, 115 U. S. 566, 569; N. O. Gas Co. *v.* Louisiana L. Co., *id.* 650, 658; N. O. W. W. Co. *v.* Rivers, *id.* 674, 680; Railroad Commission Cases, 116 U. S. 307, 325; Seibert *v.* Lewis, 122 U. S. 284, 294; N. O. Waterworks *v.* La. Sugar Co., 125 U. S. 18, 30; Williamson *v.* New Jersey, 130 U. S. 189, 197; Hunt *v.* Hunt, 131 U. S. clxv; Morley *v.* L. S. R'y Co., 146 U. S. 162, 166; Hamilton Gas Co. *v.* City, *id.* 258, 265; N. Y. & N. E. R'd Co. *v.* Bristol, 151 U. S. 556, 567; Central Co. *v.* Laidley, 159 U. S. 103, 109; Pearsall *v.* G. N. R'y Co., 161 U. S. 646, 659; Barnitz *v.* Beverly, 163 U. S. 118, 121; Douglas *v.* Kentucky, 168 U. S. 488, 490; Chicago &c. R'd *v.* Nebraska, 170 U. S. 57, 67.

[1] Brown *v.* Maryland, 12 Wheat. 419, 437; License Cases, 5 How. 504, 594; Mager *v.* Grima, 8 How. 490, 494; Cooley *v.* Board, 12 How. 299, 313; Crandall *v.* Nevada, 6 Wall. 35, 41; Hamilton Co. *v.* Mass., *id.* 632, 639; Waring *v.* Mayor, 8 Wall. 110, 121; Woodruff *v.* Parham, *id.* 123, 131; Cook *v.* Penn., 97 U. S. 566, 570; Turner *v.* Maryland, 107 U. S. 38, 41; People *v.* Compagnie, *id.* 59, 61; Brown *v.* Houston, 114 U. S. 622, 628; Turpin *v.* Burgess, 117 U. S. 504, 506; Pittsburg Coal Co. *v.* Bates, 156 U. S. 577, 584; Same *v.* Louisiana, *id.* 590, 597.

[2] Cooley *v.* Board, 12 How. 299, 313; Steamship Co. *v.* Portwardens, 6 Wall. 31, 34; State Tonnage Tax Cases, 12 Wall. 204, 211; Cannon *v.* New Orleans, 20 Wall. 577, 580; Inman S. S. Co. *v.* Tinker, 94 U. S. 238, 242; Packet Co. *v.* Keokuk, 95 U. S. 80, 84; Transportation Co. *v.* Wheeling, 99 U. S. 273, 276; Wiggins Ferry Co. *v.* St. Louis, 107 U. S. 365, 375; Transportation Co. *v.* Parkersburg, *id.* 691, 695; Morgan *v.* Louisiana, 118 U. S. 455, 461; Huse *v.* Glover, 119 U. S. 543, 549; Ouachita Packet Co. *v.* Aiken, 121 U. S. 444, 448.

[3] Green *v.* Biddle, 8 Wheat. 1, 85; Virginia *v.* West Virginia, 11 Wall. 39, 55; Virginia *v.* Tennessee, 148 U. S. 503, 517; Wharton *v.* Wise, 153 U. S. 155, 167.

ARTICLE. II.

SECTION 1. The executive Power shall be vested in a President of the United States of America. He shall hold his Office during the Term of four Years, and, together with the Vice President, chosen for the same Term, be elected, as follows

Each State shall appoint, in such Manner as the Legislature thereof may direct, a Number of Electors, equal to the whole Number of Senators and Representatives to which the State may be entitled in the Congress: but no Senator or Representative, or Person holding an Office of Trust or Profit under the United States, shall be appointed an Elector.[1]

[The Electors shall meet in their respective States, and vote by Ballot for two Persons, of whom one at least shall not be an Inhabitant of the same State with themselves. And they shall make a List of all the Persons voted for, and of the Number of Votes for each; which List they shall sign and certify, and transmit sealed to the Seat of the Government of the United States, directed to the President of the Senate. The President of the Senate shall, in the Presence of the Senate and House of Representatives, open all the Certificates, and the Votes shall then be counted. The Person having the greatest Number of Votes shall be the President, if such Number be a Majority of the whole Number of Electors appointed; and if there be more than one who have such Majority, and have an equal Number of Votes, then the House of Representatives shall immediately chuse by Ballot one of them for President; and if no Person have a Majority, then from the five highest on the List the said House shall in like Manner chuse the President. But in chusing the President, the Votes shall be taken by States, the Representation from each State having one Vote; A quorum for this Purpose shall consist of a Member or Members from two thirds of the States, and a Majority of all the States shall be necessary to a Choice. In every Case, after the Choice of the President, the Person having the greatest Number of Votes of the Electors shall be the Vice President. But if

---

[1] McPherson *v.* Blacker, 146 U. S. 1, 24.

there should remain two or more who have equal Votes, the Senate shall chuse from them by Ballot the Vice President.[1]]

The Congress may determine the Time of chusing the Electors, and the Day on which they shall give their Votes ; which Day shall be the same throughout the United States.

No Person except a natural born Citizen, or a Citizen of the United States, at the time of the Adoption of this Constitution, shall be eligible to the Office of President ;[2] neither shall any Person be eligible to that Office who shall not have attained to the Age of thirty five Years, and been fourteen Years a Resident within the United States.

In Case of the Removal of the President from Office, or of his Death, Resignation, or Inability to discharge the Powers and Duties of the said Office, the Same shall devolve on the Vice President, and the Congress may by Law provide for the Case of Removal, Death, Resignation or Inability, both of the President and Vice President, declaring what Officer shall then act as President, and such Officer shall act accordingly, until the Disability be removed, or a President shall be elected.

The President shall, at stated Times, receive for his Services, a Compensation, which shall neither be encreased nor diminished during the Period for which he shall have been elected, and he shall not receive within that Period any other Emolument from the United States, or any of them.

Before he enter on the Execution of his Office, he shall take the following Oath or Affirmation : — " I do solemnly swear (or affirm) that I will faithfully execute the Office of President of the United States, and will to the best of my Ability, preserve, protect and defend the Constitution of the United States."

SECTION. 2. The President shall be Commander in Chief of the Army and Navy of the United States, and of the Militia of the several States, when called into the actual Service of the United States ;[3] he may require the Opinion, in writing, of the principal Officer in each of the executive Departments, upon any Subject relating to the Duties of their respective

[1] This clause was amended by the 12th Amendment, *post.*

[2] United States *v.* Wong Kim Ark, 169 U. S. 649, 715.

[3] Cross *v.* Harrison, 16 How. 164, 190; Texas *v.* White, 7 Wall. 700, 729; The Grapeshot, 9 Wall. 129, 132; Stewart *v.* Kahn, 11 Wall. 493, 506; Johnson *v.* Sayre, 158 U. S. 109, 115.

Offices, and he shall have Power to grant Reprieves and Pardons for Offences against the United States, except in Cases of Impeachment.[1]

He shall have Power, by and with the Advice and Consent of the Senate, to make Treaties, provided two thirds of the Senators present concur;[2] and he shall nominate, and by and with the Advice and Consent of the Senate, shall appoint Ambassadors, other public Ministers and Consuls, Judges of the supreme Court, and all other Officers of the United States, whose Appointments are not herein otherwise provided for, and which shall be established by Law: but the Congress may by Law vest the Appointment of such inferior Officers, as they think proper, in the President alone, in the Courts of Law, or in the Heads of Departments.[3]

The President shall have Power to fill up all Vacancies that may happen during the Recess of the Senate, by granting Commissions which shall expire at the End of their next Session.

SECTION. 3. He shall from time to time give to the Congress Information of the State of the Union, and recommend to their Consideration such Measures as he shall judge necessary and expedient; he may, on extraordinary Occasions, convene both Houses, or either of them, and in Case of Disagreement between them, with Respect to the Time of Adjournment, he may adjourn them to such Time as he shall think proper; he shall receive Ambassadors and other public Ministers; he shall take Care that the Laws be faithfully executed,[4] and shall Commission all the Officers of the United States.

SECTION. 4. The President, Vice President and all civil Officers of the United States, shall be removed from Office on Impeachment for, and Conviction of, Treason, Bribery, or other high Crimes and Misdemeanors.

---

[1] *Ex parte* Wells, 18 How. 307, 309; *Ex parte* Garland, 4 Wall. 333, 380; Ill. Cent. R'd *v.* Bosworth, 133 U. S. 92, 99; Brown *v.* Walker, 161 U. S. 591, 601.

[2] Am.'Ins. Co. *v.* Canter, 1 Pet. 511, 542; Fong Yue Ting *v.* United States, 149 U. S. 698, 713.

[3] *Ex parte* Hennen, 13 Pet. 230, 257; United States *v.* Le Baron, 19 How. 73, 78; United States *v.* Germaine, 99 U. S. 508, 509; *Ex parte* Siebold, 100 U. S. 371, 397; Parsons *v.* United States, 167 U. S. 324, 328; United States *v.* Eaton, 169 U. S. 331, 343.

[4] Kendall *v.* United States, 12 Pet. 524, 612; State *v.* Johnson, 4 Wall. 475, 499; *In re* Neagle, 135 U. S. 1, 63.

## ARTICLE. III.

SECTION. 1. The judicial Power of the United States, shall be vested in one supreme Court, and in such inferior Courts as the Congress may from time to time ordain and establish. The Judges, both of the supreme and inferior Courts, shall hold their Offices during good Behaviour, and shall, at stated Times, receive for their Services, a Compensation, which shall not be diminished during their Continuance in Office.[1]

SECTION. 2. The judicial Power shall extend to all Cases, in Law and Equity, arising under this Constitution, the Laws of the United States, and Treaties made, or which shall be made under their Authority;[2] — to all Cases affecting Ambassadors, other public Ministers and Consuls;[3] — to all Cases of admiralty and maritime Jurisdiction;[4] — to Controversies to which the United States shall be a Party;[5] — to Controversies between two or more

[1] Hayburn's Case, 2 Dall. 409, 410; United States v. Peters, 5 Cranch, 115, 136; Martin v. Hunter's Lessee, 1 Wheat. 304, 330; Am. Ins. Co. v. Canter, 1 Pet. 511, 546; Jackson v. Lamphire, 3 Pet. 280, 289; Livingston v. Story, 9 Pet. 632, 656; Benner v. Porter, 9 How. 235, 243; United States v. Ferreira, 13 How. 40, 48; United States v. Todd, *id.* 52; Murray's Lessee v. Hoboken Co., 18 How. 272, 275; State v. Johnson, 4 Wall. 475, 499; United States v. Eckford, 6 Wall. 484, 488; Mechanics' &c. Bank v. Bank, 22 Wall. 276, 294; Gordon v. United States, 117 U. S. 697, 702.

[2] Martin v. Hunter's Lessee, 1 Wheat. 304, 331; Robinson v. Campbell, 3 Wheat. 212, 221; Cohens v. Virginia, 6 Wheat. 264, 378, 413; Parsons v. Bedford, 3 Pet. 433, 447; M'Bride v. Hoey, 11 Pet. 167, 172; Bennett v. Butterworth, 11 How. 669, 675; Teal v. Felton, 12 How. 284, 292; Neves v. Scott, 13 How. 268, 272; State v. Wheeling &c. Bridge Co., *id.* 518, 563; Irvine v. Marshall, 20 How. 558, 564; The Moses Taylor, 4 Wall. 411, 428; Mayor v. Cooper, 6 Wall. 247, 250; United States v. U. P. R. R. Co., 98 U. S. 569, 602; Tennessee v. Davis, 100 U. S. 257, 262; Ellis v. Davis, 109 U. S. 485, 497; Barron v. Burnside, 121 U. S. 186, 197; Interstate Comm. v. Brimson, 154 U. S. 447, 475.

[3] United States v. Ravara, 2 Dall. 297, 298; Börs v. Preston, 111 U. S. 252, 256.

[4] Slocum v. Mayberry, 2 Wheat. 1, 9; United States v. Bevans, 3 Wheat. 336, 387; The Thomas Jefferson, 10 Wheat. 428, 430; Am. Ins. Co. v. Canter, 1 Pet. 511, 545; United States v. Coombs, 12 Pet. 72, 76; Waring v. Clarke, 5 How. 441, 454; N. J. Nav. Co. v. Bank, 6 How. 344, 385; The Genesee Chief v. Fitzhugh, 12 How. 443, 451; Smith v. State, 18 How. 71, 76; Jackson v. Magnolia, 20 How. 296, 300; Allen v. Newberry, 21 How. 244, 245; Morewood v. Enequist, 23 How. 491, 493; The St. Lawrence, 1 Black, 522, 526; The Commerce, *id.* 574, 578; The Hine v. Trevor, 4 Wall. 555, 564; Steamboat Co. v. Chase, 16 Wall. 522, 530; The Lottawanna, 21 Wall. 558, 574; The City of Panama, 101 U. S. 453, 457.

[5] Cotton v. United States, 11 How. 229, 231; United States v. Texas, 143 U. S. 621, 641.

States;[1] — between a State and Citizens of another State;[2] — between Citizens of different States,[3] — between Citizens of the same State claiming Lands under Grants of different States, and between a State, or the Citizens thereof, and foreign States, Citizens or Subjects.[4]

In all Cases affecting Ambassadors, other public Ministers and Consuls, and those in which a State shall be Party, the supreme Court shall have original Jurisdiction.[5]  In all the other Cases before mentioned, the supreme Court shall have appellate Jurisdiction, both as to Law and Fact, with such Exceptions, and under such Regulations as the Congress shall make.[6]

The Trial of all Crimes, except in Cases of Impeachment, shall be by Jury;[7] and such Trial shall be held in the State where the

[1] Rhode Island v. Massachusetts, 12 Pet. 657, 720; Commonwealth v. Dennison, 24 How. 66, 95; Virginia v. West Virginia, 11 Wall. 39, 53; United States v. Texas, 143 U. S. 621, 639.

[2] This clause was amended by the 11th Amendment, post; Chisholm v. Georgia, 2 Dall. 419, 430; Hollingsworth v. Virginia, 3 Dall. 378, 382; Wisconsin v. Pelican Ins. Co., 127 U. S. 265, 286; Plaquemines Fruit Co. v. Henderson, 170 U. S. 511, 513.

[3] Bingham v. Cabot, 3 Dall. 382, 383; Abercrombie v. Dupuis, 1 Cranch, 342, 343; Hepburn v. Ellzey, 2 Cranch, 445, 452; Bank v. Deveaux, 5 Cranch, 61, 86; New Orleans v. Winter, 1 Wheat. 91, 94; Osborn v. Bank, 9 Wheat. 738, 823; Gassies v. Ballon, 6 Pet. 761, 762; Brown v. Keene, 8 Pet. 112, 115; Bank v. Earle, 13 Pet. 519, 586; McNutt v. Bland, 2 How. 9, 14; Louisville R'd Co. v. Letson, id. 497, 553; Sheldon v. Sill, 8 How. 441, 448; Dodge v. Woolsey, 18 How. 331, 347; Dred Scott v. Sandford, 19 How. 393, 403; Covington Co. v. Shepherd, 20 How. 227, 232; Barber v. Barber, 21 How. 582, 592; O. & M. R'd Co. v. Wheeler, 1 Black, 286, 295; Payne v. Hook, 7 Wall. 425, 429; Paul v. Virginia, 8 Wall. 168, 177; Ins. Co. v. Morse, 20 Wall. 445, 453; R'd Co. v. Mississippi, 102 U. S. 135, 140; St. L. & San F. R'y v. James, 161 U. S. 545, 554.

[4] Cherokee Nation v. Georgia, 5 Pet. 1, 15; United States v. Kagama, 118 U. S. 375, 378.

[5] Marbury v. Madison, 1 Cranch, 137, 174; Osborn v. Bank, 9 Wheat. 738, 820; United States v. Ortega, 11 Wheat. 467, 468; Davis v. Packard, 7 Pet. 276, 281; Ex parte Barry, 2 How. 65; State v. Wheeling &c. Bridge Co., 13 How. 518, 559; 18 How. 460, 462; Florida v. Georgia, 17 How. 478, 491; Ames v. Kansas, 111 U. S. 449, 462; Wisconsin v. Pelican Ins. Co., 127 U. S. 265, 286.

[6] Durousseau v. United States, 6 Cranch, 307, 313; Cohens v. Virginia, 6 Wheat. 264, 413; Osborn v. Bank, 9 Wheat. 738, 820; Ex parte McCardle, 7 Wall. 506, 512; The Alicia, id. 571, 573; Ex parte Yerger, 8 Wall. 85, 98; Murdock v. City, 20 Wall. 590, 618.

[7] Murray's Lessee v. Hoboken Co., 18 How. 272, 276; Ex parte Milligan, 4 Wall. 2, 119; Callan v. Wilson, 127 U. S. 540, 547; Cook v. United States, 138 U. S. 157, 181.

said Crimes shall have been committed; but when not committed within any State, the Trial shall be at such Place or Places as the Congress may by Law have directed.[1]

SECTION. 3. Treason against the United States, shall consist only in levying War against them, or in adhering to their Enemies, giving them Aid and Comfort. No Person shall be convicted of Treason unless on the Testimony of two Witnesses to the same overt Act, or on Confession in open Court.

The Congress shall have Power to declare the Punishment of Treason, but no Attainder of Treason shall work Corruption of Blood, or Forfeiture except during the Life of the Person attainted.[2]

### ARTICLE. IV.

SECTION. 1. Full Faith and Credit shall be given in each State to the public Acts, Records, and judicial Proceedings of every other State. And the Congress may by general Laws prescribe the Manner in which such Acts, Records and Proceedings shall be proved, and the Effect thereof.[3]

SECTION. 2. The Citizens of each State shall be entitled to all Privileges and Immunities of Citizens in the several States.[4]

---

[1] United States *v.* Jackalow, 1 Black, 484, 486; Cook *v.* United States, 138 U. S. 157, 181.

[2] Jenkins *v.* Collard, 145 U. S. 546, 552; United States *v.* Dunnington, 146 U. S. 338, 346.

[3] Mills *v.* Duryee, 7 Cranch, 481, 483; Hampton *v.* M'Connel, 3 Wheat. 234, 235; M'Elmoyle *v.* Cohen, 13 Pet. 312, 324; Mitchell *v.* Lenox, 14 Pet. 49, 50; Bank *v.* Dalton, 9 How. 522, 527; D'Arcy *v.* Ketchum, 11 How. 165, 174; Bacon *v.* Howard, 20 How. 22, 25; Christmas *v.* Russell, 5 Wall. 290, 301; Green *v.* Van Buskirk, 7 Wall. 139, 147; Caperton *v.* Ballard, 14 Wall. 238, 241; Public Works *v.* Columbia College, 17 Wall. 521, 528; Thompson *v.* Whitman, 18 Wall. 457, 461; Bonaparte *v.* Tax Court, 104 U. S. 592, 594; Embry *v.* Palmer, 107 U. S. 3, 9; Hanley *v.* Donoghue, 116 U. S. 1, 2, C. & A. R'd *v.* Wiggins Co., 119 U. S. 615, 622; Reynolds *v.* Stockton, 140 U. S. 254, 264; Huntington *v.* Attrill, 146 U. S. 657, 666; Laing *v.* Rigney, 160 U. S. 531, 539.

[4] Bank *v.* Earle, 13 Pet. 519, 586; Conner *v.* Elliott, 18 How. 591, 592; Dred Scott *v.* Sandford, 19 How. 393, 412; Paul *v.* Virginia, 8 Wall. 168, 178; Downham *v.* Alexandria, 10 Wall. 173, 175; Ward *v.* Maryland, 12 Wall. 418, 428; Slaughter-House Cases, 16 Wall. 36, 75; Bradwell *v.* State, *id.* 130, 138; Chemung &c. Bank *v.* Lowery, 93 U. S. 72, 77; McCready *v.* Virginia, 94 U. S. 391, 395; Pembina Mining Co. *v.* Penn., 125 U. S. 181, 187; Kimmish *v.* Ball, 129 U. S. 217, 222.

A Person charged in any State with Treason, Felony, or other Crime, who shall flee from Justice, and be found in another State, shall on Demand of the executive Authority of the State from which he fled, be delivered up, to be removed to the State having Jurisdiction of the Crime.[1]

No Person held to Service or Labour in one State, under the Laws thereof, escaping into another, shall, in Consequence of any Law or Regulation therein, be discharged from such Service or Labour, but shall be delivered up on Claim of the Party to whom such Service or Labour may be due.[2]

SECTION. 3. New States may be admitted by the Congress into this Union; but no new State shall be formed or erected within the Jurisdiction of any other State; nor any State be formed by the Junction of two or more States, or Parts of States, without the Consent of the Legislatures of the States concerned as well as of the Congress.[3]

The Congress shall have Power to dispose of and make all needful Rules and Regulations respecting the Territory or other Property belonging to the United States; and nothing in this Constitution shall be so construed as to Prejudice any Claims of the United States, or of any particular State.[4]

SECTION. 4. The United States shall guarantee to every State in this Union a Republican Form of Government, and shall protect each of them against Invasion; and on Application of the Legislature, or of the Executive (when the Legislature cannot be convened) against domestic Violence.[5]

---

[1] Commonwealth v. Dennison, 24 How. 66, 98; Robb v. Connolly, 111 U. S. 624, 628; Ex parte Reggel, 114 U. S. 642, 648; Roberts v. Reilly, 116 U. S. 80, 94; Lascelles v. Georgia, 148 U. S. 537, 540.

[2] Prigg v. Commonwealth, 16 Pet. 539, 611; Jones v. Van Zandt, 5 How. 215, 229; Strader v. Graham, 10 How. 82, 94; Moore v. People, 14 How. 13, 17; Dred Scott v. Sandford, 19 How. 393, 411.

[3] Virginia v. West Virginia, 11 Wall. 39, 55.

[4] United States v. Rice, 4 Wheat. 246, 253; M'Culloch v. Maryland, id. 316, 422; Am. Ins. Co. v. Canter, 1 Pet. 511, 542; Wilcox v. Jackson, 13 Pet. 498, 516; United States v. Gratiot, 14 Pet. 526, 537; Cross v. Harrison, 16 How. 164, 193; Dred Scott v. Sandford, 19 How. 393, 432; Irvine v. Marshall, 20 How. 558, 566; National Bank v. County, 101 U. S. 129, 132; Murphy v. Ramsey, 114 U. S. 15, 44; United States v. Kagama, 118 U. S. 375, 379; Mormon Church v. United States, 136 U. S. 1, 42; McAllister v. United States, 141 U. S. 174, 179; Koenigsberger v. Richmond Min. Co., 158 U. S. 41, 48; Thompson v. Utah, 170 U. S. 343, 347.

[5] Luther v. Borden, 7 How. 1, 42; Texas v. White, 7 Wall. 700, 730.

### ARTICLE. V.

The Congress, whenever two thirds of both Houses shall deem it necessary, shall propose Amendments to this Constitution, or, on the Application of the Legislatures of two thirds of the several States, shall call a Convention for proposing Amendments, which, in either Case, shall be valid to all Intents and Purposes, as Part of this Constitution, when ratified by the Legislatures of three fourths of the several States, or by Conventions in three fourths thereof, as the one or the other Mode of Ratification may be proposed by the Congress; Provided that no Amendment which may be made prior to the Year One thousand eight hundred and eight shall in any Manner affect the first and fourth Clauses in the Ninth Section of the first Article; and that no State, without its Consent, shall be deprived of it's equal Suffrage in the Senate.

### ARTICLE. VI.

All Debts contracted and Engagements entered into, before the Adoption of this Constitution, shall be as valid against the United States under this Constitution, as under the Confederation.

This Constitution, and the Laws of the United States which shall be made in Pursuance thereof; and all Treaties made, or which shall be made, under the Authority of the United States, shall be the supreme Law of the Land; and the Judges in every State shall be bound thereby, any Thing in the Constitution or Laws of any State to the Contrary notwithstanding.[1]

The Senators and Representatives before mentioned, and the Members of the several States Legislatures, and all executive and judicial Officers, both of the United States and of the several

---

[1] Calder v. Bull, 3 Dall. 386, 392; Martin v. Hunter's Lessee, 1 Wheat. 304, 340; M'Culloch v. Maryland, 4 Wheat. 316, 405; Gibbons v. Ogden, 9 Wheat. 1, 210; Brown v. Maryland, 12 Wheat. 419, 448; Foster v. Neilson, 2 Pet. 253, 313; License Cases, 5 How. 504, 573; Dodge v. Woolsey, 18 How. 331, 348; Ableman v. Booth, 21 How. 506, 517; Sinnot v. Davenport, 22 How. 227, 242; Mayor v. Cooper, 6 Wall. 247, 250; Hepburn v. Griswold, 8 Wall. 603, 611; The Cherokee Tobacco, 11 Wall. 616, 620; Hauenstein v. Lynham, 100 U. S. 483, 488; Head Money Cases, 112 U. S. 580, 599; The Chinese Exclusion Case, 130 U. S. 581, 600; Horner v. United States, 143 U. S. 570, 578; In re Debs, 158 U. S. 564, 578.

States, shall be bound by Oath or Affirmation to support this Constitution; [1] but no religious Test shall ever be required as a Qualification to any Office or public Trust under the United States.

## ARTICLE. VII.

The Ratification of the Conventions of nine States, shall be sufficient for the Establishment of this Constitution between the States so ratifying the Same.[2]

[1] Dodge v. Woolsey, 18 How. 331, 348; Ableman v. Booth, 21 How. 506, 524.
[2] Owings v. Speed, 5 Wheat. 420, 421.

# AMENDMENTS TO THE CONSTITUTION OF THE UNITED STATES.

The Conventions of a number of the States having at the time of their adopting the Constitution expressed a desire, in order to prevent misconstruction or abuse of its powers, that further declaratory and restrictive clauses should be added: And as extending the ground of public confidence in the government will best insure the beneficent ends of its institution —

*Resolved,* By the Senate and House of Representatives of the United States of America in Congress assembled, two thirds of both Houses concurring, That the following articles be proposed to the legislatures of the several states as amendments to the constitution of the United States, all or any of which articles, when ratified by three fourths of the said legislatures, to be valid to all intents and purposes, as part of the said Constitution, namely:

Articles in addition to, and amendment of, the Constitution of the United States of America, proposed by Congress and ratified by the Legislatures of the several States, pursuant to the fifth article of the original Constitution.[1]

## ARTICLE I.

Congress shall make no law respecting an establishment of religion, or prohibiting the free exercise thereof;[2] or abridging the freedom of speech, or of the press;[3] or the right of the people peaceably to assemble, and to petition the Government for a redress of grievances.[4]

[1] 1 St. 97; Rev. St. p. 28, note.
[2] Permoli *v.* Municipality, 3 How. 589, 609; Reynolds *v.* United States, 98 U. S. 145, 162; Davis *v.* Beason, 133 U. S. 333, 342.
[3] *In re* Rapier, 143 U. S. 110, 134.
[4] United States *v.* Cruikshank, 92 U. S. 542, 551.

### ARTICLE II.

A well regulated Militia being necessary to the security of a free State, the right of the people to keep and bear Arms, shall not be infringed.[1]

### ARTICLE III.

No Soldier shall, in time of peace be quartered in any house, without the consent of the Owner, nor in time of war, but in a manner to be prescribed by law.

### ARTICLE IV.

The right of the people to be secure in their persons, houses, papers, and effects, against unreasonable searches and seizures, shall not be violated, and no Warrants shall issue, but upon probable cause, supported by Oath or affirmation, and particularly describing the place to be searched, and the persons or things to be seized.[2]

### ARTICLE V.

No person shall be held to answer for a capital, or otherwise infamous crime, unless on a presentment or indictment of a Grand Jury,[3] except in cases arising in the land or naval forces, or in the Militia, when in actual service in time of War or public danger;[4] nor shall any person be subject for the same offence to be twice put in jeopardy of life or limb;[5] nor shall be compelled in any Criminal Case to be a witness against himself,[6] nor be deprived of life, liberty, or property, without due process of law; nor shall private property be taken for public use, without just compensation.[7]

[1] Presser *v.* Illinois, 116 U. S. 252, 264.

[2] *Ex parte* Milligan, 4 Wall. 2, 119; Boyd *v.* United States, 116 U. S. 616, 621; *In re* Chapman, 166 U. S. 661, 668.

[3] *Ex parte* Wilson, 114 U. S. 417, 422; *Ex parte* Bain, 121 U. S. 1, 5; Talton *v.* Mayes, 163 U. S. 376, 382.

[4] Dynes *v.* Hoover, 20 How. 65, 78; *Ex parte* Milligan, 4 Wall. 2, 118, 136; *Ex parte* Mason, 105 U. S. 696, 700; Johnson *v.* Sayre, 158 U. S. 109, 115.

[5] United States *v.* Perez, 9 Wheat. 579, 580; *Ex parte* Lange, 18 Wall. 163, 168; Simmons *v.* United States, 142 U. S. 148, 154; *In re* Chapman, 166 U. S. 661, 671.

[6] Boyd *v.* United States, 116 U. S. 616, 633; Counselman *v.* Hitchcock, 142 U. S. 547, 559; Brown *v.* Walker, 161 U. S. 591, 593.

[7] Barron *v.* Baltimore, 7 Pet. 243, 247; Murray's Lessee *v.* Hoboken Co., 18

## ARTICLE VI.

In all criminal prosecutions, the accused shall enjoy the right to a speedy and public trial, by an impartial jury of the State and district wherein the crime shall have been committed, which district shall have been previously ascertained by law,[1] and to be informed of the nature and cause of the accusation; to be confronted with the witnesses against him; to have compulsory process for obtaining Witnesses in his favor, and to have the Assistance of Counsel for his defence.[2]

## ARTICLE VII.

In suits at common law, where the value in controversy shall exceed twenty dollars, the right of trial by jury shall be preserved, and no fact tried by a jury, shall be otherwise re-examined in any Court of the United States, than according to the rules of the common law.[3]

## ARTICLE VIII.

Excessive bail shall not be required, nor excessive fines imposed, nor cruel and unusual punishments inflicted.[4]

How. 272, 275; Withers *v.* Buckley, 20 How. 84, 89; *Ex parte* Milligan, 4 Wall. 2, 119, 137; Twitchell *v.* Commonwealth, 7 Wall. 321, 325; Hepburn *v.* Griswold, 8 Wall. 603, 623; Miller *v.* United States, 11 Wall. 268, 304; Legal Tender Cases, 12 Wall. 457, 551; Pumpelly *v.* Green Bay Co., 13 Wall. 166, 176; Kohl *v.* United States, 91 U. S. 367, 372; Davidson *v.* New Orleans, 96 U. S. 97, 101; Sinking Fund Cases, 99 U. S. 700, 718; Langford *v.* United States, 101 U. S. 341, 343; Barrett *v.* Holmes, 102 U. S. 651, 655; United States *v.* Lee, 106 U. S. 196, 218; *Ex parte* Wall, 107 U. S. 265, 288; United States *v.* Jones, 109 U. S. 513, 518; Monongahela Co. *v.* United States, 148 U. S. 312, 324; Bauman *v.* Ross, 167 U. S. 548, 574; Wilson *v.* Lambert, 168 U. S. 611, 613.

[1] *Ex parte* Milligan, 4 Wall. 2, 119; Reynolds *v.* United States, 98 U. S. 145, 154; Callan *v.* Wilson, 127 U. S. 540, 547; Cook *v.* United States, 138 U. S. 157, 181; Thompson *v.* Utah, 170 U. S. 343, 346.

[2] Twitchell *v.* Commonwealth, 7 Wall. 321, 325; Reynolds *v.* United States, 98 U. S. 145, 158; Mattox *v.* United States, 156 U. S. 237, 240; Rosen *v.* United States, 161 U. S. 29, 34; United States *v.* Zucker, *id.* 475, 481.

[3] Bank *v.* Okely, 4 Wheat. 235, 240; Parsons *v.* Bedford, 3 Pet. 433, 446; Hiriart *v.* Ballon, 9 Pet. 156, 166; Webster *v.* Reid, 11 How. 437, 460; Murray's Lessee *v.* Hoboken Co., 18 How. 272, 276; The Justices *v.* Murray, 9 Wall. 274, 277; Edwards *v.* Elliott, 21 Wall. 532, 557; Baylis *v.* Ins. Co., 113 U. S. 316, 321; Arkansas Co. *v.* Mann, 130 U. S. 69, 72; Scott *v.* Neely, 140 U. S. 106, 109; Cates *v.* Allen, 149 U. S. 451, 456; Thompson *v.* Utah, 170 U. S. 343, 346.

[4] *Ex parte* Watkins, 7 Pet. 568, 573; Pervear *v.* Commonwealth, 5 Wall. 475, 480; *In re* Kemmler, 136 U. S. 436, 442; O'Neil *v.* Vermont, 144 U. S. 323, 331.

ARTICLE IX.

The enumeration in the Constitution, of certain rights, shall not be construed to deny or disparage others retained by the people.[1]

ARTICLE X.

The powers not delegated to the United States by the Constitution, nor prohibited by it to the States, are reserved to the States respectively, or to the people.[2]

ARTICLE XI.

The Judicial power of the United States shall not be construed to extend to any suit in law or equity, commenced or prosecuted against one of the United States by Citizens of another State, or by Citizens or Subjects of any Foreign State.[3]

ARTICLE XII.

The Electors shall meet in their respective states, and vote by ballot for President and Vice-President, one of whom, at least, shall not be an inhabitant of the same state with themselves; they shall name in their ballots the person voted for as President, and in distinct ballots the person voted for as Vice-President, and they shall make distinct lists of all persons

[1] Barron *v.* Baltimore, 7 Pet. 243, 249; Lessee *v.* Moore, *id.* 469, 546; Loan Assoc. *v.* Topeka, 20 Wall. 655, 662; Giozza *v.* Tiernan, 148 U. S. 657, 661.

[2] Martin *v.* Hunter's Lessee, 1 Wheat. 304, 325; Dodge *v.* Woolsey, 18 How. 331, 352; Hepburn *v.* Griswold, 8 Wall. 603, 613; Collector *v.* Day, 11 Wall. 113, 124; Inman Co. *v.* Tinker, 94 U. S. 238, 244.

[3] This Amendment, adopted as a result of the decision in Chisholm *v.* Georgia, 2 Dall. 419, was declared ratified 8th January, 1798. Rev. St. p. 30. Hollingsworth *v.* Virginia, 3 Dall. 378, 382; United States *v.* Peters, 5 Cranch, 115, 139; Cohens *v.* Virginia, 6 Wheat. 264, 403; Osborn *v.* Bank, 9 Wheat. 738, 849; United States Bank *v.* Planters' Bank, *id.* 904, 906; Governor *v.* Madrazo, 1 Pet. 110, 122; *Ex parte* Madrazzo, 7 Pet. 627, 632; Briscoe *v.* Bank, 11 Pet. 257, 321; Rhode Island *v.* Massachusetts, 12 Pet. 657, 731; Louisiana *v.* Jumel, 107 U. S. 711, 720; N. H. *v.* Louisiana, 108 U. S. 76, 86; Virginia Coupon Cases, 114 U. S. 269, 285; Hagood *v.* Southern, 117 U. S. 52, 67; *In re* Ayers, 123 U. S. 443, 487; Christian *v.* A. & N. C. R'd, 133 U. S. 233, 243; Lincoln Co. *v.* Luning, *id.* 529, 530; Hans *v.* Louisiana, 134 U. S. 1, 9; Pennoyer *v.* McConnaughy, 140 U. S. 1, 9; *In re* Tyler, 149 U. S. 164, 190; Reagan *v.* F. L. & T. Co., 154 U. S. 362, 388; Tindal *v.* Wesley, 167 U. S. 204, 209; Smyth *v.* Ames, 169 U. S. 466, 518.

voted for as President, and of all persons voted for as Vice-President, and of the number of votes for each, which lists they shall sign and certify, and transmit sealed to the seat of the government of the United States, directed to the President of the Senate; — The President of the Senate shall, in the presence of the Senate and House of Representatives, open all the certificates, and the votes shall then be counted; — The person having the greatest number of votes for President, shall be the President, if such number be a majority of the whole number of Electors appointed; and if no person have such majority, then from the persons having the highest numbers not exceeding three on the list of those voted for as President, the House of Representatives shall choose immediately, by ballot, the President. But in choosing the President, the votes shall be taken by states, the representation from each state having one vote; a quorum for this purpose shall consist of a member or members from two-thirds of the states, and a majority of all the states shall be necessary to a choice. And if the House of Representatives shall not choose a President whenever the right of choice shall devolve upon them, before the fourth day of March next following, then the Vice-President shall act as President, as in the case of the death or other constitutional disability of the President. — The person having the greatest number of votes as Vice-President, shall be the Vice-President, if such number be a majority of the whole number of Electors appointed, and if no person have a majority, then from the two highest numbers on the list, the Senate shall choose the Vice-President; a quorum for the purpose shall consist of two-thirds of the whole number of Senators, and a majority of the whole number shall be necessary to a choice. But no person constitutionally ineligible to the office of President shall be eligible to that of Vice-President of the United States.[1]

## ARTICLE XIII.

SECTION 1. Neither slavery nor involuntary servitude, except as a punishment for crime whereof the party shall have

[1] This amendment was declared ratified, 25th September, 1804, amending the third paragraph of section 1, article II. Rev. St. p. 30.

been duly convicted, shall exist within the United States, or any place subject to their jurisdiction.[1]

SECTION 2. Congress shall have power to enforce this article by appropriate legislation.

ARTICLE XIV.[2]

SECTION 1. All persons born or naturalized in the United States, and subject to the jurisdiction thereof, are citizens of the United States and of the State wherein they reside. No State shall make or enforce any law which shall abridge the privileges or immunities of citizens of the United States; nor shall any State deprive any person of life, libertv, or property, without due process of law; nor deny to any person within its jurisdiction the equal protection of the laws.

SECTION 2. Representatives shall be apportioned among the several States according to their respective numbers, counting the whole number of persons in each State, excluding Indians not taxed. But when the right to vote at any election for the choice of electors for President and Vice President of the United States, Representatives in Congress, the Executive and Judicial officers of a State, or the members of the Legislature thereof, is denied to any of the male inhabitants of such State, being twenty-one years of age, and citizens of the United States, or in any way abridged, except for participation in rebellion, or other crime, the basis of representation therein shall be reduced in the proportion which the number of such male citizens shall bear to the whole number of male citizens twenty-one years of age in such State.

SECTION 3. No person shall be a Senator or Representative in Congress, or elector of President and Vice President, or hold any office, civil or military, under the United States, or under any State, who, having previously taken an oath, as a member of Congress, or as an officer of the United States, or as a member of any State legislature, or as an executive

---

[1] This amendment was declared ratified 18th December, 1865. Rev. St. p. 30. Osborn *v.* Nicholson, 13 Wall. 654, 662; Slaughter-House Cases, 16 Wall. 36, 66; *Ex parte* Virginia, 100 U. S. 339, 344; United States *v.* Harris, 106 U. S. 629, 640; Civil Rights Cases, 109 U. S. 3, 20; Robertson *v.* Baldwin, 165 U. S. 275, 280.

[2] See *ante,* p. 1.

or judicial officer of any State, to support the Constitution of the United States, shall have engaged in insurrection or rebellion against the same, or given aid or comfort to the enemies thereof. But Congress may by a vote of two-thirds of each House, remove such disability.

SECTION 4. The validity of the public debt of the United States, authorized by law, including debts incurred for payment of pensions and bounties for services in suppressing insurrection or rebellion, shall not be questioned. But neither the United States nor any State shall assume or pay any debt or obligation incurred in aid of insurrection or rebellion against the United States, or any claim for the loss or emancipation of any slave; but all such debts, obligations and claims shall be held illegal and void.

SECTION 5. The Congress shall have power to enforce, by appropriate legislation, the provisions of this article.

### ARTICLE XV.

SECTION 1. The right of citizens of the United States to vote shall not be denied or abridged by the United States or by any State on account of race, color, or previous condition of servitude — [1]

SECTION 2. The Congress shall have power to enforce this article by appropriate legislation —

[1] This Amendment was declared ratified 30th March, 1870. Rev. St. p. 32. Slaughter-House Cases, 16 Wall. 36, 71; Minor *v.* Happersett, 21 Wall. 162, 175; United States *v.* Reese, 92 U. S. 214, 216; United States *v.* Cruikshank, *id.* 542, 555; Neal *v.* Delaware, 103 U. S. 370, 388; *Ex parte* Yarbrough, 110 U. S. 651, 664; McPherson *v.* Blacker, 146 U. S. 1, 37.

# INDEX TO CONSTITUTION.

# INDEX TO CONSTITUTION.

## A.

I.

# O.

# P.

PEACE. See Breach of.                                          Art. Sec. Page
   time of, soldiers not to be quartered in house . . (amd.) III    202
   time of, state not to keep troops or ships, except . . . . I 10  191
PENSIONS. See Debts.
PEOPLE. See Powers; Right.
PETITION. See Right.
PIRACY,
   Congress to define and punish . . . . . . . . . . I  8  188
PLACES. See Congress, Power.
PORTS. See Congress, Limitations on.
POST,
   offices and roads, Congress to establish . . . . . . . I  8  187
POWERS. See Congress; Courts; President.
   not delegated to U. S. or prohibited to states, reserved to
      states and people . . . . . . . . . . . (amd.) X    204
PREFERENCE. See Congress, Limitations on.
PREJUDICE,
   constitution does not, claim to territory . . . . . . . IV  3  198
PRESIDENT,
   to be thirty five years of age, and a natural born citizen . II  1  193
   commander in chief of army, etc. . . . . . . . . . II  2  193
   compensation of. . . . . . . . . . . . . . . . II  1  193
   death, etc., of . . . . . . . . . . . . . . . . II  1  193
   duty of,
      to adjourn Congress on certain occasions. . . . . . II  3  194
      to commission all officers of U. S. . . . . . . . . II  3  194
      to convene Congress on extraordinary occasions . . . II  3  194
      to inform Congress of state of union . . . . . . . II  3  194
      to recommend measures to Congress . . . . . . . II  3  194
      to receive ambassadors and public ministers. . . . . II  3  194
      to see that laws are faithfully executed . . . . . . II  3  194
      to sign bills, resolutions, etc., or return with objections . I  7  184
      to take oath . . . . . . . . . . . . . . . II  1  193
   election of . . . . . . . . . . . . . (amd.) XII    204
   executive powers vested in . . . . . . . . . . . II  1  192
   impeachment of . . . . . . . . . . . . . . . II  4  194
   power of,
      to appoint certain officers . . . . . . . . . . . II  2  194
      to fill certain vacancies . . . . . . . . . . . . II  2  194
      to grant reprieves and pardons . . . . . . . . . II  2  194
      to make treaties . . . . . . . . . . . . . . II  2  194
      to require written opinion of cabinet officers . . . . II  2  193
   removal of, from office . . . . . . . . . . . . . II  4  194
   who is ineligible for . . . . . . . . . . . . . . II  1  193
PRESIDENT,
   *pro tempore*, Senate to choose . . . . . . . . . . I  3  183
   of Senate, Vice President to be . . . . . . . . . . I  3  183

## Q.

## R.

### S.

### W.

### Y.

# INDEX.

(For Analytical Index of the Constitution, see page 211.)

## DATE DUE